ENGLISH RECUSANT LITERATURE
1558–1640

Selected and Edited by
D. M. ROGERS

Volume 217

PHILIPPE D'OUTREMAN
The True Christian
Catholique
1622

PHILIPPE D'OUTREMAN
The True Christian
Catholique
1622

The Scolar Press
1974

ISBN 0 85967 201 8

Published and printed in Great Britain by
The Scolar Press Limited, 59-61 East Parade,
Ilkley, Yorkshire and
39 Great Russell Street,
London WC1

NOTE

THE TRVE
CHRISTIAN
CATHOLIQVE
OR
THE MANER HOW
TO LIVE CHRISTIANLY.

GATHERED

Forth of the holie Scriptures, and ancient Fathers, confirmed and ex-
plained by sundrie Reasons, apte
Similitudes, and Examples.

By the Reuerend Father F. PHILLIP
DOVLTREMAN, *of the So-*
cietie of Iesus.

And turnd out of Frenche into Englishe
By IOHN HEIGHAM.

AT S. OMERS, *With permission*
of Superiors. Anno 1622.

TO THE RIGHT

WORTHY LADY, THE
LADY ELIZABETH
WILLOVGHBY, DAVGHTER
to I. Thornbrough, Lord Bishopp of
Worcester.

ADAM

The Sonne of God, the supreame wisdome of the Father, setting vp his diuine conclusions, and daring (as it were) the greatest wittes of all the worlde, to enter in dispute against them, saith. *Doe men gather grapes of Thornes, or Figges of thistles?* What shall we say to this demande? Must it needes be granted, and can it no way be denied? Surely yes, me thinkes it may. First therfore I say (with my Lord and masters leaue) that

A 2   he

he himselfe being perfect man, doth gather from many sinful men sonnes and daughters, of whom he maketh glorious Saints: but this is to gather grapes of Thornes, ergo. Secondly, who may better helpe me to maintaine this assertion, (Madam) then your selfe? For from whence hath he gathered your selfe (so worthie a grape) but of a Thorne? A grape so rare (albeit gathered of a very Thorne) that hauing bene pressed by him in his sacred presse, hath yelded such store & plentie of pretious liquor, as hath not only filled his house with the odor therof, but hath further kindled and enflamed, yea plainly inebriated the harts of many cold ones in his burning loue.

The presse wherin this Lord doth presse such pretious grapes,

as

as your selfe, what other is it then the preſſor of perſecution. The pretious iuyce which is preſſed out of theſe excellent grapes, are thoſe moſt pretious and excellent Chriſtian virtues, which manifeſt thē ſelues amidſt perſecutions. The glorious Apoſtle S. Paul, deſirous to giue vnto vs, a proofe and taſt of that pretious liquor which was preſſed out of him ſelfe, after his conuerſion to the faith of Chriſt, ſaith. *Vntill this houre, we doe both hungar and thirſt, and are naked, & are beaten with buffets, and are wanderers, and labor working with our owne handes.* And which is there of all theſe, that you may not truly ſay as well as he? Verely it ſeemeth to me, that God would in ſome ſort, paragonize you Lady-ſhipp, with this glorious Apoſtle,

A 3   and

and make you a spectacle, or rather patterne to women, as he was to men, in eache of these probations and persecutions.

First therfore, in hungar and thirst as well as he, hauing bene reduced to that extremitie, as to be forced to send to the Spanish and Venetian Embassadors to beg your bread: and on Fridayes and Saturdayes, to be taxed to the allowance of three pence a day, for the maintenance of your selfe, your man, & your maide. In nakednes as well as he, as being not only despoiled of your plate, iewells, and rich apparell, but also to be stript so nere, euen of necessaries, as to be forced to set in your chamber in your naked sleeues, not able to goe out of doores, for lack of clothes. In being beaten with buffets as well as he, pitti-

pittifully swollen with black and blue, yea trailed by the haire of the head, and trodden vnder foote: treatment truly fitter for a dog, then for a Christian Lady: which yet for the loue you still beare to your abuser, I ommit to enlarge. In wandring as well as he; who haue bene forced to trauell many miles (not in the day time, and in your Coache, as your custome was, and your ranck requireth) but on foot, in the dead of the night, and to flit from place to place, thorough vncoth and vnknowen wayes: and last of all, to flie the lande, to liue in a strange and forrein contrie. In labor and working with your own handes to get your liuing: wherof many gentlemen of worth can yet beare witnes, who coming to visit you in that poore estate, found you

A 4 la-

labouring with your handes to get your liuinge.

But to fay in a word with what incredible patience and inward confort you fuſtained and fuffered the preſſures aforſaid , let this remaine for an euerlaſting memory, that to as many of your acquaintance as you met with all , with great pleaſure and contentment you faid, that you could tell them great good newes , to wit, that you were now no more a Proteſtant , but were become a Roman Catholique; Which you vttered to all with ſuch alacritie of minde , that many who heard you, deemed you mad for making that anſwer; like as the Apoſtles , for their enflamed feruor in the faith of Chriſt , were eſteemed drunke. But o happie foode which

which causeth such a happie fren-
sie! And o happie drinke, which
so makes drunke!

I neede not (Madam) the pre-
misses considered, frame any apo-
logie for my selfe in this place, why
I made choise of your Lady-ship,
to protect and patronize this present treatise, intituled, *The true
Christian Catholique*: for eache one
may easily iudge, that a booke of
this title, meriteth to be dedicated
to none other, then to such a true
and virtuous Christian Catholique, as you haue manifested your
selfe to be by so euident triall:
assuring my selfe, that of all
the bookes which euer you saw,
you neuer met with anie of so
smale a bulke, which doth ex-
presse with more liuelye examples, the virtues meete for a

A 5   true

true Christian Catholique , nor
yet set forth with more fearful pre-
sidents the punishments inflicted
by God, vpon such as are vicious.
Receiue the same then , I doe be-
seeche you, into the armes of your
protection, and I shall neuer cease
to pray, that you may become pee-
reles in the practise of the virtues
and be perpetually preserued from
the vices: and finally of a Thorne
in this life, you may become an e-
uerlastinge Lillie in the life to
come. Amen .

*Your Ladyships euer humble seruant
in our Lord and Sauiour Iesus*

IOHN HEIGHAM.

THE PREFACE.

His Title of a True Christiā Catholique, is not of so base & of so smale a reckning as perhaps (my friendly Reader) thou doost account it: for I finde, that the greatest and renowned of the world, haue glorified more therof, then of all their other titles of honor and nobilitie. Non principis, non terrenæ, &c. *We are not honored (saith Saint Chrisostome, Hom. 8. in* Ioan. *circa finem, with the name of Prince, or of some earthly power, not of Angell not of Archangell, but with the name of the Kinge of the whole worlde. That valorous martyred Deacon, called Sanctus (as Eusebius writeth l. 5. hist. Eccl. c. 1.) being asked*

of

of the tyrant vvhat his name vvas, ansvvered . I am a Christian. Of vvhat familie art thou? I am a Christian, quoth he. Of vvhat quallitie, free, or a bondman? To all the demandes vvhich vvere made him, he returned no other ansvvere but, I am a Christian. The same author vvriteth, that S. Blandinas martyr, in her confession of faith, and in the midst of all her torments, as often times as she pronouced these vvordes, I am a Christiã, so many times she felt her selfe streghtned anevv, & reioyced. And vvhat shall I say of S. Greg. Nazianzen. Who speaking of him selfe and of S. Basil, saith (in the funeral ortion of S. Basil.) Nobis magna res, &c. that is to say: We esteemed it for a great thinge, and held it for a great and noble name; indeed to be, and to be called Christians: wherof

wherof we glorie more, then euer Gi-
gas did of the change of the stone of
his ring (if notwithstanding it were
not fabulous) by the which he possest
himselfe of al Lidia. Thou shalt further
see in the first chapter of this booke,
that which the great Kinge Lewis
of France also iudged of this name.

Consider then the excellencie of
this booke, sith it beareth a name so
loftie and so honorable ; But yet behould rather (ô Christian) the glorious name which thou doest beare, &
if the life ought to answere to the excellencie of the name , hast thou not
cause to make account of this booke,
which teacheth thee in a few leaues,
how to liue Christialy, that is to say,
conforme to the life of Iesus Christ,
whose name thou bearest? Christia-
nismus est imitatio diuinæ naturæ
&c (saith S. Gre. Naz. tra. de nomine
& pro-

professione Christiani. *Christiani-*
tie is the imitation of the diuine na-
ture. If then thou be a Christian, imi-
tate Iesus Christ thy God. Beware
thou beare not a name emptie and vai-
ne, but complete. Employ then the
measure of so great a name, vpon wor-
kes worthie of the name. For this it
is that thou art Christian (saith S.
Iohn Chrisostome , orat. 5. in Iud.*)*
& that thou hast receiued this name,
to the end that thou imitate Iesus-
Christ, and fulfill by worke his coman-
dements. Briefly , Nemo Christia-
nus verè dicitur &c. *(* saith S. Cyprian *) No mã is rightly called a Chri-*
stian, who endeuoureth not to become
like vnto Iesus Christ by his Chri-
stian workes. Now to imitate Iesus
Christ , one must doe two thinges.
The first is , to roote vp all the sin-
nes and vices that are in his soule.
The

*The second, to plant virtues in
their places : for our Lord is not
come into this worlde, but to destroy sinne (1. Ioan. 3.) and to teache
vs by examples, (1. Pet. 2. 21.
Ioan. 13. 15. Heb. 10. 20.) and
wordes, the exercise of virtues, and
of good workes.*

*Behould here the summe and a-
bridgement of all Christian iustice,
saith S. Prosper with S. Aug. (in
sent. 98. ex Aug.) to fly from euill,
and to doe good. And to this it is,
that also Isay, Dauid, and the Apostle doth exhorte vs. (Isay 1. 16,
Psal. 33. 15. Rom. 12. 9. Colos. 3.
9. Ephes. 4. 22. 23.) This also is the
whole subiect of these twoo bookes,
wherin as in a most cleare miroir,
thou shalt finde these twoo pointes
taught vnto thee, by the holy Scriptures, and holie Fathers, with
sundry*

sundry notable reasons, rare similitudes and examples. And note that I haue serued my selfe of examples, because I see that the Sonne of God him selfe serued him selfe thereof, as also the holy Fathers did, especiallie S. Aug. and S. Greg. vvho in one of his homilies saith (38. in Euang. vvherin he bringeth sundry examples) that it hapneth oftentimes, that the hartes of the hearers, are more conuerted and moued, by the examples of the faithfull, then by the vvordes of the preachers. Nonnunquam mentes audentium, plus exempla fidelium, quam docentium verba conuertunt. *Which sith it is so, I assure my selfe that this litle booke, vvill bringe vnto thee both profit and contentment, if vvith a serious and attentiue lecture, thou ioynest together the*

practise

practise and good vvorkes . God grant, that both thou and I, may so vvell practise these profitable Documents , that after vve haue by the meanes hereof, led a life Trulie Christian and Catholique, *vve may one day haue the recompence promised to all good Christians; life and glorie euerlasting,* Amen .

Of

Of the true Christian Catholique
or
The maner how to liue Christianly.

THE I. BOOKE.

Of the flight from sinne.

THE I. CHAPTER.

Of the name Christian.

1. HIS word Christian, comes of Christ, and signifies him, who beinge Baptised, doth beleeue in Iesus-Christ, and maketh profession of the true and wholsome doctrine taught in his Church. *Canis. t. 1. de fide & simb q. 1.* Or else, it is like a soldiour, who hauing left the diuels banner, *2.Tim.2.* hath willingly enrolled him selfe by Baptisme, vnder the standart & banner of

of Iesus Christ, making profession to
follow him wherfoeuer, with his weapons in his hande, and to fight incef-
fantly against the worlde, the flesh,
and the diuell, vntill such time as hauing gott the victorie, he enter triumphantly into h̄eauen, there to receiue
an immortall crowne of glorie, and of
eternall contentment. (1. *Cor.* 9.)
What honor will it be, to be enrolled
vnder such a captaine, how happie an
houre to arriue at such a triumphe,
and at such a crowne! You are they
which expect and hope for all these
thinges, whofoeuer carry by good and
true tokens, the name of Chriftians.
But what shame and confusion shall it
be to him, who belying a name fo honorable, and despising a recompence
of fo incomparable a price, addicteth
him felfe to none but to thinges vile
and vnworthie of a man ? nor occu-
pieth him felfe, but only about that
which is of earth, of flesh and blood?
nether thinketh nor dreameth, but of
eating

eating and drinking, and to ftuffe top
full like a beaſt, his brutall appetites?
depriuing him felfe by this meanes of
this crowne of glorie, and opening to
him felfe by the fame meanes, the
way and path to a lamentable confu-
fion of paines and torments which are
eternall. 2. S. Paul (2. Tim. 3. 34.) faith.
Labour thou as a good foldiar of Chriſt
Ieſus, *no man being a foldiar to God, in-*
tangleth him felfe with fecular buſineſſes,
(vnderſtand by fecular, the affembly of
the wicked:) and then he addeth. No
foldiour, *that ſtriueth for the maſterie*
is crowned, vnles he ſtriue lawfully; that
is to fay, vnles he haue exactly obferued all the lawes of the combat. And
in the 4. chapter. 7. 8. *I haue fought a*
good fight, I haue confumate my courſe.
Concerning the reſt, there is laid vp for
me a crowne of iuſtice, which our Lord
will rendar to me in that day, a iuſt iudge,
and not only to me, but to them alfo that
loue his cominge. And 1. Cor 9. 25. *Eue-*
rie one that ſtriueth for the maſtrie, refrai-
neth

neth him selfe *from all thinges,* and *they certes, that they may receiue a corruptible crowne, but* We (Christians) *an incorruptible.* I therfore so runne, *not as it* were *at an vncertaine thinge :* so I fight, *not as it* were beating *the ayre, but* I chastce *my bodie, and bringe it into seruitude.* S. Peter 1. cap. 4. 15. *Let none of you suffer as a murderer, or a theefe, but if as a Christian, let him not be ashamed, but let him glorifie God in this name.*

3. Sainct Augustin explicating the name of a Christian, saieth. He who maketh him selfe a Christian only to escape the fier of hell, and to come to heauen with Iesus Christ, countergarding him selfe against all tentations, and not suffering him selfe to be corrupted by prosperity, nor beaten downe with aduersity, and who arriueth to this perfection, that he more loueth God, then he feareth hell. Who though God him selfe should say vnto him, vse and enioy the pleasures of the world, commit all the sin-

nes

nes thou wilt, thou shalt not be damned, would not for all this commit
sinne, for feare of offending almighty
God, such an one is truly Christian.
lib. de Catech. rud. c. 16. & 17. tom 4.
Acknowledge thy dignitie, o Christian
(saith S. Leo) and take good heede
that thou returne not by a degenerate
and vnworthy conuersation, to thy
wonted vilenes and basenes. *Ser. 1.*
de Nat.

EXAMPLES.

1. S. Lewis kinge of France, went
more willingly to Poissi, then to any
other place in all his kingdome, for
that he had bene there baptised and
made a Christian: and was wont to
say, that he had receiued more dignitie
and honor in that place, then in any
other in the whole world. *Nicol. Aegid.*
& Franc de Belleforest vpon his life. Behould (o Christian) the dignitie thou
hast, sith such a Kinge preferreth the
same

same before his crowne!

2. Now to be a true Christian, one must first flie and detest all sinne, as well mortall as veniall; as well that of will only and of thought, as of wordes and worke.

3. And touching wordes, to keepe him selfe from swearing without necessitie and reason: from blaspheming: cursing and wicked imprecations: from speaking wordes of contumelie, detracting, lying, vttering of dishonest songes or wordes.

4. As touchinge sinnes of worke, parents ought to take heede, that they be not negligent, both to instruct and correct their children: and children not to disobey their parents.

5. Aboue all, the sinne of Pride, Couetousnes, Luxurie, Enuie, Gluttonie, Drunkenes, Anger and Sloth, is to be auoided.

6. The most effectual remedies are, to fly the occasion ; the memorie of the presence of almightie God; of the
passion

paſſion of Ieſus Chriſt; of death, Iudgement, Hell, and the kingdome of Heauen: thus much concerninge the flight of ſinne.

7. Secondly, one muſt addict himſelfe to the exerciſe of virtues and of good workes, as;

8. To make the ſigne of the Croſſe, in riſing vp, and lying downe; before eating, and drinking; before worke, and in euery neceſſitie.

9. To pray to God, and to giue him thankes both morning and eueninge, both before and after meate, and to inuoke the aſſiſtance of our B. Ladie, his Angell Guardian, and of the Saintes, namly of him whoſe name he beareth.

10. To ſprinkle him ſelfe with holie water, and to beare about him an Agnus Dei.

11. To learne the moſt neceſſarie pointes of faith, and of Chriſtian religion.

12. To haue a diſtruſt of him ſelfe, and a great truſt and confidence in almightie

mightie God.

13. To loue God aboue all thinges, and his neighbour for God.

14. To heare Maſſe, both with reuerence and attention.

15. To Confes often, gaine Indulgences, and to pray for the ſoules that are in Purgatorie.

16. To faſt, pray, and willingly to giue almes vnto the poore.

17. To receiue often the holy Communion, to heare gladly ſermons, and to beare a ſingular deuotion to our B. Ladie.

Loe theſe are the moſt neceſſarie pointes, to liue and die a good Chriſtian, whereof I pretend to treate, thorough all the chapters that doe enſue.

THE II. CHAPTER.

Of mortall and veniall ſinne.

1. A Mongſt all the euills that raigne in the world, the greateſt,

B

teſt, and moſt to be deplored is, that
men know not nor apprehend not, the
euills and miſeries of the ſoule, regarding none but thoſe of the body. The
Aſſe falleth into the myre (ſaith S.Ber-
nard) and both the maſter , and the
neighbours runne with ſpeed to pull
him forth: the ſoule falleth into ſinne,
and perdition,& none at all takes care
thereof.

2. *What doth it profit a man* , ſaith
our Lord, *if he gayne the whole worlde,
and ſuſtaine the damage of his ſoule?* Mat.
16.26. O yee fathers & mothers, apprehend this point , and teache it betimes vnto your children , make them
to ſuck it with their milk, whilſt they
are yet in their infancie, and often ſinge
vnto them this goulden ſentence of
our Sauiour. *Feare yee not them that kill
the body , and are not able to kill the
ſoule, but rather feare him that can deſtroy both ſoule and body into hell.* Mat.
10.28. which nether is , nor neuer
ſhall be, but for ſinne.

§. What

§. W*hat mortall sinne is , and what de-*
triments it bringeth to the soule.

1. S. Augustin speaking of sinne in
generall saith , that it is a word,
thought, or deede, against the law of
almightie God. *lib.* 22. *cont. Faustum,*
cap. 27.

2. Diuines say, that it is a foulenes
and deformitie of the reasonable creature, wherby it is made displeasing to
God, and wherwith it can not see God
in his glorie.

3. To be mortall , it must be committed freely and voluntarily, against
some commandement of God, or the
Church in a matter of importance.

4. It is called mortall , because it
depriueth vs of our spirituall life, and
bringeth death vnto the soule , sepa-
rating it by this death from the kingdome of God , and making it
worthie of fire and paines that are
perpetuall.

5. *The soule that shall haue sinned,*
shall dye the death. Ezech. 18. If I doe

this

this (said the chaft Sufanna, being fo-
licited vnto finne) *it is my death. Dan.3.*
And the father of the prodigall child,
faid vnto his eldeft fonne, *thy brother*
was dead, and is reuiued. Luc.15.32.

6. Befides the fpirituall life, that is
to fay, the grace of God which is loft
by mortall finne, he likewife loofeth
all the merits he had got. Ezech. 18.
24. All the giftes, and the familiaritie
of the holy Ghoft, and his virtues.
Sap.1. 4. & 5. Abdias 5.6. He loofeth
the right of the children of God, that
is to fay, euerlafting life. The efpeciall & particular protection of God.
Pfal. 32. 18. The protection of his
good Angell. S.Bafil in pfal.33. Com-
munication in the merits of all the
Saints, that is to fay, of all good
Chriftians. He becometh in an inftant the flaue of the deuill, prickt &
gnawen côtinually with the remorce
of confcience, it being the greateft of
all torments that are in this life. *S.*
Auguft. in Pfal.45. Iob. 15. 21. Pro.28.
                                    1. tha

1. *thoroughout. Sap.* 17. *Pſal.* 50. He
meriteth nothing in doing any good
worke . *Iſay.* 59. *Luc.* 5. 5. But that
which is the greateſt of al miſchiefes,
he remayneth obliged to euerlaſting
paines. *Eccleſ.* 21. 10. 11. *Iis procella te-*
nebrarum ſeruata eſt in æternum. Cath.
ep. of S. Iude, to whom the ſtorme of
darknes is reſerued for euer . Bleſſed
Lord, how many euills doth one only pleaſure bringe!

E X A M P L E S.

1. Lyſimachus kinge of Thracia,
rendring him ſelfe, with his whole
kingdome vnto his enimie , for the
thirſt which he could no longer ſuffer, after he had drunk a glaſſe of water; Good God(ſaid this poore Pagan)
how great a miſerie is it for me, to
looſe a whole kingdome, for ſo litle
a pleaſure! *Plutarch.* Ah ſinner, thou
dooſt the ſame for leſſe , when for a
pleaſure, but of a momēt, of a wicked
B 3   worke,

worke, of a diſordered word, or of
conſent to ſome euill thought, thou
looſeſt in an inſtant, the whole kingdom of heauen,& thine owne ſoule?

2. What a ſubiect of griefe was it
to accurſed Eſau,to haue loſt for a litle
diſhe of pottage, all his birth-right?
Gen. 25.

3. Suſanna ſeeing her ſelfe ſolicited
to the ſinfull concupiſcence of two
ould men of Babilon, who threatned
her in caſe of refuſall, to accuſe her of
adulterie, ſhe ſighing ſaid. *Perplexities*
are to me on euery ſide, for if I ſhal doe this,
it is death to me : and if I doe it not, I
ſhall not eſcape your handes. But it is bet-
ter for me, without the act, to fall into
your handes, then to ſinne in the ſight of
our Lord. Dan. 13.22.

4. Eleazer, one of the princes of
the Scribes, being fourſcore and ten
yeares ould, being vrged to eate ſwines fleſh againſt the commandement
of God,or elſe to die, anſwered. That
he would *rather be ſent vnto hell,* that
                                   is to

is to ſay, that he had rather die: *For* (quoth he) *although at this preſent time, I be deliuered from the torments of men, yet neither aliue nor dead, ſhal I eſcape, the hande of the almightie God:* & ſo at the laſt was put to death. *2. Mac. 6.*

5. Seauen bretheren alſo, together with their mother, being taken and moſt cruelly ſcourged for the ſame cauſe, one of them, which was the firſt ſaid. W*hat ſeekeſt thou, and what wilt thou learne of vs? we are ready to die, rather then to tranſgreſſe the lawes of God, coming from our fathers.* ibid. cap. 7.

6. All the martyrs, both of the ould and the new Teſtament, haue they not choſen rather to die, then to ſinne?

7. This alſo was that which S. Blanche ſo greatly recommended vnto S. Lewis Kinge of France, ſaying vnto him. That ſhe had rather to ſee him die, then to ſee him offende God mortallie, which point he imprinted ſo deepely in his pious hart, that it is houlden for certaine, that in his whole

life he neuer committed any mortall
finne.

8. And the fame S. Lewis, in the
inftruction which he gaue to his fonne
Phillip at the houre of his death, faid
vnto him. My fonne, take heede to
thy felfe, that thou offende not God
mortallie, although thou fhouldeft
fuffer all the torments in the worlde.

9. S. Thomas of Aquin faid, that
he knew not how a man who faw
him felfe in mortall finne, could
ether laughe or be merry in any time
whatfoeuer. *Ribad. 7. of March.* And
the kinge of Spaine Philip the third,
could not comprehend, how fuch an
one could euer fleepe.

10. S. Stillites of Edeffa, obtained
this fauor of almightie God, as to fee
his Angell gardian, and that of others,
but differently: for thofe which were
in the grace of God, he faw them accompanied with their good Angells,
who guided them with a torche a-
lighted; but thofe which were in
mor-)

mortall ſinne, he ſaw them detained in chaines by the diuells, and their Angells which followed them a far off, heauilie weeping. *Ex Patrico Grecorum M. S. Biblioth. Reip. Auguſtana. Raderus in virid. ſanct. pag. 2. cap. 6.*

Weepe, weepe yee, ô yee bleſſed Spirits, ſith the ſinner him ſelfe is ſo vnfortunat as not to ſee nor deplore his owne ill fortune. Deſire you to ſee yet more, reade the §. that doth enſue.

§. 2. *Hovv much mortall ſinne is deteſtable, horrible, and ſtinking.*

1. *Fly from ſinne* (ſaith the wiſe man) *as from a ſerpent. Eccle. 21. 2.* One may well ſay of a ſoule fallen into mortall ſinne, that which the Prophet Ieremie ſaid, of the ſonnes and daughters of Ieruſalem, during the time of their affliction. *From the daughter of Sion, all her beautie is departed. Thren. 1. 6.*

2. And againe. *Hovv is the gold darkned, the beſt color changed   the ſtones of the ſanctuarie diſperſed, in the head of all*

B 5   *ſtreetes?*

streetes? The noble children of Sion, and they that were clothed with the principall gold, how are they reputed as earthen vessels, the worke of the potters handes? Her Nazarits whiter then snowe, purer then milke, ruddier then the ould yuorie, fairer then the saphire, their face is made blacker then coales, and they are not knowen in the streetes. Ibid. cap. 4.

3. They are become abhominable, like to the thinges which they loued. *Osee.* 9. Aske (faith S. Ambrose) the confcience of the finner, if it be not more ftinking then all the fepulchers of the dead. *lib.* 1. *offic. cap.* 12.

4. Euen as the rottenes taketh away all the beautie, color, fent and fauor of the apple: euen fo finne taketh away the beautie of the foule, the odor of her good name, the goodnes of grace, and the fauor of glorie. *S. Bon. in Dieta falutis c.* 2.

EXAMPLES.

1. The Sonne of God, hauing taken
vpon

vpon him selfe the sinnes of men, lost
in such wise his excellent beautie, that
of the fairest that he was amongst all
men, he became so disfigured, that the
prophet behoulding him, said. *There is
no beautie in him , nor comelines , and we
haue seene him, and there was no sightli-
nes.* I *say 53.* 2. Now if the only paine
of sinne , hath so disfigured our B.
Lord, what shall the guilt it selfe doe
vnto vs?

2. The diuel is most horrible gastly,
but mortall sinne is yet much more;
for a holy hermit, seeing him selfe honored for the miracles which he did,
in driuing diuells forth of bodies , for
feare of falling into vaine glorie, he
instantly asked of almightie God , to
be him selfe possest of the diuell, as he
was. *Seuer. Sulpit. in the life of S. Martin
c. 1.* Doe you see how this holie man
was more afraid of sinne, then of the
diuell ?

3. Our B. Ladie appeared to S. Catharine virgin and martyr, before such
B 6   time

time as she was baptised, houldinge
her litle Sonne betwixt her armes, and
she recommended Catharin vnto him:
our Lord turned his face from her, saying that she was too il fauored. Which
was the cause that she made haste to
be baptised, and within awhile after,
our Lord bethrothed him selfe vnto
her, in the presence of his holy mother, and of an infinit number of B.
Angells, and put a ringe vpon her fingar, the which she kept during her
life. *Pet. de natal. l. 10. c. 105. & Ribad.
in her life.*

4. S. Catharine of Sienna, discoursing with a gentlewoman which was
defiled with the sinne of the flesh,
stopt her nose. And when father Raimond her confessar was amazed therat,
she said vnto him, that vnles she should
haue done so, she should haue been
forced for to vomit, because of the
stinke which came forth of the soule
of the same woman.

5. S. Anthonie relateth the like of
an

an Angel, who paſſing with an Hermit hard by an effeminat youngſter, ſtopt his noſtrils, which he had not done, paſſing by a dead carion. And when the Hermit was aſtoniſhed therat, he ſaid vnto him: that young man, by reaſon of his ſinnes, was much more ſtinking and abhominable vnto him, then was the moſt corrupted carion. *D. Antonij 4. p. ſum. tit. 14. c. 6. §. 1.* O ſinne how horrible, deteſtable, cruell, gaſtly, and ſtinking art thou &c? Let vs fly, from a monſter ſo abhominable.

6. S. Edmond had an exceedinge horror therof, ſith he ſaid, that he had rather caſt him ſelfe into a burning fornace, then to fall into one mortal ſinne. *Sur. in his life. c. 29. Nou. 16.*

7. Yea S. Anſelme ſaid, that he had rather fall into hell, then into ſinne. *S. Anſel. de ſimilit. & Sur. 2. of Aprill.* See hereafter *lib. 2. c. 3. §. 1.* the like anſwere of an old Iaponian.

§. 3. By mortall ſinne, we crucifie againe Ieſus Chriſt.

1. O

1. O the full meafure of all mif-chiefe! that finne is not only extremly iniurious to him who committeth it, but euen to God him felfe, the author of health. It is the fentence of S. Paul Heb. 6. 6. faying that finners, *crucify againe to them felues the Sonne of God, and make him a mocquerie*. And in the 10. c. 29. he faith, that *they tread the Sonne of God vnder foote, and efteeme the blood of the teftament polluted, wherin they had bene fanctified*. By one mortall finne, we crucifie againe the Sonne of God, becaufe we doe that which was the caufe of his crucifixion. And if his death had not bene fufficient for the ranfome of all the finnes of the world, he muft for the expiation of euery finne which we commit, haue againe bene crucified and put to death.

2. With great reafon then faid that good doctor Ioannes Taulerus, if God would fuffer fome one to fee his owne finnes, as they are feene of God him felfe, he would burft a funder with

very

very forrow at the fame inftant, perceiuing the iniurie and contempt that
he hath done by them, to his Creator
and Redeemer. *lib. de vita & paff.*
Chrifti c. 7.

EXAMPLES.

1. At the time that the Albigenfian
heretiques ranfacked France, our Lady
appeared vnto S. Leutgarde with a fad
and weeping countenance. The faint
hauing enquired the caufe of her hea-
uines, fhe anfwered vnto him, that it
was becaufe that the heretiques and
euil Chriftiãs, crucified againe by their
finnes, her deare Sonne Iefus Chrift.
Sur. tom. 3. ex Tho. Cantiprat.

2. S. Bridgit of Sueede, haueing
heard preached vpon a day, the paffion
of our B. Sauiour, the night enfuinge
our Lord appeared vnto her, al bloody
and full of dolors, as when he was faftned to the Croffe, and faid vnto her.
Behould my woundes. The Saint beleeuing

leeuing that they were fresh, said vnto
him in weeping wise. Alas my Lord,
who hath hurt thee in this maner.
They (quoth he) that doe contemne
and make none account of my charity.
*Sur . to . 4. Ribad. in her life the 23. of
Iuly.*

3. See more in the 2. booke c.7. §.
3. Example 4. of S. Collect. O execrable malice of mortall sinne ! Let vs
now speake of veniall sinne.

§. 4. Of veniall sinne.

1. Veniall sinne, doth not exclude
the grace of God, nor charitie ; it diminisheth notwithstanding the feruor
thereof, and as S. Paul speaketh
Ephes.4. *doth contristat the holy Ghost*,
obfuscat the conscience, and hinder
the aduancement in virtues, and by
litle and litle, draweth a man to mortall sinne. *He that contemneth smale thinges, shall fall by litle and litle*, saith the
wiseman. *Eccles. 19. 1.* S. Aug. compareth veniall sinnes vnto the itche,
which spoyle the beautie of the face,
and

and diſguſteth the beholders : feare them not, ſaith he , becauſe they are leſſer then the others, but becauſe they are in greater nombre . The gnattes and flies are litle beaſtes, which yet if they be many in number, are able to take from a man his life . Graines of Sande being multiplied, doe ſinke the Shippes : and droppes of waters gathered together, make riuers ſwell, and ruine houſes.

2. Veniall ſinne is like to a thrid, tied to the foote of the ſoule , which hindreth it to fly to perfection. It is a mothe, which eateth by litle and litle beames and ſummer poſtes, which not able at the laſt to ſupport the waight that is laid vpon them, doe cauſe the fall of the whole houſe.

No polluted thinge ſhall enter into the celeſtiall Ieruſalem, ſaith S. Iohn. Apoc. 21. 27. vnles therfore veniall ſinnes be blotted forth in this life, they traile a man to the fire of Purgatorie, a fire ſo terrible, that in reſpect therof, the

the paines of this life are in a maner
nothinge, as both S. Aug. and S. Greg.
say (in psl. 37. & ser. 41. in 3. psl. pænit.
And our Lord him selfe saith. *That*
euery idle word that men shall speake, they
shall render an account for it in the day of
iudgement. Mat. 12. 36. And doost thou
set so light by veniall sinne?

EXAMPLES.

1. The Abbot Moises, was posessed
with the diuell, for hauing thorough
impatience spoken a litle ouer roughly
vnto another. Cassian Colat. 7. c. 27.
Another Monke was also possest, for
hauing drunke with too much sensual-
litie, a glasse of water. S. Greg. dial. l.
1. c. 4. And another, for hauing bene
distracted voluntarily in his prayer.
Ibid. l. 2. c. 1. Is not this enough to
giue to vnderstand, that veniall sinnes
are not so litle before God, as men
imagin?

2. S. Marie of Ognia, was so cir-
cumspect,

cumspect, and so aduised in her actions, euen in the very least of all, that none could euer obserue, the least idle word to issue out of her mouth, nor anie other vncomely cariage: and was accustomed to confes her selfe of her least faultes, with as much contrition, as if they had beene mortall sinnes. *Iac. de vitriaco Card. in her life l. 1. c. 6.*

3. Eusebius Monke, casting once his eye thorough curiositie, vpon the the workmen which laboured in the fieldes whilst Amyan read the gospels vnto him, & for this cause not hauing well vnderstood a certaine passage, whereof the other asked him the explication, had so great repentance for it, that he euer after mortified his sight, duringe the time of his whole life, carying continually his head enclined towards the earth, by meanes of a great iron chaine, which tyed his neck vnto his girdle: and this for the space of forty yeares, so great esteemed he this litle fault. *Theodore in hist. sanct.*

sanct. pat.sect. 4. & Sophron. in prato
spirit.

4. The B. Mother Teresa of Iesus,
foundresse of the discalceat Carmelits,
makes métion in her writinges of her
sinnes, with such excesse of exaggera-
tion (albeit they were but very litle)
as if they had bene exceeding greuous,
If in reciting any lesson in the quire,
she chanced to fayle but a litle, she pre-
sétlie prostrated her self vpó the groúd
in the midst of the quire: which all the
other sisters seeing, could not abstaine
from teares, and were constrained to
interrupt their seruice, for the great
feeling they had therof. *Ribera in her*
life : and in the 10. *c. of that which she*
wrote with her owne hande.

Now if the Saintes haue so apprehended the malice of veniall sinne,
what great horror had they of mortall
sinne?

THE

THE III. CHAPTER.

Of sinnes of will only, and of thought.

1. THere is a great abuse, ignorance, and blindnes, which raigneth amongst simple people and such as are idiots, to thinke that one offendes not God, vnles by worke, and by worde, and not with the wil alone: for he that hath forbidden to commit the sinne of the flesh and adultrie, hath likewise forbidden to couet his neighbours wife.

You haue heard that it was said to them of old, thou shalt not commit aduoutrie: but I say to you, that whosoeuer shall see a woman to luste after her, hath already committed aduoutrie with her in his hart. Mat. 5. 28. And the like is, of euery other euill will.

Concupiscence, when it hath conceiued, bringeth forth sinne, but sinne when it is consummate, ingendreth death. Iac. 1. 15.

Bles-

Bleſſed is he, that shall dashe his litle ones (that is to ſay, his firſt thoughtes) *againſt the rock.* (that is to ſay, Ieſus Chriſt. psl. 136. 9.

Whilſt your enemie is but litle, kill him (ſaith S. Herom) *and crush malice in the very ſeede.* Epiſt. 12. ad Euſtoch.

Man ſeeth thoſe thinges which appeare, but our Lord behouldeth the hart. 1. Reg. 26. 7.

EXAMPLES.

1. Kinge Pharao, for hauing coue-ted Sara the wife of Abraham, albeit he touched her not in any ſort, both he himſelfe, and all his familie were out of hande chaſticed of God moſt rigorouſly, with diuers great and ſharp afflictions.

2. A Iew, gotten into a temple by night, ſaw a troupe of diuells, which gaue account to one who ſeemed to be the chiefe of the reſt, of all their comportment towardes men: and heard one who bragged, that he had

indu-

induced Andrew Biſhop of Fonda, to embrace a diſhoneſt thought. S.Greg. l.3. Dial.c.7.

3. At Coſma, a towne of Itallie, a cittizen giuen for a long time to follow a concubine, felt him ſelfe at laſt to be brought to the point and pinche of death. A father of the Societie of Ieſus, was called to heare his Confeſſion. At the firſt begining being informed of his life, as he was before, he repreſented vnto him, that the houre was now come, that he muſt needes depart this worlde, and therfore exhorted him to forſake his harlot. The obſtinat and accurſed wretch, hauing death in his face, replied that he could not be without her in that extremitie, but that ſhe would ſerue him very well. The father preſſed him againe, caſt him ſelfe at his feete, and beſought him with teares to take compaſſion on his ſoule, cauſing all the fathers and brothers of his colledge, to pray to this effect and purpoſe. At the laſt, our Lord

Lord touched him, he caused this shee
wolfe to depart his lodging, confest
him selfe with exceeding sorrow, and
with other signes of true repentance,
and the very day after this confession,
he dyed. Vpon the morrow, as this
father went from his chamber to the
sacristie to say Masse for his soule, he
felt him selfe scuffeld with al and thrust
back, and heard a voice most distinctly
which said vnto him. Whether goest
thou? The father went on his way,
and being arriued at the vestrie doore,
he felt him selfe pusht back more for-
ceibly then before, and was constrained to recoyle, two or three great
steps. He ommitted not for all this to
inuest him selfe, and to goe vnto the
Altar. As he descended thence, he that
asisted him being come to the Confiteor, behold a horrible monster most
gastfull and fearfull, shewed him selfe
visiblie vpon the Altar, on that side
where the Epistle is read, and looking
vpon the priest, said. Pray not for me,
                                    beware

beware thou dooſt not. The father replied, why not, art not thou ſuch an
one? Didſt thou not confes thy ſelfe
to me yeſterday, with ſo great contrition and with teares? Hadſt thou not
pardon of thy ſinnes? What then is
betided of new vnto thee? Yea (quoth
the Spirit) I am euen he in very deed,
I confeſt my ſelfe, it is true, and that
entirely, and withall receiued pardon
of my ſinnes; But after that thou waſt
departed, that accurſed ſtrumpet that
had kept me captiue all my life, entred
againe into my houſe, drew nere vnto
me to doe ſome ſeruice, and forthwith
the accuſtomed fancies awaked in me,
I yelded entrie to a wicked thought,
ſtayed therein, and conſented; and
therupon I died. For which I now
burne, and ſhall burne for all eternitie.
Extracted out of the annuall hiſtories
of the Societie, and alleadged by Val-
lad. in the ſermon vpon the Thurſday
of the paſſion, who aſſureth to haue
learned it of a religious mã, who knew

the father that heard the confeſſion of
this miſerable man , and had it from
his owne ſelfe . Good God, what a
tragicall example ! And ſhall we then
ſay, that euill deſires, are no ſinnes?

THE IV. CHAPTER.

Of the ſinnes of the Tongue.

Death and life , are in the hande
of the tongue , ſaith the wiſe
man. Prou. 18. 21.

*Out of the mouth proceedeth bleſſing
and curſing . The tongue is certes a litle
member and vanteth great thinges . Behould how much fire, what a great wood
it kindleth: and the tongue is fire, a whole
worlde of iniquitie .* Finally he concludeth, ſaying . *If any man offend not in
worde, this is a perfect man.* Iac. 1. 2. 10.
5. That is to ſay, according to Hugo
of S. Victor, it is a ſigne , that he hath
a great care to keepe his hart, & therfore hath a great inward perfection.
In

In cap. 13. ep. ad Rom.

Philo faith, that the worde is as the hande of the diall, which giues to vnderftand the eftate of the inward fpringe, and of the wheeles, that is to fay, of the good or bad conftitution of the foule. And our Sauiour faith. That out of the aboundance of the hart, the mouth fpeaketh. Mat. 12. Luc. 6.

EXAMPLES.

1. Nicephorus writeth that a certaine learned man, went vpon a day to vifit S. Pambonus Abbot, one very holie, but fomwhat fimple, and laboured to perfwade him, to ioyne & linke, learning with his virtu. And when the Saint had fhewed him that he was well content as he was, this Doctor tooke the Bible, and openinge the fame, expounded vnto him the firft paffage that he feil vpon, which was out of the 36. Pfalme. *I haue*

said, I will keepe my wayes, that I offend not in my tongue. Enoughe (quoth the Saint) you shall teache me the rest, when I shall haue first well learned & practised this. Geuing to vnderstande, that the first and principalest point of a spirituall life , is to refraine and bridle the tongue. Niceph. & Socrat. l. 4. hist. ecclef. c. 18. hist. trip. Cassiod. l. 8. c. 1.

§. 1. of Swearing.

The second commandement of the first table is. *Thou shalt not take the name of thy Lord thy God in vaine , for God wil not hould him guiltles that taketh his name in vaine.* Exod.20. Deut.5.11.

Thou shalt not sweare at all , nether by heauen , becaufe it is the throne of God: nether by the earth, becaufe it is the foot-stoole of his feete &c.but let your talke be,yea,yea, no, no, and that which is ouer and aboue these,is of euill. Mat.5. 37.

Yet must we vnderstand these wordes of swearing, vsed without any necessi-

ceſſitie: for our Lord in Ieremie cap. 2.
permitteth to ſweare, *with truth, iudge-*
ment and iuſtice: that is to ſay, touching
a thinge that one knoweth for truth,
and that one iudgeth that there is neceſſitie: and if it be an oath promiſſiue,
that it be of a thing iuſt and lawfull.

Let not thy mouth be accuſtomed to
ſwearing, ſaith the wiſe man; and verſ.
12. *A man that ſweareth much, shall be*
filled with iniquitie, and plague shall not
depart from his houſe. Eccl. 23. 9.

Is it not a thinge abſurde, ſaith S.
Iohn Chriſoſt. that if we haue one
pretious garment, we vſe it not but
once a weeke, and yet that we dare,
raſhlie vſurpe vpon eache occaſion,
the moſt pretious and ſacred name of
almightie God? Hom. 9. ad pop. Antioch.

I had a cuſtome to ſweare euery
day, ſaith S. Aug. but hauing read how
great a ſinne it was, I was afraid to
commit the ſame; I haue combatted
againſt this euill cuſtome, and in this

C 3　　　　combat

cuſtome, I had recourſe vnto God, and he hath giuen me the grace to ſweare no more, now nothing is more eaſie vnto me, then not to ſweare; I tell you this, to the ende that you may ſee that it is not impoſſible, euen to one that is accuſtomed to ſweare, to ſweare no more; the feare of God, o-uercometh all. Aug.ſer. 10. de ſanctis.

To ſweare, is to call God for a wit-nes of that truth which we auerre; If then it be a great ſinne to ſweare raſh-lie and without neceſſitie, it is a great deale more when one knoweth well, that which one auerreth to be falſe, or that one douteth of the truth: for this is to call God, to witnes a lie, and ſo to make him the author and defender of our owne malice: & what impietie can be more enorme then this?

For this reaſon, all ſortes of nations, euen the moſt barbarous, haue had per-iuries in great horror.

The Egiptians and Scithians, put them to death. Iohn. Boemus, in the

def-deſcription of Egipt.

The Indians cut off the toppes of their feete and handes : and in ſundry places of Europe, they cut off their hande. Couuarruuias in c. *quamuis pactum.* p. 1. §. 7. n. 2.

According to the decrees of the Canon law, periured perſons are infamous. c. *infames* 6. a. q. 1.

They ought to faſt fortie daies with bread and water, and after for the ſpace of ſeauen yeares, performe ſome penance a litle milder: nor neuer may be admitted for witnes. c. *quicunque* 6. 9. 1.

S. Lewis kinge of France, cauſed their tongues to be pierced thorough. S. Antonin. 3. p. chron. tit. 19. c. 9. §. 4. Paul. Æmil. l. 7. hiſt. Franc. Ribad. in his life.

Charles the good Count of Flanders, made them to faſt fortie dayes. Hiſt. Fland. Behould the apprehention which theſe great perſonages had of this ſinne.

C 4   EXAM-

EXAMPLES.

1. In the cittie of Tours, a certaine person being entred into our Ladies church to auouche by oathe, a thinge that was falſe, he had no ſooner laid his hande vpon the Altar to ſweare, but that he fell backward, and was grieuouſly woũded. S. Greg. of Tours, the firſt miracle c. 20.

2. Another hauing ſet a houſe a fire, ſware in S. Martins church, that he did it not, and at the ſelfe ſame inſtant he was ſmitten with a reuenginge fire which fell from heauen, which ſlew him out-right vpon the place. The ſame author l. 8. of the hiſt. of France c. 16.

3. A litle after the death of S. Omer, a burgeſſe of the ſame cittie, hauinge receiued a ſomme of mony lent him of another, and ſwearing to repay it him againe vpon a certaine day, the creditor demanded his mony, but he denied

nied to haue receiued it, and went to
take his oathe vpon the tombe of S.
Omer. As they came neere to the
Church, his creditor ſaid vnto him:let
vs not goe to prophane the ſacred
tombe of the Saint, ſweare here that
thou receiuedſt nothing, and I ſhall be
ſatisfied. The other preſently lifted vp
his hande, & beginneth to pronounce
his periurie, hauing his face turned
towards the church of the Saint: but
before he was able to vtter one worde,
he fell to the grounde, with his eyes
rowling in his head, depriued of the
vſe of all his members, and ſo dyed
within three daies after. Surius in the
life of S. Omer c. 26. Sept. 9. and Vincent of Beauuais, in his miror, hiſt. l.
23. c. 109.

4. Two ſiſters, the daughters of a
Duke, wragling for their goods againſt
their brother, came frō France to Va-
lenciē there to finde king Charlemaigne, to haue redres of the wronge their
brother did them in detayninge their
C 5   goods?

goods. And as he denied the fact, the kinge made him to fweare vpon the body of S. Sauue, that he owed them nothing. The which he did, but to his coft, for at the fame inftant, he burft afunder in the midft, rendred al his intralls, caft great aboundance of blood forth of his mouth, eyes, eares, and noftrills, and two houres after gaue vp the ghoft. Vincent of Bauuais in the fame hift. l. 24. c. 24.

5. But behould here of a frefher date. In the yeare 1599. the 26. of Nouember, at Grandmount in Flanders, at the figne of the Ship, two gatherers of impoft, giueing vp their accounts before their magiftrats, the one of thé called Peter Clippel, and the other Antonie Haek, this Peter faid, that Antonie had receiued of him twentie french crownes more then he owed him. Which Antonie denied, faying that he was contented to be fried in his owne fat, and to be reduced to afhes, if it were fo as the other faid.

The

The magiſtrates & other which were
preſent, trembling at ſuch terrible ex-
ecrations, withdrew them ſelues deferring this affaire vntill the morrow.
Antonie remayned alone in his chamber, and after he had ſupped merrily
with the hoſte & hoſtis, they bid him
god night. On the morrow morning
about eight a clock, his brother came
to ſpeake with him, and hauing knoc-
ked ſundry times at his chamber
doore, receiuing no anſwere, he cauſed the hoſte to open the doore. Good
God, what a ſpectacle! they had no
ſooner ſet their foote within the
chamber, but that they ſaw a forme
ouerwhelmed and halfe burned, and
the two feete of the man, with ſome
two handfulls of his legges betwixt
the anckles, yet hauing on his ſhoes
and hoſe, all the reſt of his body, and
his apparell entirely burnt and reduced to aſhes : the chamber pot was
alſo melted: the ſtoole likewiſe wheron he had ſet by his beds ſide, was

alſo

also wholy burnt, excepting to endes
only of the feete. His budget also was
there founde, and the gold and siluer
that was therin, all turned to ashes,
saue only the twentie crownes which
he denied to haue receiued, which
were found al whole amidst the ashes.
Of this, information was since taken
by our most Excellent Archdukes of
Brabant, and the whole found to be
most true. Herrie Culens licentiat in
diuinitie, pastor of the said Grandmount, and an eye witnes, in his
booke of New-years gifts. O the terrible iudgement of God against per-
iurers!

6. An hoste in Germanie, hauinge
receiued a great somme of mony *in de-*
positum, of a certaine soldiar who lay
sick in his house, denyed it afterwards
impudently, and said in the presence
of the magistrates, that he would that
the diuell should carry him away, both
in soule and body, if it were true :
which he repeating, the diuell (dispu-
ting

ting against him visible) tooke him,
and lifted him vp in the sight of all,
and was neuer seene after : and whether
thinke you? but to the eternall
fires and flames. This is that which
God threatneth to periured persons in
Malachie 3. 5. and vnto lyers in the
Apoc. 21. 8. This historie is written
by one I. C. German, in the
3. booke of Fairees c. of the malice
of the diuell. And by P. M. Delrio.
lib. 3. of his disq. mag. p. 1. q. 7.
ſ. 1.

7. In Saxonie, a very wealthy maiden
promiſed mariage to a younge
man, of a meaner condition then her
ſelfe, ſwearing that ſhe would that the
diuell ſhould carry her away the day
of her mariage, if ſhe gaue her ſelfe to
any other. Notwithſtanding this, ſhe
married another, and vpon her wedding
day, two diuels, diſguiſed like
gentlemen, came & knockt at the gate
of her houſe, & deſired to ſpeake with
her. Being brought into the chamber
where

where they danced, one of them danced a dance with the bride, and the dance ended, carried her in body and foule vnto hell. The fame author, in the fame place.

8. The yeare a thoufand fix hundred and ninteene, in the month of Auguft, a younge man, a Shoomaker by trade, playinge at Barleduc in Lorraine, towardes the euening, tooke a teftron from the table, & hid the fame within his fhoe. When they came to count, they founde this teftron to be wanting, eache one affuring that he faw it not. At the laft, this fhoomaker being asked, waxt very angrie, and faid. The diuell breake my neck, if I tooke it. No fooner faid, but it was as foone done, for behould at the fame inftant, he fell to the grounde, hauing his head wrefted and turned to his back. His companions affrighted hereat, called his mafter and his miftris, they ftroue to fet his head ftraight, but all in vaine, vntill fuch time as

pul-

pulling off his ſtockinginges to lay
him on the bed, they found the te-
ſtron in his ſhoe, which hauing taken forth, the head ſuffred it ſelfe to
be turned againe vpon the ſhoulder.
A father of the ſocietie of Ieſus was
called for to heare his Côfeſſion, who
founde the youngman ſpeechles, his
eyes open, his head turned vpon his
ſhoulder, all trembling and terrible
gaſtly: and not finding him in eſtate
to be confeſſed, fell to prayers, and
read the Litanies: after he applied
vnto him certaine reliques of S. Ignatius, which hauing done, the younge
man by litle and litle came to himſelfe, and was confeſt. His Confeſſion ended, he ſaid to the father, that
hauing pronounced theſe wordes.
The diuell breake my neck if I tooke it,
he ſaw the diuell enter in forme of a
great maſtife, walkinge like a man v-
pon his hinder feete, hauing thoſe before, like to the handes of a man,
wherwith he caſt him ſelfe vpon him,
threw

threw him to the ground, and brake his neck. All this was certified by the teſtimonie of his companions, who ſubſigned the authenticall atteſtation of this accident, before publique Notaries:and was printed at Tournay the yeare 1620. with approbation. Bleſſed Lord, how dangerous is it, to pronounce ſuch damnable execratiõs,againſt him ſelfe, or againſt others!

§.2. *Of Blaſphemie.*

Blaſphemy,is a contumely pronoũced againſt God himſelfe, or againſt his Saintes : as to ſay. By Gods hart. &c. As true as God:God hath no kind of care ouer me. He ſees me not &c.

Curſed ſhall they be, that ſhall contemne thee, and damned ſhall they be, that ſhall blaſpheme thee. Tobie. 13. 16.

He that ſhall blaſpheme againſt the Holy Ghoſt, he hath not forgeuenes foreuer, but ſhall be guilty of an eternall ſinne. Marc. 3. 29.

Dareſt thou (ſaith S. Ephrem) open thy mouth, and caſt forth oathes and blaſ-

blaſphemies againſt heauen, and dooſt thou not feare, that that burning ſight, which the prophet ſaw, remayne in thy houſe, and cut thee in two, thou who art ſo hardy as to open thy mouth againſt the almightie, vpon whom the Angells, Archangels, Cherubins and Seraphins, dare not lift vp their eyes? S. Ephrem Paræneſi 43.

Euen as there is nothing better then thankſgiuing: euen ſo there is nothing worſe then blaſpheming, ſaith S. Iohn Chriſoſtom Hom. 1. ad pop. Ant. The reaſon is, for that by blaſphemie, God is touched in his proper perſon, and not in the thinges created, as in theft, manſlaughter, and adulterie &c. S. Iohn alſo ſaith, that blaſphemy is proper to the damned. Apoc. 16. 10.

EXAMPLES.

1. In Leuiticus 24. God commanded, that he who had blaſphemed, ſhould be ſtoned to death.

2. Se-

2. Senacharib, kinge of the Aſſyrians, hauing blaſphemed againſt God, was kild by his owne daughters, hauing firſt loſt, a hundred and eightie fiue thouſand of his people, which an Angell cut in peeces in one night. Iſay 37. 4. of Kinges 19.

3. A childe of the age only of fiue yeeres, vomiting forth blaſphemies againſt God betwixt the armes of his father, was ſnatched from him, & carried away by a deuill, in the forme of a black a More, or Ethiopian. S.Greg. Pope, l.4.dial.c.18.

4. Another likewiſe blaſpheming S. Hierom, of the age of twelue yeares old, playing at dice with his father, was carried away by the deuill. S. Ciril of Hieruſ. in his epiſtle of the miracles of S. Hierom, written to S. Aug. and is to be found amongſt the epiſtles of S. Aug. ep. 206.

5. In the territorie of Bullen the fat, two fellowes being at table, the one hauing cut and diſmembred a roſted

ſted Cock, and poured theron a ſpi-
ced ſauce, the other ſaid. Thou haſt ſo
cunningly cut aſunder this Cock, that
S. Peter cannot ioyne him together.
Tut (quoth he that had cut him) God
himſelfe, although he would, can not
make him a liue againe : and thereupon they burſt out into laughing . A
ſtrange caſe ! They ſcarcely had con-
cluded theſe wordes , but that the
Cock ioyned him ſelfe together a-
gaine, ſtood vp in his fathers., and all
aliue , beating his winges, began to
crow, and with beating them in the
platter, ſpatterd the ſauce againſt the
faces of the blaſphemers, who at the
ſelfe ſame inſtant, became couered all
ouer with leproſie , and their whole
poſteritie , were ſince infected alſo
with the ſame . *Bleſſed Petrus Damia-*
nas Cardinall, hath left this in writing,
in his epiſtle to Deſiderius Abbot of mount
Caſſin.l.2. ep. 17.And S. Antoninus doth
relate it likewiſe, in the 2. p. of his Summe
tit.8.c 7.§.3.and Vincent in his hiſtorie.

6. A

6. A wicked man, hauing by mayne force conſtrained an Indian woman to lie with him, behould how at midnight, a tempeſt aroſe with a terrible thunder. The woman ſtricken with feare, cryed out ſaying. O bleſſed virgin Marie keepe me. Which this diſſolut companion hearing, he ſaid vnto her. That it was needles to call vpon our Lady, for that ſhe had not the meanes how to helpe her. Scarce had he vttered the laſt wordes, but a thunderbolt caried him out of the bed into the mideſt of the chamber, & burnt all his ſhirt. The woman lept forth of the bed, and puld him by the feete, but his feete remayned in her hādes, as if they had not held to his body. She endeuored to draw him out of the chāber, but a flame entring at the doore, hindred him that he could not get forth. She cryed for helpe, and the neighbours runne, and finde this accurſed caytiffe ſtarke dead, with his mouth open in a horrible maner, without teeth, without

out tongue, and all his members bru-
sed and grounden in such a sort, that in
pulling of them thovgh neuer so litle,
one deuided and rent them from the
body. *Franciscus Bencius in the Annales
of Col. of Pacen, of the societie of Iesus in
Peru. in the yeare 1588. And Matheus Tim-
pius in the Theatre of the diuine vengance.*

Happie was this poore wenche,
that she called vpon our B. Lady so
luckelie : but cursed was this hoore-
master, and blasphemer, so to haue
mocked her.

§. *3. Of Malediction, and of wicked Imprecation.*

To curse any one, is to wishe him
some euill, as the plague, death, the diuel to take him, or the like.

In the old law, he that cursed father
or mother, was to be put to death. *Le-
uit. 20. 9. & c. 24. 15.*

*The mothers curse, rooteth vp the foun-
dation. Eccles. 3. 11.* that is to, say,
ouerthrowes her whole familie.

Maledictiõ, according to S. Thomas,
is

is of its nature mortall sinne, becaufe it repugneth vnto charitie: and is fo much the more greuous, as the perfon which one curfeth, ought to be more loued and reuerenced, as for example God, Saints, Superiors and our parents. *S.Thom.2.2.q.76.a.3.*

EXAMPLES.

1. Surius vpon the life of S. Zenobius martyr, writeth, that a mother angrie with her childe (who afflicted with a terrible ague, asked her drinke vnto the fourth time in one night) faid vnto her childe in choller, in giuinge him the goblet. Hould, drinke, and fwallow downe the diuell and all together: & at the fame inftant, the childe was poleffed of the diuell.

He writeth likewife of another mother, who being beaten of her children, fent them all vnto the diuell: and that forthwith they were feafed and poffeffed, in fuch fort, that they fell a
bytinge,

bytinge , and tearing of one another.
The mother repenting her of her faɛt
(albeit a panim)brought them vnto S.
Zenobius, who by the ſigne of the holy Croſſe deliuered them,and baptiſed
them,together with their mother,and
all the houſhold. Ioannes Archipreſbi-
ter Aretin. in the life of S. Zenobius,
and Surius 25. of May.

3. S. Aug. in his 22. booke of the
cittie of God, *& de diuerſ. ſer.* 94. writeth, that a certaine woman in Capa-
docia, hauing ſeauen ſonnes , and
three daughters, was ſtricken of her
eldeſt ſonne, with the conſent of all
the others . Which ſhe ſupported ſo
impatiently,that ſhe went to Church,
to curſe them vpon the holy Font,
wherein they had bene baptiſed. As
ſhe was in the way,the diuel appeared
vnto her, in the likenes of her huſ-
bands brother; who hauing aked her
whither ſhe went, ſhe anſwered that
ſhe went to curſe her ſonne . The diuel tould her , that ſhe ſhould curſe
them

them all . When ſhe was come to
the place of the Font, all in a furie ſhe
touſed her haire, and diſcoueringe her
breaſtes,beſought God that he would
ſende vpon her children the puniſhment of Cain , making them all trembling and rogues. This being ſaid, ſhe
retourned , and behould inſtantly her
eldeſt ſonne was ſtricken with a trembling of all his members ; and before
the end of the yeare , all the others
were in the like perplexitie ; The mother ſeeing the vnfortunat diſaſter of
her children , conceiued ſo great ſorrow therfore,that ſhe hunge and ſtran-
gled herſelfe, her children became va-
gabound rogues here and there about
the contrie,wherof two bretheren and
ſiſters were ſeene of S. Aug. at Hippo,
who healed them at the reliques of S.
Steuen. Learne here, you fathers and
mothers,to reſtraine your choller, and
to bridle the intemperance of your
tongue,that you become not the cauſe
of ſuch diſaſter vnto your children.
4. That

4. That famous poſeſſed perſon at Laon in Lannois in France, anno 1566. fell ſhe not into the power of the diuell, thorough the wicked imprecation of her parents, which hath likewiſe hapned to ſo many others?

§. 4. *Of contumelious wordes.*

To giue one ſome euill name, or to obiect vnto him ſome vice, ether of body or minde, as, to cal him lyer, dolt, theiſe, drunkard, or the like, is a contumelie, which of its nature is a mortall ſinne.

Whoſoeuer ſhall ſay to his brother. Thou foole, ſhall be guiltie of the hell of fire. Mat. 5. 23.

And the Apoſtle S. Paul Rom. 1. 30. rancketh the cōtumelious, with thoſe that doe deſerue death.

EXAMPLES.

1. As the holy prophet Eliſeus went vp to Bethell, certaine children came foorth of the cittie, who ſeeing

D   him

him with his head balde, mockt him, saying. Goe vp bald-pate, which the Saint hearing, he turned him towards them, and curſed them, and behould at the ſelfe ſame inſtant, two Beares which came forth of the forreſt, ran vpon theſe children, and deuoured of them, fortie two. *4. Reg. 2.*

2. The Chamberlaiu of the Emperor Valens, hauing vomited forth a number of iniurious & contumelious wordes againſt S. Aphrates, went to prepare the Emperors bayne, but he was come no ſooner in, but he became ſtark madde, and caſt him ſelfe into the ſcalding water, wherin he dyed. *Theodoret. l. 4. hiſt. eccleſ. c. 26. Card. Barron. tom. 4. of his eccleſ. Annales, in the yeare of our Lord 370.*

3. Iohn Aratus, a great fauorer of the Iewes in Lacedemonia, after he had diſgorged a many of contumelies againſt S. Nicon, was in the night time whipt in his ſleepe of two venerable old men: who hauing ſharply rebuked him

him for his sinne, cast him into a
deepe prison. Hereupon he awaked,
and found him selfe taken with a
stronge ague, and knowing that this
was a punishment from God, arose,
and went and sought forth the Saint,
and asked him forgiuenes. S. Nicon
forgaue him, but withall told him,
that God had decreed to take him
out of this life, and that therfore he
should dispose him selfe for his death.
Hereupon he returned to his house,
layes him downe on his bed, and
three dayes after gaue vpp the ghost.
Baron. tom. 10. of his annales, anno 982.

See you not by these examples, that
contumelie is a great sinne! You shall
then be chasticed, ether in this life or
in the other (you fathers and mothers)
who hearing your children to pronounce the like wordes, doe not punish nor reprehend them:yea, doe oft-
times excite them to vtter them by
your euill example.

§.5.Of Detraction.

Contumelie takes away the honor
of persons present, but Detraction takes away the good name of the absent.
Now to detract in that which may
diminish notably the renowne of
another, is mortall sinne, as saith S.
Thomas 2. 2. q.7. a. 2.and much more
greuous then to steale his goods.

Haue care of a good name (saith the
wiseman) *for this shall be more perma-*
nent to thee,then a thousand treasures pre-
tious and great. Eccles. 4.1. 15.

Better is a good name, then much ri-
ches: aboue siluer, and gold,good grace. *Pro.22.1. Detractors are odible to God,*
and men. Rom. 1. 30. Pro.24. 9.

Detractors were of old represented
by those Locusts which S. Iohn saw,
hauing the faces of men, and teeth of
Lyons . *Apoc.* 9.3. for as much as vnder pretext of humanitie and compassion, they teare with faire teeth, the
good renowne of other persons.

They haue againe bene represented,
by

by the fourth terrible beaſt which Daniel ſaw, which hauing teeth of iron, deuoured al he met with all, trampling the reſt vnderfoote. *Dan. 7.*

By the Crow, which flying forth of the Arke, went and fell vpon the carions. Gen. 8.

The ſcripture doth compare them alſo, to open ſepulchers, from whence cometh forth nothinge but filthe and abhomination. psl. 13. 3.

To Serpents, which giue their venim in ſecret. Eccl. 10. 11. psl. 139.

They be compared alſo vnto hogges, which tread vnderfoote the faire flowers, and haue their ſnowt alwaies groueling in the durt.

To flies, which leauing the faireſt parts of the body, ſetle them ſelues no where elſe but vpon the ſcabbes.

To the Hen, which ſcraping in the dirt, caſteth from her the pearles and diamonds, and taketh nothinge but wormes and vermin.

To the Spider, for that inſteede of

D 3   draw-

drawing of honnie from the flowers
of virtues of their neighbour, they
draw venim, wherwith they kil them
selues and others.

Is it any maruell then if Dauid said.
*One secretly detractinge from his neigh-
bour, him did I persecute.* psal. 100. 5.

S. Peter was wont to say, that the
mansleyar, and the detractor, were e-
quall in malice, according as S. Clement recounteth; *in his Epistle to S. Iames, and by Gratian de penit. dist.1.*

What doth the detractor meritt
(saith S. Basill) and he that harkneth
to him? And he answereth. They must
be both chased and banished away,
from the conuersations of others.
Reg. 26.

He that detracteth, and he that
harkneth, doe both of them beare the
diuel; the one in his mouth; the other
in his eares. *S. Bern. in serm.*

And it is to be noted, that in this
sinne, as also in theft, it sufficeth not
that one confes him, vnles withall he
make

make reſtitution.

EXAMPLES.

1. Marie the ſiſter of Moyſes, ha-uing detracted from her brother, our Lord God, was ſo angrie therat, that the cloude which couered the Taber-nacle, withdrew it ſelfe, and Marie became inſtantly, couered all ouer with leproſie. *Num. 12.* The cloude (ſaith Origen) withdrew it ſelfe: to ſignifie, that the grace of the Holie Ghoſt, withdrawes it ſelfe from the detractor, and that his ſoule remaynes all full of the leproſie of ſinne. *Hom. 7. vpon Num.*

2. At another time the Iſraelites detracted Moyſes, and God puniſhed them by the meanes of Serpéts, which deuoured the greateſt part of them. *Num. 21.*

3. Core, Dathan, and Abiron, did likewiſe detract Moyſes, and within a while after, were ſwallowed vpp of
D 4 the

the earth, and descended quick into hell: and two hundred and fiftie of their complices, were consumed with a fire which came forth frō our Lord. *Numb. 16.*

4. A detractor of S. Vincent Ferrier after his death, albeit he had satisfied in the fire of Purgatorie, yet could not enter into heauen, till first he had bene to make restitution to the good name of the Saint, to those before whom he had taken it away: as him selfe said vnto S. Vincent, appearing vnto him a litle before he went to heauen. *S. Vincent serm. Dom. in albis.*

5. Donatus an African by nation, & a priest of Milan, setting at the table with certaine religious, began to detract S. Ambrose who whas dead: & at the same time, almightie God strook his tongue with such a soare, as laid him on his bed, and in his sepulcher.

6. A while after, at Carthage, Mauranus bishop of Bolitan, did as much: and was also punished with the

the ſame chaſticement, and ſelfe ſame
death. Paulinus vpon Baron. tom. 5.
anno 397.

7. A certaine detracting Prieſt falling ſick, became as out of his witts
before his death, tearing him ſelfe, &
cutting out his owne tongue. Thomas
à Cantip. l. 2. ap. c. 37. p. 3.

Loe the effects of the threatning of
God againſt detractors, in the 24. 21.
of the Prouerbes, where he ſaith.
*With detractors medle not, becauſe their
perdition ſhall ſodenlie riſe, and the ruine
of both, who knoweth?* that is to ſay,
of the detractor, and of him that
harkneth to him.

§. 6. *of Lying.*

To lye, is to ſpeake againſt ones
thought, or to ſpeake otherwiſe then
one thinketh: which neuer is permitted, no not to conſerue a whole cittie,
nor which is more, not to conſerue the
whole worlde. *S. Aug. l. de mendacio ad
Conſentium c. 3. Innocentius 3. c. ſuper eo.
de vſura:* & it is the common opiniō of

all the holie fathers and Doctors, *in 3. d. 37. & 38.*

When the diuell speaketh a lie, saith our Lord, *he speaketh of his owne, because he is a lyer, and the father thereof.* Iohn 8. 44. And Dauid saith. *Thou wilt destroy at all that speake lies.* Psal. 5. 7.

Six thinges there are which our Lord hateth, and the seauenth his soule detesteth. Loftie eyes, a lying tongue, handes that shed innocent blood. Pro. 6. 16.

The mouth that lyeth killeth the soule. Sap. 1. 11.

A false witnes shall not be vnpunished, and he that speaketh lyes shall not escape. Pro. 19. 5.

To all lyers, their part shall be in the poole burning with fire & brimstone, which is the second death. *Apoc.* 21. 8.

The holie fathers affirme no lesse, S. Basil saith. The most mightie thinge of all is the truth : and the extremitie of malice, is lying, *In proemio de Spir. Sanct.* And in another place he saith,
that

that lyinge is the proper fruit of the diuell. *ep. 63. & 79.*

And B. Ceſarius ſaith, that euery
lyer, hath within him the malignant
ſpirit. *Hom. 16.*

S. Hierom ſaith, that a virgin eſtee-
mes it ſacriledge for to lie.*ep. 7. ad Latã.*

Haſt thou heard, thou wretched
lyer, the orracles of holie ſcriptures,
and doctors of the Church? Heare
now then the examples that follow.

EXAMPLES.

1. A certaine woman accuſed
wrongfully to haue committed adul-
tery with a young man, was taken
with him, and both put vpon the tor-
ture. The young man not able to ſupport the paines, confeſt to haue committed the fact, which yet notwithſtanding he had not done. But ſhe, not
able to lift vp her handes which the
hangman had tyed, lifted vp her eyes
to heauen, with riuers of teares, and

said . Thou art witnes my Lord Iesus
Chrift (thou who fearcheft the reynes
and hart) that I will not deny the adulterie for feare to die, but that I will
not lie, for feare of offending thee.
But thou o wretch (quoth fhe, turning her felfe to the younge man, who
for feare of the torments, had tould a
lie) if thou doe haften thee for to pe-
rifh, yet why wilt thou kill two inno-
cents? I am ready to die, but not as an
adultres, I will carry myne innocencie together with me . To conclude,
fhe was condemned with the young
man to haue her head cut off; At the
firft ftroke that the hangman gaue to
the young man, his head was deuided from his body: but to her, feauen blowes were giuen, and yet the
fword did her no hurt : which the
Emperor feeinge, he knew the innocencie of the woman, and therupon fet her at libertie . See you,
how lyinge was the caufe of the
young mans death, and how main-
tayning

tayning of the truth . gaue life vnto this good woman ? This hiſtorie
is related by S. Hierom , *ep. 45. ad
Innocent.*

S. Anthimus Biſhop of Nicomedia,
during the perſecution of the Emperor Maximian , was ſought for by the
Seargeants;He ſeing that they ſought
for him , receiued them , and treated
them right curteouſly, making them a
good dinner: and in the end ſaid vnto
them , that he was he whom they
ſought for. They not able ſufficiently
to admire his charitie , ſaid that they
would make report to the Emperor,
that they could not finde him . No
(quoth the B. Saint) it is not lawfull
for Chriſtians to lie, to ſaue the life of
whom ſoeuer : and this being ſaide,
put him ſelfe into their handes , and
after diuers great torments,endured
death . Surius 27. of Aprill , out of
Metaphraſt.

O great Saint, who had rather that
his body ſhould be kild by the handes
of

of the hangman , then conseruing his
body, to kill his soule by a lye.

§. 7. *Of songes, and of dishonest wordes.*

Fornication and all vncleanes , let it not so much as be named amongst you, as it becometh Saintes , or filthines , or foolish talke, or scurrillitie. Ephes.5.3.4.

Theodoret infers from this prohibition of the Apostle, how execrable fornication is, sith he will not that it be so much as spoken of, nor that it be at all remembred.

*Be not seduced , euill communications corrupt good maners.*1. *Cor.*15. 34. And S. Clement Pope , forbids the same amongst Christians. *l.5.const.Apost.*

Dishonest talke , saith S. Isidore, hath oftimes more force to gayne harts, and to perswade them to vice, then the sight , then euill example, and then all other deceits and allurements.

Euen as a stone, saith S. Basill, cast
into

into the water of a Cesterne, doth not
only stir that parte of the water which
it toucheth, but also doth stir vp cir-
cles, which continually multiplied, arriue at the last to the edge and brimme: euen so lasciuious talke , falling
into a chast hart and soule, as it were
within a pure water, doe excite diuers
dishonest thoughtes , which multi-
plying them selues, make the soule to
be all to tossed with the waues of vo-
luptuousnes , and carnall thoughtes.
lib. de vera virginitate.

The philosophers say, that the
worde, is the shadowe of the action,
and deed. Now when one seeth some
shadow approache him , he may well
iudge that the body is not far off: euen
so maist thou say , that from whence
dishonest wordes proceede, the worke
of the flesh is not far. *Plutarch. in the
treatise how children are to be nourished.*

If a dishonest worde hath so much
force of it selfe to spoyle a soule, what
will it haue then sunge and pronounced

ced with a sweet inchantment of the
voice?

The sweetnes of the voice, saith S.
Basil, renders the soule wholie encli-
ning to lubricitie. It is better, saith S.
Cyprian, to heare the venemous
whistle of a Basiliske, then to heare
the wanton and lasciuious voice of a
woman.

EXAMPLES.

1. The sister of B. Petrus Damia-
nus Cardinall, was in purgatorie fifteene dayes, for hauinge conceiued
pleasure in hearing certaine maides to
sing as they were a dancing. Flor. Har-
lemus Carthus. Institut. Christiana l.
2. c. 25.

S. Bernard, being yet but a younge
youth in the worlde, as soone as he
heard any filthie word to be pronounced, he felt the same in such sort, that
for very shame al his face was set a fire,
as if had receiued some box on the
eare. Which his playfellowes perceiuing,

uinge, as soone as euer they saw him come, they said one vnto another. Lets hould our peace, loe where Bernard comes. *Ribad and Surius the 20. of May* The like is read of B. Lewis of Gonzaga of the societie of Iesus.

S. Edmund Archbishop of Canterburie, studying at Paris, and walking on a day in the Clarkes medow with his companions, who sunge there a number of songes, he went aside from them, not able to suffer them. Then our Lord appeared vnto him, in the forme of a faire childe, such as the espouse doth paint him in the Canticles. *White and ruddy, chosen amongst thousands,* and said vnto him with a smyling countenance. I salute thee my wel beloued. S. Edmond was astonished at the first, and waxt ashamed at those wordes; But our Lord said vnto him; Doost thou not know me? I set hard by thee euery day in the schole: and then made him both to see & to reade, that which was written in his in his fore-head ; and he perceiued written in letters of gold. *Iesus of Nazareth, kinge of the Iewes.* *Surius tom.6. Ribad, 6. Nou.*

4. S. Vallery Abbot, returninge vpon a day into his Abby in the winter time, entred with his people into a Priests house to warme him selfe: as he approached to the fire, the Priest and the Mayor of the place, began to vtter great store of dishonest wordes; from which they not desistinge for ought the Saint could say vnto them, he went forth of the place, shakinge off against them the dust of his shoes. And behould, at the same instant the Priest became blinde, and the Mayor was stricken with a shamfull disease. They perceiuing that this was in punishment of their euill tongues, ran after the Saint, and besought him to returne againe: but he refused. Thus the Priest remained blinde his whole life, and all the members of the other rotted by litle and litle, and in the end

dyed

dyed moſt miſerably . *Surius vpon the life of S. Vallery. 1. of Aprill.*

Durannus , of an Abbot made a Biſhop, was diuers daies in purgatory, for hauing ſomtimes tould tales to excite and make others to laugh : and could not get thence , till firſt ſeauen religious perſons had kept ſilence for him , for the ſpace of ſeauen dayes. Vincent Bellouac. ſpec. hiſt. l. 26. c. 5. Now if one goe to purgatory for light wordes and only of laughter, what puniſhment then doe diſhoneſt wordes deſerue?

5. The very Pagans are aſhamed to ſpeake of diſhoneſt things: for Agellius a Roman hiſtorian, writeth of Socrates, that finding him ſelfe enforced to mixe amidſt his diſcourſe ſome one point but litle honeſt, he couered his face for very ſhame . O Chriſtian , learne honeſtie of this Pagan: & you aboue all, fathers and mothers.

Hitherto haue we ſpoken of ſinne in generall, mortall, veniall, ſinnes of
thought,

thought, & of the tongue. As touching
that which followes after of sinnes of
worke, to the end that this litle dif-
course do not enlarge it selfe too lōge,
I wil contēt my selfe to speake of capitall, to wit, of those which are the
springe and fountaine of all. Saue only
before I come therto, I wil insert this
alone.

THE V. CHAPTER.

Of the sinnes of parents and their children.

L Et not fathers and mothers thinke
it strange, if I addresse my selfe
more oft and more particularly to thē
in this litle discourse, and that I set before them particularly, this litle chapter: *sith all the good or euill fortune of a
common welth, proceedeth from no other
cause, then from their good institution, or
negligence to frame their children as they
ought, and to bringe them vp in the feare
of God. See the last chap. of the 3. booke of
the life of our B. Father Ignatius, by Ribadeneira.*   As

As God hath commanded children, to honor, loue and helpe their parēts. (Exod.20.11.) and to obey them in all that is reaſon, ſo will he, that parents loue their children (Eccl. 7. 25. 26.) nouriſhing them, and bringing them vp according to their power and qualitie, in all that which is needfull for them, as well for body, as for ſoule. *Et Epheſ.6.4.1.Tim.5.8.S.Chriſt.to.6.ho.27*

§.1.*Of the negligence of parents to correct their children from their tendre youth, and to inſtruct them in matters of faith, and of good maners.*

Can I conceale from Abraham the thinges that I will doe, wheras he ſhall be into a nation great, and very ſtronge, and in him are to be bleſſed, all the nations of the earth? For I knowe that he wil cōmand his children, and his houſe after him, that they keepe the way of the Lord, and doe iudgement and iuſtice. Gen.18.18.

Forget not the wordes that thine eies haue ſeene, and let them not fall out of thy hart,

hart, all the dayes of thy life: thou shalt teach them thy sonnes and thy nephewes. Deut. 4. 9. And in the 11. Chapter. *Teache your children my commandements, when thou sittest in thy house, and walkest on the way, and lyest downe and risest vp, that thy dayes may be multiplied, and the dayes of thy children. Deut.11.19.*

Hast thou children? instruct them, and bow them from their childhood. Ecc. 7.25.

The notable negligence of parents to see that their children know and vnderstand the contents of the Creed, the Pater, Aue, Commandements, & the vse of the holy Sacraments, is mortall sinne, saith Nauar. Man. cap. 14. num. 17.

He that spareth the rod, hateth his childe, but that loueth him, doth instantly nurture him. Pro. 13. 24.

The childe that is left to his owne will, confoundeth his mother. Pro.29.15.

An vntamed horse, becommeth stubburne, and a dissolute childe wil become heady. Pamper thy sonne, and he will make thee

thee aſraid: play with him he will make thee ſorrowfull. Laugh not with him, leſt thou be ſorrie, and at the laſt thy teeth ſhal be on edge. Giue him not power in his youth, & contemne not his cogitations. Curbe his neck in youth, and knock his ſides whiles he is a childe, leſt peshaps he be hardned and beleeue thee not. O beautifull ſentence! Eccl. 30. 8.

He that loueth ſonne or daughter aboue me, is not worthie of me. Mat 10. 37.

If the childe by the conniuencie or winking of the parents, come to fall into any ſinne, his parents ſhall be anſwerable for his ſoule. *S. Clement ſucceſſor to S. Peter. conſt. Apoſt. l. 4. c. 20.*

S. Baſil ſaith, that children are like vnto ſoft wax, wherein one printeth what he liſt, and with the ſelfe ſame fingars, one formes an Angell or a deuill. *Reg. fuſ. diſp. interrogat. 7.*

Thoſe parents (ſaith Saint Chriſoſtome) which care not to correct their children (I teli them the truth and without paſſion) are more wicked

then

their paracides, for thefe doe but feperat the bodie from the foule, but fuch parents by their conniuence, fend both the bodies and foules of their children, to eternall flames : and he that is kild as touching the body, muft of neceffitie haue once died, but thefe poore children, might haue efcaped the fire of hell, if the negligence of their fathers and mothers had not fent them thither. *l. 3. aduerf. vituperat vita monaft.*

This is that which the wifeman faith. Withdraw not difcipline from a childe; thou fhalt ftrike him with the rod, and deliuer his foule from hell. Pro. 23. 13. 14.

EXAMPLES.

1. Helie the high Prieft (albeit a Saint as S. Hierom writeth in c. 6. ad Ephef.) not hauing reprehended his children, as he ought to haue done, for their finnes of Gluttonie, and Lubricitie, God called the prophet Samuell,

muell, and said vnto him. *Behould I doe
a thinge in Israel, which whosoeuer shall
heare, both his eares shall tingle. In that
day will I raise vp against Helie, all thinges which I haue spokē touching his house,
I will begin and accomplish it, for I haue
foretold him, that I would iudge his house
for euer, because of iniquitie, for that he
knew that his sonnes did wickedly, and
hath not correĉted thē.1.Reg.3 11.&c.* And
what betided then vnto him? 1. He became blinde. 2. His soule melted. 3.
The life of his posterity was shortned.
4. He lost the battaile against his enemies, thirtie thousand of his foote
men, remayning slaine vpon the place.
5. The Arke of God was taken and carried from them. 6. His two sonnes,
Ophin and Phinees, were likewise killed the same day. 7. He hearing the
newes, fell backward and broke his
neck. 8. His daughter in law, at the
rehearsall of so strange a fortune, was
deliuered before her time, and so died.
How many mischifes doth the conni-

E   uence

uence of a father, trayle after it!

.2. You haue feene a litle before, a childe of fiue yeares old, borne away by the diuels forth of his fathers armes, for his blafphemies: (c. 4. §. 2. Ex. 3.) what a hart breaking was it to this father. to fee his childe carried to hell, from whence he might haue deliuered him, with three or four ierkes of a rod?

3. S. Auguftine, preaching to the religious of the defert, tould them, that that very day wherin he preached vnto thē, the fonne of Cyrillus, one of the moft notable bourgeffes of Hippo, hauing bene alwaies ouer well beloued of his father, yea more then God, and therfore left to all kinde of libertie, ether to fay, or to doe whatfoeuer he lift: after he had wafted all his wealth in diffolutenes, cominge drunke in a doores, had forced his mother great with childe, and ftroue to violate one of his fifters, had kild his father, and deadly wounded his two fifters.

sisters. *Aug. ser. 33. ad fratres in eremo.*
Deare God, what greater disaster could
possibly befall vnto a familie!

4. A certaine woman, damned for
hauing taught her daughter all sortes
of mondanitie, appeared to S. Bridgit,
as coming forth of some darksome
lake, with her hart torne forth of her
bellie, hir lippes cut off, her nose all
eaten, her eyes puld out of her head,
hanging downe vpon her cheekes, her
breast couered with great wormes, and
with most fearfull and lamentable
cries and lamentations, complaining
of her daughter, and saying as if she
had spoken to her. Vnderstand my
daughter and venimous Newte, accursed be I, that euer I was thy mother,
for as often as thou doost imitate and
follow the workes of my wicked cu-
stomes, that is to say the sinnes which
my selfe haue taught thee, so oft my
paine is renewed. S. Bridgit in her reuelations l. 6. cap. 52.

5. A certaine person, saw vpon a
day

day hell open, and in the midſt of the
flames the father and the ſonne, which
bitterly curſed one another: the father
ſaid. Curſed be thou my ſonne, who
art cauſe of my damnation, for to en-
riche thee, I haue done a thouſand in-
iuſtices. The ſonne on the contrary
ſaid; It is thou curſed father, who art
the cauſe of my damnatiõ, becauſe for
feare to diſpleaſe thee, I haue remayned in the worlde. *Dioniſ. Carib. l. de*
4. noiuſ. art. 42. towards the end. Loe
here a goodly looking glaſſe, for thoſe
which hinder their children to enter
into religion, principally when one
ſeeth that God doth call them.

6. A certaine crack-rope led to the
galloes, cald for his father, and making as if he would tel him ſomewhat
in ſecret, approached with his mouth
vnto his eare, and then tore it off with
his teeth, ſaying. Auant wretch, if
thou hadſt whipt me in my youth, I
had not now bene where I am. *S. Ber-*
nardinus ſer. 17. de euang. æterno.

7. An-

7. Another called Lucretius, being likewiſe led vnto the galloes, and hauing called for his father to bid him farwel, tore off his noſe with his teeth, ſaying vnto him as the other did. *Boetius de diſciplin. ſcholarium. Ioan. Hieroſo. ſerm. 16.*

8. Pretextat a Roman Lady, by the commandement of Hymettius her husband, ouncle to the virgin Euſtochium, for hauing changed the habit and dreſſe of this mayden, and renewed her head-geare, after the model of ſuch as were ſecular, contrary to the minde both of the virgin, and the deſire of her mother Paula, ſaw the ſame night in her ſleepe, her Angell addreſſe him ſelfe vnto her, threatning her with a terrible voice. Dareſt thou to touche the heade of the virgin of God, with thy prophane and ſacriledgious handes? the which ſhall wither from this very houre, and fiue monthes hence, thou ſhalt be carried into hell: and if thou perſeuer in thy ſinne, thou ſhalt

be

be depriued both of thy husband and
thy children altogether. The succes
wherof enfued in ordre, for fodaine
death, made euident the late repentance of this wretched womā. S. Hier.
l. 2. ep. 15.

All thefe examples, proue they not
apparantly, that the negligence and
conniuence of the parents, is both
their owne, and their childrens ruine?
Thus the Ape, making ouermuch of
her litle ones, doth ftifele them.

§. 2. *Of the finnes of Children, towards*
their parents.

The firft commandement of the fecond table is. *Honor thy father and thy*
mother, that thou mayeft be long liued
vpon the earth. Exod. 20. 12.

Three obligations are comprifed in
this commandement. The firft, to loue,
honor, and reuerence our parents. The
fecond, to obey them in that which is
reafon. The third, to afift and fuccour
them in their neceffities. *S. Tho. 2. 2.*
q. 101. a. 2.

Cur-

Cursed be he that honoreth not his father and mother. *Deut* 27. 16.

If *a man beget a stubburne and froward sonne*, that will not heare the commandments of his father and mother, and being chastned, contemneth to be obedient, they shall take him and bringe him to the ancients of his cittie, and to the gate of iudgment, and shall say to him. This our sonne, is froward and stubburne, he contemneth to heare our admonitions, he giueth himselfe to commessation, and to ryot and banquetinges. The people of the cittie shall stone him, and he shall die, that you may take away the euill out of the midest of you, and all Israel hearing it may be afraid. *Deut*. 21. 18.

He that curseth his father and mother, his lampe shall be extinguished in the middest of darknes. *Pro*. 20. 20.

He that curseth his father and mother, dying let him die. *Exod*. 21. 17.

The eye that scorneth his father, and that despiseth the trauaile of his mother in bearing him, let the Rauens of the

E 4   tor-

torrent pick it out , *and the younge of the Eagle eate it. Pro 30. 17.*

It is moſt certaine, that whoſoeuer curſeth father or mother , or vttereth againſt them iniurious threatninges, or ſmiteth them , or wiſheth them dead, or pronoũceth wordes which of them ſelues may greatly put them into choler; or being in honor, deſpiſeth his father or his mother that are poore, or ſhall accuſe them before a Iudge , or ſhall not obey them in a point of importance touching the gouerment of their famillie , eſpeciallie if it be done by contempt or ſelfe opinion, or doth not aſiſt them in their great neceſſitie, offendeth God mortallie . *Toletus l. 5. Inſtruct. c. 1. S. Tho. 22. q. 101. art. 4. ad 4. Silueſt. verbo filius Nauar. c. 14. n. 11.*

EXAMPLES.

1. Cain was curſed, and all his poſteritie , becauſe he mockt his father Noe. *Gen. 19.* nor would receiue the
in-

inftructiōs which he gaue him to ferue
God. *Lactuntius.*

2. Efau, for takinge a wife againſt
the will of father and mother. *Gen.*
26. 34.

3. Ruben fell from his birth-right,
for hauinge wrought ſhame to his father Iacob. *Gen. 49. 3. 4.*

4. Abſalon was hanged in a chaine
made of his owne haire, and perced
with three ſtrokes of a ſpeare, becauſe
he had taken armes againſt his father
Dauid. *2. Reg. 18. 9. & 14.*

5. The yeare of our Lord 873. and
the firſt yeare of Iohn the 8. Pope, in
the aſſemblie of Biſhops and Lords
which was made in Francfort, by the
commandement of Lewis kinge of
Germany. Charles his younger ſonne,
was thorough the iuſt iudgment of
God, poſeſt of the diuell, for that he
had conſpired againſt his father, as he
him ſelfe confeſt being deliuered, ſaying. That as oft as he conſented to
this deliberation, ſo oft was he ſeaſed

E 5   on

on by the diuell. *Taken out of the An-*
nales of France by Pitheus , and of Amo-
nius l. 5. c. 30. and of Card. Baron , the
yeare aboufaid.

6. A boy of eighteene yeares old
being hanged , at the fame inftant a
beard grew forth of his chinne al gray,
and his haire alfo became white, God
manifefting by this miracle, till what
age he fhould haue liued, if he had not
bene difobedient to father and mother . *S. Bernardinus to. 2. dom. 40.*
fer. 17.

7. A Young maried man, feing his
father cominge, hid a rofted Goofe,
which he had made to be fet on the table , to the end he fhould haue none
thereof, but bidding it afterwards to
be fet on the borde , as he went a-
bout to breake it vp, a Toade appeared vpon the fame, which leapt vpon
his face, and ftuck faft therto in fuch
maner , that it was neuer poffible to
pluck it away, vntill fuch time as he
was dead : and which was yet more,
what-

whatſoeuer the Toade endured in his
body , the miſerably man did endure
the ſame alſo. This was to preache
without ſpeaking a worde,to all thoſe
that ſaw the ſame, the honor and affection which children owe vnto their
parents. *S.Bon.l.de 10.precept ſer.5.Tho.
a Cantip. l. 2.ap.c. 7.art. 4.*

8. A certaine marchant, not furnis-
hing two of his ſonnes with as much
mony as they deſired, was ſet vpon by
them as he went to a certaine faire in
Germanie, and was ſlaine. And hauing made them ſelues riche by meanes of his horſe and of his purſe, they
went to the Tauerne to play who
ſhould haue the whole.As the one ſaw
that he loſt all , in a rage he puld out
his poyniard , and threw the ſame a-
gainſt the floore , ſaying to God. If
could pierce thee, I would doe it . At
this helliſh worde , the earth and hell
did both open at the ſame inſtant, and
ſwallowed him vp all aliue. The other
more then halfe dead , departed that

houſe, went to Geneua, preſented him ſelfe vnto the Magiſtrates, confeſt his faƈt, and was put to death. *Ioannes Honthemius Leod. S. Hieronimi relig.*

9. A young gentleman natiue of Fleſche in France, ſeing that his father ſent him not as much mony as he would ſpend, wrote a letter vnto him full of reproaches, contumelies, and greuous curſes. But he had no ſooner ſent the ſame, but that he founde him ſelfe ſtricken with ſo great a deafnes, that he could not heare ſo much as the noiſe of a Canon; He tried the art and remedies of the moſt part of the Phiſitiens and Doƈtors that were in France, but all in vaine. At laſt he aduiſed him ſelfe, to haue recourſe to our B. Lady of Loretto; He went then, and hauing made a generall Confeſſion, he continued ſo nine daies, with a great deale of deuotion. The night of the feaſt of the Aſſumption, as he was laid in his bed, behould how he ſaw a venerable and dreadfull matrone enter
his

his chamber, accompanied with his father and mother, and asked them if that were their sonne; who answered, I. She asked them moreouer, if they were willinge to haue him healed; They answered, that they had no other desire. Then approaching to the beds side, she put one of her fingars within the eare of the young gentleman, and puld out a paper, which she shewed vnto him. He read it, and saw, that they were all the wordes of his letter, and then she presently disappeared, he finding him selfe entirely healed of his deafnes, saue only a paine of that eare, from whence the paper was taken forth, which lasted him diuers daies. Then he arose, and went and sought forth presently, father Henrie Campege of the societie of Iesus, his Confessar, who led him to the holy chamber of the virgin, and made him there to sweare, that the matter had passed, as I haue here put it downe: and the one & the other gaue thankes to to God, and to the holy virgin Marie. This hapned in the yeare 1613. and was related vnto me, by the selfe same father Henrie, the yeare 1616. Is not this a very notable and rare example?

10. A young youth, vpon a day caſt his mother forth of a Chariot with a kick or blow of his foote ; Within a while after, he had ſome quarell with his maſter, who without any reaſon, cut off one of his feete. Whereof a holy Ermite complaining to God, an Angell came and tould him, that God had permitted the ſame, in puniſhment of a blow of the foote, which he had ſomtimes giuen to his mother. *Raderus in virid. ſanct. in anot. ad vitam S. Fphrem, ex Ioſepho Balardino l. 3. c. 47.* O God, how iuſt and admirable are thy iudgments, againſt rebellious children towards their parents?

§. 3. *Other conſiderations for the fathers of families, touching the gouuerment of their houſhold: and particularly towards their men and women ſeruants.*

Euen

Euen as God commandeth, men & women seruants to obey their masters and mistrisses, in all that which is reason, *with feare and tremblinge, in the simplicitie of hart, as to Christ: not seruing to the eye, as it were pleasing men, but as the seruants of Christ, doing the will of God from the hart.* Ephes. 6. 5. euen so will he, that masters and mistresses haue care of them, as well in that which concernes the body, as the soule.

And as touching the body. First giuing them conuenient nourishment, and paying them faithfully, and with the soonest, for their seruice: for it is a sinne which cryeth for vengeance from heauen, to defraude the labourer of his hyer. Hearken to S. Iames. *You haue stored to your selues wrath in the last dayes, behould the hire of the workmen that haue reaped your fieldes, which is defrauded of you, cryeth, and their cry hath entred into the eares of the Lord of Saboth.* c 5. 4. Secondly, not ouer-

burde-

burdening them, nor moleſting them. Thirdly, if they be ſick, nether turning them away, nor ſending them vnto the hoſpitall, but keeping them with them, and hauing a care of them, after the example of the Centurion, with all charitie, as members of Ieſus Chriſt, and their Chriſtian brothers.

As touching the ſoule, inſtructing them, or cauſing them to be inſtructed in pointes of faith, and not to diſſemble hearing them ſweare or ſpeake vnſeemely wordes, or ſeeing them commit any kinde of ſinne.

2. Making them to hante the Sacraments, heare Maſſe, and as much as they may Catechiſing, or ſermons.

3. Recommending often vnto them, the examine of the Euening, and neuer to goe to bed, nor yet to riſe, without thanking and praying to God, in the maner that we ſhall ſhew in the booke enſuing.

Loe here the duties of good and Catholique maſters, for as the Apoſtle ſaith.

faith. *If any man haue not care of his own, and especially of his domesticalls, he hath denied the faith, and is worse then an infidell.* 1. *Tim.* 5. 8.

EXAMPLES.

1. The good Centurion of Caphernaum, albeit a Panim, hauing his seruant lying sick, so far was he from turning him out of doores, that he went him selfe to seeke our Lord, to beseech him for to heale him : which he performed so well, that he obtained his perfect healing. *Mat.* 8.

S. Elzearus Count of Arie in Prouence, had a maruellous care of his seruants, and to the end that euery one should studdie and aduance him selfe in the way of virtu, he ordained.

1. That euery one should euery day heare a whole masse.

2. He would not that any should eate of his bread, which he knew to be in mortall sinne, for feare least he should spoyle the others, and that he
should

should seeme to feede and nourish sinne.

3. That all should confes them once a weeke: and once a month, should receiue the B. Sacrament.

4. That none should be so bould, as to speake any blasphemy, othes, or dishonest wordes. And if any one were fallen in to ether of these thinges, he made them to sit vpon the ground, whilst the others dined, not giuing him ought for his dinner but bread and water.

5. He would not suffer, that anie should play at dice in his house, or at other forbidden game.

6. He was carefull, that all agreed well together, and if he perceiued any quarrell to be moued amongst them, he endeuored that they should forthwith be reconciled.

7. After dinner, or towards the euening, he made them in his presence to speake of spirituall thinges. *Sur.27. of Sept.c.18.vpon his life.*

8. The

8. The mother of S. Marie of Ognies, appeared vnto her vpon a day, as ſhe prayed for her in the time of Maſſe, and ſaid vnto her, that ſhe was damned, for that ſhe was careles of that which was done in her houſe againſt God, by thoſe of her famillie. *Iacobus de Vitr. Card.* in the life of S. Marie of Ognies, *lib. 3. c. 11. Thomas à Cantip. lib. 2. ep. c. 54. p. 18.*

O that God would be pleaſed to giue to famillies, a great many of Cēturions, and Elzears, and preſerue them from ſuch mothers or fathers of families, as this wretched womā was. What great good would enſue thereof, not only to famillies, but to the whole common welth?

THE VI. CHAPTER.

Of the Seauen capitall ſinnes.

THe ſinnes of Pride, Couetouſnes, Lecherie, Enuie, Gluttonie, Anger,

ger, Slouth, are called capitall, becauſe they are as the heades and fountaines, from whence as from a corrupted roote, doe proceede the peſtiferous fruites of all ſortes of ſinnes and vices. *Caniſ. Hic.*

§. *1. Of Pride and Superbitie.*

Pride (*a*) is a diſordinate appetite of ones proper excellence ; and is as the (*b*) mother and Queene of all vices. Her principall daughters (c) are, diſobediéce, boaſting, hipocriſy, debates, pertinacitie, diſcord and curioſitie.

(a) *Chriſoſtome hom. 43. ad pop. Bernard. de grad. humil. Greg. 34. mor. c. 17. & ſeq. & l. 23. c. 7. Iſidor de ſum. bo. l. 2 c. 38.* (b) *Greg. l. 13. mor. c. 31. Proſper l. 3. de contemplat. c. 2. Auguſt. ep. 56. Bern. ſer. 3. ex paruis. & ſer. 4. de Aduent.*

(*c*) Deut. 17. Sap. 5. Mat. 23. Pro. 13. Gen. 49. Pro. 6. 1. Tim. 5. 5. Tob. 4.

Neuer permit pride to rule in thy word, for in it all perdition tooke its begininge. Tob. 4. 6.

God

God reſiſteth the proud, and giueth grace to the humble. Iac. 4. 6. 1. Pet. 5. 5.

He that exalteth him ſelfe, ſhal be humbled, and he that humbleth him ſelfe, ſhall be exalted. Mat. 23. 12.

Pride is odious before God, and men. Eccl. 10. 7.

S. Bonauenture compareth the proud man, to the winde: for that, euen as the winde putteth out the light, drieth vp the dew, and ſturres vp the duſte; euen ſo the proud man, putteth out the light of wiſdome, drieth vp the dew of grace, and ſtirreth vp the duſt of vanitie.

2. He compares it next vnto the ſmoke, for as much as the ſmoke, the more it ariſeth, the more it vaniſheth and ſcattereth it ſelfe.

3. To the ſpider, for that as the ſpider emptieth out his owne bowells weauing his cloth to catch a flie, euen ſo the proud man looſeth all the good he hath in his ſoule, to catch a litle honor and humain praiſe. *Iſay 59.*

4. To

4. To the henne, who as soone as she hath laid an egge, she makes it knowen to all the house by her cackling, which is the cause her egge is taken away, as S. Chrisostome saith. And so doth the proud man, for as soone as he hath done any good thinge, he makes it knowen and publisheth it abroad, desiring that euery one should know it. *S. Bon. in dieta salut.tit.1. c.5.*

And of such persons our Lord saith, *that they haue receiued their reward in earth,* and that therfore they shall haue none in heauen. Mat. 6. 2.

EXAMPLES.

1. Lucifer the noblest and fairest amongst the Angels, for his pride, hath lost heauen, and hath encurred an eternitie of paines. *Isay* 14. 12. *& seq.*

2. Pharo kinge of Egipt, after diuers most horrible chasticements, was swallowed vp with all his troope, chariots, and baggage, within the waters

ters of the fea. *Exod. 14.*

3. Chore, Dathan, and Abiron, were fwallowed vpp aliue of the earth, which gaue way vnto them, to lett them finke downe in to hel. *Num. 16.*

4. Kinge Senacherib was flaine of his owne children. *4. Reg. 19. 37.*

5. Nabuchodonofer became like a beaft, and for fuch, liued for the fpace of feauen yeares, of nothinge elfe but of graffe and hey, *Dan. 4. 30.*

6. Holofernes had his head cut off with his owne fword, by the hande of a woman. *Iudith 13. 10.*

7. Aman was hanged vpon the fame gallous, which he had caufed to be made for humble Mardocheus, and he exalted to honor in his place. *Efther 7. 10.*

8. Kinge Antiochus, hauing firft endured a worlde of dolors, was at the laft eaten vp of lice. *2. Mach. 9.*

9. Kinge Herod dyed of the fame death. *Act. 12. 23.*

10. Iefabell was caft downe headlong

long from a windoe, and eaten of dogges. *4. Reg. 9.33.37.*

Of all which , that may be verefied
which Dauid said of all the proud . *I*
haue seene the impious highly exalted, and
aduanced as the Cedars of Libanus, and I
passed by , and behould he was not , and I
sought him, and his place was not founde.
psal. 36.35.

11. About the yeare of our Lord
1570. in a certaine conuent after Com-
plin , appeared in the refectorie at all
the tables certaine religious , which
being coniured by the Prior of the
Conuent, in virtu of the most holy Sacrament which he helde in his handes, to tell who they were ; He that
seemed to be chiefe of the rest answered, that they were all religious of the
same ordre , and the greater part of
them, Doctors, Bachelors, Priors, Sub-
priors, Readers, and al of them daned
for theire pride and ambition. Which
hauing said , they opened all their robes, and appeared all in fire. Anno 1599.
Bro-

Brother Tiberius, a holy man, entring into the same refectorie, saw and vnderstoodthe same. This fearful history, is recounted by brother Anthonie of Sienna, in the Chronicles of the brothers preachers, anno 1570.

Loe here the end of the smoke of worldly honors, to vanish sodainly away, and not to leaue to him who was addicted to them, but teares in his eyes, teares I say, & eternall confusion!

§. 2. *Of Couetousnes.*

Couetousnes, is a disordinate appetite of hauing. See touchinge this vice *S. Basil in ditesc. auar. hem.* 6. *&* 7. *S. Prosper l.* 2. *de vita contemplat. c.* 15. *&c.* 16. *Isid. de summo. bono. l.* 2. *c. 41. S. Aug. l.* 3. *de lib. arb. c.* 17. *& serm. 196. de temp. S. Amb. l. de Nabuthe Iesaraelita.*

Her daughters are, treason, fraude, deceit, periurie, vnquietnes, violence, want of mercie, or inhumanitie, and hardnes of hart. *S. Greg. l. 31. mor. c. 31.* 2. *Tim.* 3. 1. *Cor.* 6. *Eccl.* 11. *Zachar* 8. *Mat.* 6. *Pro.* 22.

F   The

The Apostle S. Paul calleth it, *the seruice of Idols. Coloſ. 3. 5. And to the Epheſ. 5. 5.*

They that will be made riche, fall into tentation, and the ſnare of the diuell, and many deſires vnprofitable and hurtfull, which drowne men into deſtruction and perdition: for the roote of all euils, is coue-touſnes. 1. Tim. 6. 9.

Nothing is more wicked then the coue-tous man. Eccl. 10. 9.

S. Bonauenture compareth the co-uetous man, vnto the hog : for euen as the hog is nothinge worth ſo long as he is a liue, and is only profitable when he is dead: euen ſo the couetous man, is nothing worth ſo long as he liueth, becauſe he keepeth all to him ſelfe, and doth no good to any body, vntil he be dead: for then he giues his ſoule to the diuells his body to the wormes, and his welth to his kinsfol-kes. *S. Bon. in diata ſalutis tit. 1. c. 6.*

The ſcripture likewiſe compares him to one ſick of the dropſie, who

the

the more he drinketh, the dryer he is:
the more he hath, the more he would
haue. *Eccl. 5. 9.*

S. Gregorie of Nazian, compares
the couetous, to the curſed Tantalus,
who is pictured by the poets, plunged
in the infernall waters as high as the
chinne, and dies for drithe; and hauing
the Apples of delight hanging nere
their noſe, can not eate them. The
couetous alſo beare their hell in their
owne boſome, and doe endure it: the
more riches they ſwallow, the more
they thirſte: the more they abound in
victualls and foode, the more are they
famiſhed. Is not this a hell in this
world, to be oppreſſed with ſleepe
vpon a bed of fethers, and to be enforced to watch? To be pinched with ex-
treame hungar, at a table full of good
meates, and not to be able to eate? To
burne with thirſt, hauing the goblets
full of delicious wine hard at his
mouth, and not able to drinke? Be-
houid the hell which the miſerable co-

uetous

uetous doe endure, is there then a more miserable sinne in the whole worlde?

EXAMPLES.

1. Giesi, Elias seruant, was for his couetousnes, punished with leprosie. *4. Reg.5.27.*

2. Iudas egged by auarice, sould his master for thirtie pence: & after hunge him selfe, burst asunder in the midst, and gaue his bowells to the earth, and his damned soule to the diuels. *Mat. 26.14.* & *27.5.*

3. Ananias and Saphira, retayning the halfe of their goodes thorough auarice, dyed both one after another with soddanie death. *Act. 5. Achan in Iosue 7. of Saul. 1. Reg. 15. 20. Of Achab and Iesabell 3. Reg. 21. & 4. Reg. 9.*

4. During the Empire of Constantine sonne of Heraclius, there was in Constantinople a riche man, who being in danger of death, gaue to the poore, thirtie pounds of gold, but re-

couering

couering after, he repented him selfe of his almes . A certaine friend of his, endeuored to take this sadnes from him, but seing that he profited not, he said vnto him . I am ready to restore you your thirtie poundes, vpon condition that you shal say in the Church in my presence. Lord, it was not I that gaue the almes of thirtie poundes, but this is he . He accepted it, and said it. But o incomparable secret of the iustice of God, as he thought to goe forth of the Church with his mony, he fell to the ground starke dead . *Baron. tom. 7. annal.an. 553. ex Cedreno, & Raderus ex Menæo Grecorum.*

5. A woman, vnder the cloke of pietie and religion, hauing made a great many of pilgrimages to holie places, she had gathered together a great deale of mony, which she fayned to be for the redeeming of prisoners, & for the necessitie of the poore: she hid the same vnder the ground within her house, that none but her

F 3   selfe

selfe should fingar the same . Her
daughter was askt , what her mother
had done with her mony? And becaufe
she could tel no tydinges, they sought
so long, that at laft they found it. The
Bishop caufed it to be carried , to the
graue of this couetous woman, and to
be caft vpon her carkas . About midnight, moft pittifull cryes were heard
to iffue forth of the hollow places of
that fepulcher, and a voice which faid
with a lamentable accent. *My gold bur-*
nes me, my gold burnes me. Thefe cryes
lafted three whole daies , at the end
wherof, they opened the graue(a fearfull thinge) and faw the gold, that had
beene there laid, all melted and in flames, to runne into the mouth of this
wicked woman . *S. Greg. of Tours re-*
ports the fame l. 1. of the glorie of Martirs
c. 106.

6. S. Atoninus writeth, that an a-
uaritious man, admonifhed of his parents and friends, being fick euen to
death, to confes him felfe, anfwered. I
haue

haue no hart, how then will you that I
confes? And that you thinke not that I
doe but ieste, goe to my coffre, & you
shall finde it amidst my gold, wherin I
haue put my whole hope. This said, he
died without any repentance. His coffre is visited, and iust as he said, his hart
was found amidst his gold: so true it is
which our B. Sauiour somtimes said.
*Where thy treasure is, there is thy hart
also. Mat. 6. S. Ant. in Summa 2. p. tit. 1.
c. 4. §. 6.*

7. Behould another like case arriue
vnto a couetous man, whose hart was
found in his coffre after his death, betwixt the clawes of a Dragon, which
lay vpon the gold and siluer, saying,
that hart was geuen vnto him by the
dead, during his life. *In Gabr. Inchinoser.
1. of the puritie of hart.*

8. Another being at the point of
death, could neuer be induced to be
confest, but as soone as he saw the
priest depart, he called his wife, and
caused a platter full of gold to be

F 4   brought

brought vnto him, to which he faid.
Thou art my gold, in thee it is that I
doe hope, let the Priefts fay what they
pleafe, thou art it that fhould'ft afift
me. Hauinge faid thefe wordes, he
bowed his head into the platter, and
there rubbing it amidft the gold,
which he kift and adored for his idoll,
he fo died miferably. *Extracted out of
the annales of the focietie.*

9. Such another alfo was he of the
cittie of Conftance, recounted by Niderus and Pinelli, who falling fick, of
fet purpofe to fpare his mony, caufed
him felfe to be carried to the hofpitall.
And feeing him felfe neere his end,
caufed to be made him fome peafe
pottage, and caft his gold into the fame, & hauing ftird it with his fpoone,
endeuored to fwallow it downe, but
he choked him felfe, and died before
he had eate it vp. *Pinelli. pag.* 1.c. 5.

10. Reginherus bifhop of Mifne,
haueing buried his treafure in his own
chamber, was found on the morrow
laid

laid theron , with his face againſt the ground, and ſtarke dead. *Lambert Schaf-nabur apud Baron. 10. 11. anno. 1067.* O ſtrange and tragicall deathes of coue-tous parſons!

§. 3. *Of the ſinne of Luxurie.*

Luxurie , is a diſordinate appetite of carnall pleaſure , her daughters are, blindnes of ſpirit, inconſideration, in-conſtancie, precipitation, ſelfe-loue, hatred of God, too great a deſire of this life, horror of death , and of the iudg-ment of God , together with diſpaire of eternall felicitie. *Greg. l. 31. Mor. 6. 31. Oſe 4. Reg. 11. Dan. 13. Pro. 13. Sap. 4. Psl. 51. Tim. 3. Pſal. 20. Iac. 4. Epheſ. 4.*

Fornication and all vncleanes , let it not ſo much as be named among you, as it becometh Saints , that is to ſay , Chri-ſtians. Epheſ. 5. 3.

Know you not, that your bodies are the members of Chriſt? Taking therfore the members of Chriſt , ſhall I make them the members of an harlot? God forbid. 1. Cor. 6. 15. 19.

F 5

Doe not erre, nether fornicators, nor adulterers, nor the effeminate, shall possesse the kingdome of God. ibid. 10.

If you liue according to the flesh, you shall die. Rom. 8. 13.

You haue heard, that it was said to them of old, thou shalt not commit adulterie: but I say to you, that whosoeuer shal see a woman to lust after her, hath already committed adulterie with her in his hart. Mat. 5. 28.

S. Bernard saith, that Luxurie is one of the chariots of Pharao, who pursued the seruants of God, and carries them that sit thereon, to the red sea of the infernall flames. Her four wheeles are, Gluttonie, and drunkennes, curiositie of apparell, idlenes, and ardor of concupiscence. The two Coursers, or horses, are prosperitie of life, and aboundance. Vpon these two horses, doe sit, stupid ignorance, and blinded assurance. *Ser. 39. in Cant.*

EX-

EXAMPLES.

Behould the horrible pnnishments which God hath imposed vpon this sinne.

1. For the sinne of the flesh, God hath drowned all the world. *Gen.7.21.*

2. The citties of Zodome and Gomorah, and all the contrie round about, with their inhabitants, were consumed by fire sent from heauen. *Gen. 19. 25.*

3. Hemor sonne of Sichem, with all the inhabitants of the cittie of Sichem, were put to the sword. *Gen. 34.26.*

4. All the tribe of Benianim, were cut off, for the same cause. *Iudg. 20.48.*

5. Sampson was blinded with ouermuch affection towards his wife. *Iudg. 16. 21.*

6. Amnon was slaine, by his brother Absalon. *2. Reg. 13.29.*

7. Dauid was persecuted of his

F 6   sonne.

8. Salomon became an adulterer 3.
Reg. 11.

9. The husbands of Sara, were ſtran-
gled by the deuil Aſmodeus. *Tob. 3.* 8.

10. The two old men that coueted
the chaſt Suſanna , were ſtoned to
death. *Dan.* 13.

11. Four and twentie thouſand of
the people of Iſrael, were put to death.
Num. 25.

12. Marie daughter to the kinge of
Arragon, wife to the Emperor Othon
the 3. hauing ſolicited the Count of
Modena, to condeſcend to her lubricitie , and he moſt conſtantly refuſing
her, was accuſed by her calumniouſly,
that he would haue induced her to
ſinne, wherupon the Emperor cut off
his head. But before he died , hauing
declared his innocencie to his wife, he
prayed her to carry his head after his
death, vpon her bare feete into a great
fire , in witnes of the integritie of her
husband: which ſhe performed, nether
that

that head, nor yet her body, being hurt any whit at all. Which the Emperor seeing, he commanded the Empresse to be cast into the fire. Thus God permitted that this terrible chasticement, shauld befall her, not only for this calumnie and filthie desire, but also for that she had somtimes abandoned her body, to a young youth, disguised like a wenche, who serued her for a chamber maide, and was also burnet aliue by the commandement of the Emperor, but she receiued pardon by the intercession of the princes and Lordes of the court. *The 2. Chron. Gotscalcus Holenser 23. p. Hyem. Licosthemes in theatro mundi. D. Antonin. p. 2. tit. 6. c. 3. Baron anno 958. Iacobus Strada in thes. Imp. Krantz l. 4. Saxon. c. 26.*

13. Raimond of Capua, confessar to S. Catharin of Sienna writeth, that this Saint could nether see, nor abide to come neere those, which were infected with the sinne of the flesh, & that if she spake with them, she was enforced to
stop

stop her nose. *Sur. 20. of Ian.*

14. Palladius writeth, that S. Pachomus, hauing giuen a box on the eare vnto the diuell, which appeared vnto him in the forme of an Ethiopian, had his hande so infected, that he spent more then two yeares to take away the stink therof. *In his Lausiaca.*

15. S. Euthimius Abbot, as Cyrillus Monke writeth in his life, passing by one who had consented to a dishonest thought, smelt such a stinke, that he supposed him selfe to haue bene posest of the diuell.

See before a terrible and fearfull historie of this matter, in the *3. cap. example 3. and another in the 4. cap. §. 2. example 6. and in the 2. booke, cap. 2. §. 2.*

Loe here the gayne and reward which is got by this sinne, for a beastly pleasure, and which lasteth so litle, plunging ones selfe into so many euills, temporall and eternall! Let vs say with that wise Pagan Demosthenes, *I will not buy a repentance at so deare.*

deare a price. Agell. *noct.* Act. *l.* 1. *c.* 8.

§. 4. *Particular Considerations, against the sinne of voluntarie Pollution.*

It is with great griefe that I speake at ail of this sinne, yea that I doe so much as name it, because it is so enorme and detestable: yet so it is, that I cannot altogether ommit the same, for that it is (o heauie case) so cōmon and so vniuersall.

Hearken hereupon to Cardinal Toletus. The sinne of voluntarilie pollution is amongst al others the most difficult to be amended, and this by reason that one hath alwaies with him, the occasion for to fall therein: and is so vniuersall, that I beleeue that the most part of those that goe to hell, are damned for the same sinne. *l.* 5. *Instruct. sacerd. c.* 13.

Ioannes Benedictus, in his Summe vpon the 6 commandement of the decalogue, writen after Conradus Clingius, be it that the same be knowen by reuela-

uelation , or elfe by experience , that
thofe which are habituated in this finne, as many yeares as our Lord liued,
that is to fay , thirtie three, are incurable , and as it were without hope
of their faluation, vnles that God doe
fuccour them, by a maruellous, rare,
and extraordinarie grace; This is that
which this author faith. But touching
the finne it felfe , accordinge to the
minde of the Cardinall before alleadged, there is no better remedy, then to
be confeffed often, to communicate
twice, or thrice a weeke, and this vnto
the fame confeffar.

Note all this Chriftian , and if euer
thou felft into this curffed finne , refolue to rife out of it from this very inftant that thou readeft this page , for
feare left habituating thy felfe therin,
thou canft not afterwardes rid thee
thereof , and that thou twift not by
litle and litle , the netts and vnloofa-
ble lines, which draw thee in the end,
into the abiffe of mifchiefe, and eternall

nall torments. For accordinge to the
Apostle, *Effeminat, nor liers with man-*
kinde, shal not possesse the kingdom of God.
1. Cor. 6. 10.

EXAMPLES.

1. Her the eldest sonne of Iudas,
was kild (by the deuill Asmodeus,
and dyed an horrible death, as Abu-
lensis writeth) as also his brother
Onan, for that retiringe him selfe in
the coniugall act, they polluted them
selues. *Gen. 38. 7.* And the scripture
speakinge of Onan, saith. *Therfore*
our Lord strooke him (weigh well these
wordes) *because he did a detestable*
thinge. If God punished in this sort
these two bretheren in an age so rude,
wherin there was so litle knowledge
of the goodnes of God, and malice of sinne, how thinke you will
he punish those, which beinge enlightned with the light of the euan-
gellicall gospell, doe commit this
dete-

deteſtable ſinne.

2. The admirable S. Chriſtine, ſaw vpon a day in ſpirit, all the whole world repleat and crowned in this ſinne, and that for this cauſe God prepared moſt terrible ſcourges wher with to puniſh them: who to the end to auert theſe horrible ſcourges, he afflicted and chaſticed him ſelfe, with diuers horrible and ſtrange puniſhments. P. *Cornel. a Lapide in c. 38. Gen. 7.*

Take heede ſinner, for it is a horrible thinge to fall into the handes of the liuing God. Heb. 10. See the 7. cap. of this 1. booke §. 2.

§. 5. *Of the ſinne of Enuie.*

Enuie, is a ſadnes and hatred, at the good and felicitie of another: of ſuperiors, for that one is not their equall: of inferiors, for feare, leſt one be made equall to them: of like, becauſe that one is equall to them. *Caniſ. ex Aug. l. 11. de Geneſ. ad lit. c. 14. Proſper ſent. 292.*

                            Her

Her daughters are, hatred, whispering, detraction, leaping of the hart at others aduersities, and affliction of spirit for their prosperitie.

The Enuious are like vnto the diuell, for the wiseman saith. *By the enuie of the diuell death entred into the worlde, and they follow him, that are of his part.* *Sap. 2. 24.*

Where Enuie is (saith the Apostle S. Iames) there is contention, inconstancie, and all forts of wicked workes. *Iac. 3. 16.*

There is nothing more pernitious in the whole worlde then Enuie, who hurtes none but its owne author. *S. Basil Hom. 11. var. argument.*

Enuie (saith S. Cyprian) is the roote of all euills, the fountaine of all misfortunes, the schoole or seminarie of sinnes. *Serm. de zelo & liuore.*

S. Bonauenture saith, that Enuie is, as the worme to the wood, the rust to the iron, the mothe to the garment. *In diata salutis. tit. 1. c. 4.*

S.

S. Baſil compareth the Enuious to vipers, who teare and kill their owne mothers. *Supra.*

S. Chriſoſtome, vnto madde or enraged dogges. *Hom. 41. in Mat.*

EXAMPLES.

Conſider the grieuouſnes of this vice, by its effects.

1. By Enuie, Caine ſlew his brother Abell. *Gen. 4.*

2. Iacobs children ſould their own brother. *Gen. 37.*

3. Saul ſeeing that Dauid was more extolled then him ſelfe, ſought to kill him, and in the end kild him ſelfe . *1. Reg. 18. & 31.*

4. Aman enuyinge the honor which kinge Aſſuerus had done to Mardocheus, conſpired his death, and the vtter ruine of all the Iewes : but all fell vpon his owne head, for he him ſelfe was hanged vpon the ſame gibbet, which he had ſet vp for him, and all

all his race and kinred, was put to the ſword. *Heſter 7.*

5. Finally, it was this curſed Enuie, which incited the Iewes, to procure the death of the Sonne of God, the author of life. Loe from what degree of malice, this vice doth throwe downe its owne ſeruant!

§. 6. *Of Gluttonie and Drunkennes.*

Gluttonie, is a diſordered appetite of eating and drinking. *S. Greg. lib. 30. Moral. c. 27. S. Bernard. l. de paſsione Dom. c. 42.*

Her daughters are, immoderat laughter, babling, ſcurillitie, filthines, and impudicitie, with ſtupiditie of the ſences and vnderſtanding, *l. 31. morall. c. 31. Aug. l. 30. & c. afore alleadged.*

S. Gregorie declareth fiue maners or faſhions, by which one falleth into this vice.

1. Preuenting the time to eate and drinke: ſo Ionathas ſinned, the ſonne of Saul. *1. Reg. 14. 27.*

2. Seeking for delicate and exqui-
ſite

fite meates and drinkes : as did the Ifraelites. *Num. 11. 4.*

3. Commanding to prepare & feafon meates, albeit common, with extraordinary licorifh fauces, like the fonne of Hely. *1. Reg. 2.*

4. Exceeding in the quantitie and meafure: as did the Zodomites.*Ezech. 16. 49.*

5. Eating with ouer much greedines, bafe and groffe meates, as Efau did his difhe of pottage. *Gen.25.33.*

Let vs now fee what the holy fcriptures fay.

Of furfet many haue dyed, but he that is abstinent, shall adde life. Eccl. 37. 34. & 31.36.pfal. 77. 29. 30. 31. Num 11. 33. Deut. 32.15.24.32. 33. Pro. 21. 17.

Looke well to your felues, left perhaps your harts be ouer-charged with furfeting and drunkennes. Luc. 21. 34.

A workman that is a drunkard, shall not be riche. Eccl. 19. 1.

To whom is woe? to whofe father woe? to whom broyles ? to whom ditches and
dan-

dangers? to whom woundes without cause?
to whom blood shedding eyes? Is it not to
them that passe their time in wine , and
studdy to drink out their cuppes? Pro. 23. 29.
By wine, is to be vnderstood, all that
which may make one drunke.

No drunkards shall posesse the king-
dome of God. 1. Cor. 6. 10. Gal. 5. 21. Osee
4. 11. Pro 31. 4. Eccl. 19. 1. 2.

Woe *to you that rise vp early to follow*
drunkennes, and to drinke euen vnto eue-
ning. Isay 5. 11. & 22. 13. Pro. 23. 20.
Amos 6. 6. Luc. 6. 25.

Are not these thunder-darting sen-
tences which the spirit of God, doth
launche forth against drunkards ? Let
vs see if the holy fathers doe say any
lesse .

S. Basill saith, that drunkennes is, a
voluntarily deuill. *Hom. 14.*

The drunkard is worse then the
Asse, saith S. Chrisostom. For an Asse
can neuer be induced , nether by faire
meanes , nor yet by force , to drinke
more then may suffice his thirst : but
the

the drunkard burſts him ſelfe with drinking, without thirſt, or neceſſitie. *Hom. 29. in Mat.*

Where drunkennes is (ſaith this Saint in another place) there is the diuell. *Hom. 57. ad pop. Ant.*

If this vice be ſo deteſtable in a man, how much is it in a mayden or a woman?

A woman giuen to drunkennes, *is great anger* (ſaith the wiſeman. *Eccle. 26. 11.) and her contumelie and turpitude shall not be hid.*

There is nothing more villanous and infamous, then a drunken woman, ſaith 5. Chriſoſtom. *Hom. 16. in Mat. & 71. ad pop.*

EXAMPLES.

1. Noe being drunke, preſently was infamouſly vncouered, mocked, and diſhonored by his owne ſonne. *Gen. 9. 21. 22.*

2. Lot being drunke, fell into double inceſt. *Gen. 19. 33. &c.*

3. Holo-

3. Holofernes readie to burſt with wines and aboundance of other meates, had his head cut off with his owne ſword by a woman, and his ſoule caſt into the eternall flames. *Iudith* 11. 12. & 13.

4. Balthaſar kinge of Babilon, making him ſelfe drunke with his concubines and curtiſans, ſaw his ſentence of death, written with the fingar of God vpon the wall, and the ſame night it was executed. *Dan.* 5.

5. The rich glutton made good cheere euery day, but in the end, he found his graue to be made in hell. *Luc.* 16.

6. Thomas de Cantip. writeth, that in his owne time in France, two elderly religious men being ſet at table to make them ſelues drunke according to their cuſtome, one of them, at the fourth morſell which he put in his mouth, choked him ſelfe, and ſo dyed ſodainly. The other hauing ſhaken off the feare he had conceiued of ſo horri-

C ble

ble a cafe, returned to the table, and
purfued alone to eate and drinke, vntill fuch time as he could no more: and
not being able for to ftir (fo full was he
ftuft) he was borne like a beaft vnto
his bed, and there died a litle after. *l.* 2.
ap. c. 12. *n.* 15.

7. See in the 2. booke c. 2. §. 2. a
terrible example of three drunkards,
wherof the one was rofted aliue by the
diuell, in the fight of his companions.

8. Two gentlemen, all foldiars, at
Apeldorne, a village of Velue in Germanie, agreed together, to drinke fo
long till they burft afunder, and that
the firft that fhould arife from the table, fhould be in the power of the diuell (who euer heard a thinge more
execrable?) A marchant paffing by that
way, was follicited to doe the like.
Then they began to drinke after a
ftrange fafhion, but their paftime lafted not longe, for hardly had they
begun, but that in the prefence of this
marchant, the diuell brake the necks
                                    afunder

afunder of them both. O heauie and horrible end of drunkards! *Petrus Thyreus de loco infeſt. p 1. c. 19. ex Mich. ab Iſſelt an. Dom 1584.*

9. Certaine drunkards fillinge out the pots and glaſſes, moued diuers diſcourſes touching the immortallitie of the ſoule; And one of them ſaid, that he was ready to ſell his to whoſoeuer would haue it. A marchant arriued therupon (which was the diuell in the guiſe of a marchant) who prayed to haue a place in their company. He ſet him downe at the table, and hauinge heard their diſcourſe, he offred to buy the ſoule of this Athiſt, he bought it for ſome certaine pots of wine; & hauing laughed with them for awhile, he demanded if he which hath bought a horſe, ſhould not haue the bridle alſo? They all anſwered, that it was but reaſon, which was no ſooner ſaid, but he preſently ſeazed vpon his man, and carried him away both body and ſoule. *Thom. Cantip. l. 2. ap. c. 56. p. 2.*

G 2   10. In

10. In the yeare 1595. the 14. of Marche, the firft Sonday of Lent, at Baccharach, a cittie feated vpon the Rhine betwixt Conftance and May-ence, a good woman great with child, feeing her husband goe to the tauerne, to play and drinke away all that he had got the weeke before, endeuored with many wholfom reafons to diuert him, but receued nothing of him but dry blowes, and was fo fent back with her diuell (for fo he cald the fruit which fhe carried in her wombe.) Being re-turned to her houfe, thorough the paines and forrow which fhe concei-ued, fhe was deliuered before her ti-me, & brought forth a monfter, which from the head vnto the girdle, was like a man, but all the reft like to a Serpent, hauing a tayle of three elles longe. The night being come, her husband retur-nes with his purfe emptie, and his bel-lie full: but fcarce had he put his foote within the chamber, but that this di-uell incarnate leapt vpon him, wrapped
him

him within his tayle, and gaue vnto him so many prickes, that he killed him vpon the place. The poore woman in child-bed, behoulding from her bed this horrible spectacle, gaue vp the ghost, and the monster also imediatly after ceased to liue. *Mich. ab Isselt in his Merc. Gallo-belg. l. 12. an. 1595.*

11. An other, in the yeare 1583. spending all his mony at the tauerne, did likewise beate his wife in such maner, who came to shew the pouerty of her owne house, that he left her there for halfe dead. After she was returned home, she was beset with seauen litle children, which pullinge her by the coate, cryed. Mother, a litle bread, good mother a litle bread, we haue not eaten yet to day. What shall I giue you? said she vnto them, I haue nothing, your father hath eaten and consumed all. This said, all desperate, she goes and fetches a great knife from the kitchin, and kild her two litle children. The husband returning stark drunke, threw

him

him selfe vpon the bed, and as he slept, she likewise cut asunder his throate. The fact is knowen, she is apprehended, and executed for it without delay, making a goodly exhortation to husbands, to gouerne them selues better in their hous-keepinges . *Ioannes Benedicti, in the Summe of sinnes.*

§ 7. *Of the sinne of Anger.*

Anger is, an immoderate desire, to punish him, of whom one deemeth to haue receiued wronge.

Her daughters are, quarrells, arrogance, contumelie, clamor, indignation and blasphemies. *S. Greg. l. 31. Moral. c. 31.*

An angrie man, prouoketh brawles, & he that is easie to indignation, shall be more prone to sinne. Pro. 29. 22.

Whosoeuer is angry with his brother, shall be in danger of iudgment. Mat. 5. 22.

Enuie and Anger, diminisheth the daies, and thought will bringe old age before the time.

time. Eccl. *30. 26.*

Let not the sunne goe downe vpon your anger. Ephes. 4. 26. that is to say, reconcile your selues before the euening.

Blessed are the meeke, for they shall posesse the lande. Mat. 5. 4.

Loue your enimies, doe good to them that hate you &c. and you shall be the sonnes of the highest. Luc. 6. 27. & 35. & Mat. 5. 44. 45.

There is nothing more vngratefull (saith S. Chrisostome) then an angrie body, nothing more insupportable, more pernicious, and more horrible. Hom. 29.

He that is easily angrie (saith S. Bonauenture) is like vnto an emptie pot of earth, which being set nere the fire, crackes and makes a great noize: euen so he who is easilie angrie vpon eache slight occasion, euidently sheweth, that he is emptie of grace, and of virtues. In diæta salut. tit. 1. c. 5. This being conforme to that which the wiseman saith. The fornace tryeth the potters

vessels,

152   **Lib. 1.** *Of the true
vessels , and the tentation of tribulation,
iust men.* Pro. 27. 6.

EXAMPLES.

1. The Emperor Theodosius being at Theffalonica, moued to choler for a murder committed in a popular tumult againft the parfon of one of his fauorits, affembled the people in a certaine place, vnder pretext of fome fport or play to be there performed, and then caufed them all to be cut in peeces, vnto the number of feauen thoufand. But he paid dearly for his offence , for being excommunicated and fhut out of the Church by S. Ambrofe, he was enioyned to doe moft feuere penance for the fpace of a yeare : and after this receiued not his pardon , before fuch time as proftrate in the prefence of all the people , with his face vpon the earth, he often repeated this litle verfe of the prophet Dauid, with teares and fighes, faying . *My foule hath cleaued to*
the

the pauement. psl. 118.25. *Niceph. l.* 12. *hist.*
eccl. c. 40. *Sidon de occid Imp. l.* 9. *Baron.*
an. 390.

2. S. Bridgit, hauing vpon a time,
giuen some signe of impatience, our
Lord appeared vnto her, and said. I
thy Creator and thy spouse, haue endured for thee whippes and scourges,
and thou, couldst thou not endure for
me a few wordes? Being presented before the iudge, I helde my peace without so much as opening my mouth,
and thou hast answered sharplie, and
vsed reproaches, with lowdnes of voice. Thou in truth oughtest to suffer all
patiently for the loue of me, who haue
bene nayled an hunge vpon the Crosse
for the loue of thee. Be thou then for
the time to come better aduised, and
if thou be prouoked to anger, hold thy
peace and say not a word, vntill the
time thy choler be past, and then thou
maist speake with sweetnes and meek-
nes. *Lud. Blos. mon. spirit. c.* 4.

3. Sapritius Priest, after he had suf-
G 5   fered

fered much for the faith, as he was led
to his execution, he met with Nicephorus, with whom he had some former quarrel: who cast him selfe downe
at his feete, beseeching him he would
forget what was past, and receiue him
againe into grace. This he did diuers
times, and in diuers places, but all in
vaine, for the wicked wretche would
neuer forgiue him; but God punished
him by and by, taking from him the
crowne of martyrdome which was already prepared for him, and gaue the
same vnto Nicephorus. For being at
the point to be beheadded, he said he
would adore the Idolls, as he did:
which Nicephorus seeing, he declared
him selfe to be a Christian, went vp
vpon the scaffold, and was beheadded.
O what obstinacie and blindnes, rather to loose and be depriued of heauen, then for to pardon! *Surius* 9. *of
Feb* .

4. Iacobus of Vitriaco Cardinall,
preaching the expedition of Christians
in

in Brabant, it came to paſſe, that a certaine man caſt him ſelfe at the feete of
another, beſeeching him to forget their
ſurpaſſed enimitie, and to forgiue him
that wherin he had offended him :
which hauing done for three or four
ſeuerall times, and the other ſtill ſaying, that he would not forgiue him,
he turned him towards the aſſembly
and ſaid. I proteſt before you all, that I
haue done that which was my dutie, I
therfore beſeeche you all to pray vnto
God, that he would ſhew by ſome
euident ſigne, that this man doth a-
miſſe. This ſaid, he heard out the reſt
of the ſermon, and now behould a
ſtrange caſe, how this obſtinate man
fell to the grounde, his eyes rouling in
his head, and his mouth full of the
fome of blood. The holy Cardinall
fell to prayer, and takinge him by the
hande, lifted him vp, and brought him
to his perfect ſence. Then all changed
into another man, he caſt him ſelfe
vpon his enimies neck, kiſſed him, and

askt

askt him forgiuenes(in his turne)with
the teares in his eyes. *Tho. Cantipr.l.2*
ap. c. 18. p. 2.

5. Behould here another more admirable then the former. S. Bernardin
writeth to haue seene in the yeare
1419. vpon the mount of Caluarie in
Hierusalem, a woman carried quite
away by the diuel, and cast into a welle
in the sight of a great number of people, for hauing by mischance amidst a
presse of people, bene shouldred by a
young man and thrust a ground, she
neuer would vouchsafe to pardon
him, albeit he praid and besought her
sundry times with ioyned handes, and
vpon his knees. *Serm. 15. Quadrag.*

Here we see the verifying of this
euangelicall sentence. *If you will not*
forgiue men their offences, nether wil your
father forgiue you your offences. Mat. 6. 14.
Luc 6. 37. Eccl. 28. 2.

§. 8. *Of the sinne of Slouth.*
Slouth is a langor and feeblenes of
spirit

spirit to worke well:& taking it more
strictely, it is a sadnes of spiritual thinges. *Canis.*

Her daughters are, malice, despaire,
and benumdnes to fulfil the commandements of almightie God, and a wandring of spirit towards vnlawfull thinges. *S. Greg l. 31. Moral. c. 31.*

To this vice are subiect such as are
idle (*a*) and are without any arte or
knowledge, and such as the scripture
calls(*b*)luke-warme:and lastly al those
who employ in vanities, this pretious
time of grace, and day of saluation (*c*)
(*a*) *Mat. 20. 6. Pro. 6. 6. & 10. 13. 18.*
19. 20. 21. 22. 24. 25. 26. 28. and in sundry other places (*b*) *Apoc. 3. 15.* (*c*) *2.*
Cor. 6. 2.

Thou hast left thy first charitie (that is
to say, thy first feruor) *be mindfull ther-*
fore from whence thou art fallen, and
doe pennance, and doe the first workes;
but if not, I come to thee, and will moue
thy clandelstick forth of his place. Apoc.
2. 5.

I would thou were colde, or hote ; but because thou art luke-warme, and nether colde, nor hote, I will begin to vomit thee out of my mouth. *Apoc.* 3. 15.

Cursed be he who doth the worke of God negligently. *Ierem.* 48.

He that pursueth idlenes, shall be replenished with pouertie. *Pro.* 28. 19.

Idlenes hath taught much naughtines. *Eccl.* 23. 28.

Loe this was the iniquitie of Sodome thy sister, pride, fulnes of bread and abundance, and the idlenes of her , and of her daughters. *Ezech.* 16. 49.

Because of colde, the slouthfull would not plough , he shall beg therfore in the sommer, and it shall not be giuen him. *Pro.* 20. 4.

Goe to the Emmot, o sluggard, and consider her wayes, and learne wisdome: who wheras she hath no guide nor master, nor captaine, prepareth meate for her selfe in the summer, and gathereth in the haruest for to eate. How long wilt thou sleepe , o sluggard , when wilt thou rise out of thy sleepe?

ſleepe? Thou ſhalt ſleepe a litle, a litle ſhalt thou ſlumber, and penurie ſhall come to thee as a Wayfaring man, and pouertie as a man armed. Pro. 6. 6.

Euery tree that yeldeth not good fruite, ſhall be cut doWne, and ſhall be caſt into the fire. Mat. 7. 19.

And the vnprofitable ſeruant, caſt yee out into the vtter darknes, there ſhall be Weeping and gnaſhing of teeth. Mat. 25 30.

Are there not here moſt goodly ſentences, all taken forth of the booke of God, againſt ſlouthfull and lazie perſons? Let vs heare what the holy Doctors ſay to the ſame purpoſe.

If thou hadſt a ſeruant (ſaith S. Iohn Chriſoſtome) that were nether thiefe, nor detractor, nor drunkard, nor addicted to any other vice, but yet remayning whole daies together, houlding his handes one within another, wouldſt thou not baſt him? But it may be ſaid he doth no euill? He doth ill enough, when he doth not that which he ought to doe. Hom. 16. in epiſt. ad Epheſ.   S.

S. Thomas of Aquin was wont to say, that idlenes was the fishe hooke, wherwith the diuell went a fishinge, and that with it all sort of bayte was proper. *Ribad. in his life 7. of march.*

Be alwayes in action, that so the deuill may alwaies find thee occupied. *S. Hier. epist. ad Rusticum ep. 4.*

We must flie idlenes, the mother of fooleries and of fopperies, and the step-mother of virtues. *S. Ber. l. 2. de consid. ad Eugen.*

My father worketh vntill now, and I doe worke, said our Sauiour. *Ioan. 5. 18.* The Angels, are they not all occupied in their ministrie? saith the Apostle. *Heb. 1. 14.* Behould the Sunne (saith S. Aug.) the Moone, the Starres, the beastes, and all creatures, doe they not al employ them selues to doe that, for which God the Creator hath created them? And thou a man, wilt thou remayne alone doing nothinge? *Ser. 16. ad fratres in eremo.* How much is the

the litle Spider busied to catch a fly?
How dilligent the Cat, to catch a
Mouse? How longe are maydens and
women tampering to trick vp and a-
dorne them selues, to gayne the fauor
of a poore and silly mortall man? And
wilt thou doe nothinge to gayne heauen, and the grace and fauor of almightie God? *See the 6. examp. of this para-*
graphe.

EXAMPLES.

1. Idlenes caused the Israelites to fall
into the sinne of Idolatrie. *Exod.* 32. 6.

2. Those of Zodome and Gomorrha,
into the sinne of Sodomy. *Ezech.* 16. 49.

3. Dauid thorough idlenes, fel into
the sinnes, both of murder and adultrie. *2. Reg.* 11. 4.

As longe as Sampson exercised him
selfe to set vpon his enimies, he could
not be taken : but as soone as he laid
him downe and slept vpon a womans
lap, he was both taken, & made blinde.
Iudg. 16. 21.

5. Whilst

5. Whilſt Salomon employed him
ſelfe about the building of the Temple, he was not aſſaulted with the ſinne
of Leacherie. Doth he ceaſe? Behould
him ſodainly ſet on fire by his concupiſcence, courtes ſtrange women, and
becomes an idolater. 3. *Reg.* 11. *4.*
Watch then my brethren (ſaith S.
Aug.) for you are not more holy then
Dauid, ſtronger then Sampſon, nor
wiſer then Salomon. *Ser.* 16. *ſupra.*

6. Pelagia a courtlie lady of Antio-
che, paſſing vpon a day before certaine
Biſhops, mounted vpon a goodlie
Mule, all beſpangled with golde and
pretious ſtones, followed and atten-
ded vpon with a great nóber of youth-
full pages and damoſelles moſt dain-
tilie attired, and her ſelfe ſo faire, that
ſhe rauiſhed the harts of all her be-
houlders, as ſoone as the Biſhops had
eſpied her, they turned away their faces from her, only Monnus, Biſhop
of Edeſſa, looked vpon her fixedlie,
and that for a pretty ſpace of time, and
after

after asked of the others what they
suppofed. And feeing that they faid
not a worde, he bowed him downe-
wards, hid his face with his handker-
cher, weeping with moft bitter teares. Which hauing done, he errected
him felfe and faid: that he had bene
greatly recreated by looking vpon this
diffolute woman, for (quoth he) I
confidered, how many houres fhe
fpent to fpunge and beautifie her felfe
to gayne the grace and fauor of men,
and I wretch that I am, who ought to
pleafe the great God of heauen, who
promifeth me goods and pleafures
which are infinit, am yet fo negligent
and flouthfull to adorne my foule?
This faid, he drew his Deacon by the
arme, and being retyred into his
chamber, he caft him felfe vpon the
ground, lamenting before the face of
God, his tepiditie and his flouth. She
was after this conuerted to the faith,
and to a better fort of life, by a fermon
which fhe heard of this holy Bifhop,
and

and retyring her selfe into the mount
of Oliuet, disguised in the habit of a
man, passed the rest of her life most ho-
lilie, and is now placed in the catalogue of the Saints of the Church. *Su-*
rius and Ribad. 8. of October.

7. S. Antoninus Archbishop of
Florence, passing his way vpon a day
thorough the streete Ambrosienne of
the same cittie, saw Angels vpon the
top of a litle house: wherat astonished,
he entred in, and found there a good
widdow with her three daughters,
who all tottered and bare-foote, spunne with their spindell: and moued
with compassion, gaue vnto them a
good somme of mony. He past by there
againe within a while after, and saw
there diuells insteed of Angells. He
went into the house, and asked if they
had not committed some kind of sinne
since he had visited them; and vnderstood that they spunne no more, but
spent their time in doing of nothinge,
amusing the selues about naught else,
                                            saue

ſaue only to pranck and adorne them
ſelues to pleaſe men . *Vincent Mainar-*
dus in vita S. Antonini, Sur. 2. of May.

O the ſingular good to be allwayes
exerciſed in things that are good! O the
great euill, that proceedeth of idlenes!
An aduertiſement touching this vice , for
ſuch as are Magiſtrates and fathers of
families.

8. At Florence in Toſcanie, according
to the lawes & cuſtomes of the côtry,
the magiſtrates haue a very great & eſ-
peciall care, that there be not found in
the cittie, any vagrant or idle perſons:
and if they find any ſuch, they examin
them whereon they liue, whence they
got their garments, and if they anſwer
not pertinently, they are preſently puniſhed and expeld the cittie, as pernicious to the common welthe . *Sabellius*
l. 6. c. 3.

9. The Egiptians according to their
lawes, anciently puniſhed by death, al
thoſe who could not proue by what
arte they got their liuing . *Diod. Sicul.*
And

And Solon, the lawgiuer of the Greekes, made an ordonance, that the father should not be nourished of his
owne childe, to whom he had not
taught some occupation. *Laert. l. 6.*

O yee Magistrats, who ether reade
or heare this, be wise after their example, and see that youth be not nourished and entertained in idlenes in
your townes. And you, fathers and
mothers (who must rendar a most
strict account to God of your children) for Gods sake, suffer not, that
they be idle and vagabonds. Employ
them betimes, and from their youth
in some honest exercise, according to
your calling, and their capacitie. Send
them assoone as they are fiue or six
yeares old vnto the schooles, there to
learne to write & reade. Why should
you grudge them a groate a monthe,
for a thinge so necessary and profitable to them, who grudge not to giue
vnto your bellie and your guttes after dinner, all the gettinges of a
whole

whole weeke ?

After they know how to write and reade, put them to some honest exercise, ether of learning, or of some art and occupation, and take great heede of retaining them by you, doing of nothinge, for elce you lose the bridle to them, to runne headlong to all kinde of malice and mischiefe, perhaps also vnto the gallouse. I know a man, who for this only reason, saw two of his children hanged before his owne doore. O what a hart-breaking was this accident to him.

It is not the Iudge (quoth a young stripling carried vpon a day for to be hanged) that leadeth me vnto the gallouse, but it is mine owne mother. *Iansen. in Pro. 23. See touching this matter chap. 5. §. 1. examp. 6. & 7.*

THE

THE VII. CHAPTER.

Of certaine remedies and meanes, wherby not to fall into sinne.

Hitherto we haue alleadged that, which maketh for the detestation of the principall sinnes and vices, which sufficeth in myne opinion, to moue a hart, were it of stone or hardest marble; for what is there more efficacious or more energicall, then the holy scripture ? then the enflamed wordes of the holie fathers, and examples? Thou seest then (o Christian) by what hath bene said, how pernicious and horrible sinne is, and consequently what reason thou hast to detest and fly it as much as thou maist. But yet perhaps thou wouldest willingly haue some remedies, to preserue thy selfe from this accursed monster. Besides the feare and loue of God, the distrust of ones selfe, the due frequentinge of the

the Sacraments of Penance, and of the Eucharift, fpirituall lecture, daylie examen of confcience, and holy prayer, wherof we will treate by Gods afiftance in the booke enfuing: behould here feauen fingular remedies & moft effectuall.

1. To fly the occafions, as are dangerous places, and euill companies.

The memorie {
2. Of the prefence of God.
3. Of the paffió of our Lord.
4. Of death.
5. Of iudgment.
6. Of hell, and of the eternitie of the damned.
7. Of heauen, and of the eternitie of the faued.
}

§. 1. *Of flying the occafions of finne.*

The Prouerbe faith, that the occafion caufeth the thiefe. The Flies and Gnattes, houering about the candle, fall at the laft into the flame; He muft not walke nere the water, who will not be drowned. If thou

H   then

then (o Chriſtian) wilt keepe thy ſelfe
ſo as not to fall into ſinne, ſlie the occaſions, ſuch as are euill companies,
the dangerous places of tauernes, and
other houſes of diſſolute women, in
the enening and time of night. For a
maide (for example) doth put her ſelfe
in great haſard of offending God, and
of her owne honor, who vndertakes
to talke with a younge man alone, in
a place apart, in the darke, or in the
night. You ſhall rendar account fathers
and mothers, who giue ſuch libertie
vnto your daughters. *See. l. 2. c. 3. §. 4.*
examp. 3.

He that loueth danger shall perish in it
Eccl. 3. 27.

Can a man hide fire in his boſome, that
his garments burne not? Or walke vpon
hoate coales, that his ſoales be not burnt?
Pro. 6. 27.

My ſonne, if ſinners shall entiſe thee,
condeſcend not to them. If they shall ſay:
come with vs, &c. walke not with them,
ſtay thy foote from their pathes. Pro. 1. 10.

Depart

Depart from the wicked, and euill shall fayle from thee. Eccl. 7. 2.

He that toucheth pitche, shall be defiled with it: he that communicateth with the proude, shall put on pride. Eccl. 13. 1.

With the holie, thou shalt be holie, and with the innocent man, thou shalt be innocent. psl. 17. 26.

If thy right eye scandalise thee, pluck it out and cast it from thee: for it is expedient for thee, that one of thy limmes perish, rather then thy whole body be cast into hell. Mat. 5. 30.

By the eye that scandaliseth, is to be vnderstood all occasion of scandall and of offence. The master then must quit him selfe of his maide, if she giue him occasion to offende God: and, if it be the master which inciteth the maide to commit euill, then must she leaue him; and so of others.

There is no assurance (saith S. Hierom) to sleepe nere vnto a serpent: it may be that he will not bite me, but it may be also that he will bite me. *l.*

H 2   *cont.*

And writing to Furia touching her widdowhood, he saith. Fly the companie of younge youthes, let not your house admit these young courters of girles which weare their perewigges , who haue their haire frisled, their habits spruce, and their lookes lasciuious : admit not likewise neere vnto you, singers and players &c. but insteed of these, holie widdowes . *Epist.* 10.

S. Aug. bewayling the stealth of apples which he had committed in his youth, saith. If I had bene alone, I had neuer done it: it was wicked company, that caused me to doe it. O frindship too too iniust, seduction of spirit, when one saith; Let vs goe, let vs doe it, and one is ashamed, not to be without shame. l. 3. Conf. c. 8. 9.

EXAMPLES.

The children of Seth, were good before

fore they were married, but as ſoone
as they were allied with the daughters
of Caine, they became ſo wicked, that
God was conſtrained to drowne them
all by the deluge. *Gen.* 4. 6. 7.

2. Loth being retired from the holy
company of Abraham, was taken by
the Infidells, all his goods were burned in Sodome, he made himſelfe
drunke, and being drunke, violated his
two daughters. *Gen. 14. & 19.*

3. Salomõ cõuerſing with the Egiptiã
Ladies, became an Idolater. *3.Reg.11.4.*

4. S. Peter, leauing the companie
of our Ladie and the Apoſtles, and
rancking him ſelfe amongſt the wicked, denied thrice his Lord and Maſter.
Mat. 26. 70.

5. Gordiana aunt to S. Gregorie, de-
lighting ouer-much to be in company
of certaine ſecular maydes, forgot the
vow ſhe had made to ſerue God, and
by litle and litle turned all worldly: &
after the death of her two ſiſters, Thar-
ſilla & Emiliana which wẽt to heauen,

H 3 ſhe plun-

plunged her selfe entirely in vanities,
with the finall perdition of her soule.
S.Greg. 4. Dial. c. 14. *& Hom.* 38. *in Euang.*

6. A younge scholler studying in
the dioces of Mastrick, finding him self
vpon a day in the company of some
younge and dissolute libertines, was
conducted into a certaine house, where
it wanted litle, that (together with the
puritie of his hart) he lost not the
flower of his virginitie. Seing him selfe
therfore assaulted with an impudent
woman, he forsooke his companions,
and departing forth of that debauched
lodging, it being now night, he went
towards his owne dwelling, and as he
went, he began to thinke, not without
great astonishment, vpon the euident
perill which he had passed, to make an
irreparable losse of the pretious treasure of his chastitie. As he entertayned
him selfe in this thought, behould a
young man of a most maruellous beautie appeared vnto him, and gaue vnto
him

him a box on the eare, & that ſo fierce
and ſoundly ſet on, that he feld him
flat vpon the ground, ſaying vnto him.
Learne then, learne thou for another
time, to flie euill company, and ſo diſappeared ſodainly.

The ſchollar all ſhaking and trembling for very feare, got him ſelfe vp
ſome while after, and waighing more
ſeriouſly what had paſſed, knew more
clearly, that this younge man, was his
Angell gardien, which had deliuered
him that day from ſo great danger, and
had admoniſhed him ſo charitably of
the fault which he had committed: for
which cauſe he gaue thankes vnto God
and to his good Angell, makinge a
firme purpoſe, to fly for the time to
come more carefully then euer before,
all kinde of euill company. And the
better to aſſure that it was not a
dreame, the cheeke wheron the Angell ſmote, remayned ſweld ſundry
dayes after. *P. Franciſ. Albertin in his
treatiſe of our Angell Gardien. c. 7. ex*

H 4   *ſpeculo*

speculo ex dist. 10 *ex* 9. See also another
as remarkable in the treatise aforsaid
c. 19. and here before *c. 4.§. 7.examp.*
3. of S. Edmond. & in the 2. booke *c.*
3. §. 4. exampl. 3.

If we haue so great care to conserue
our body from euill ayres, and from
all that which may be hurtfull to it,
shall we not haue the same of our
soule? W*hat permutation shall a man*
giue for his soule? *Matt.* 16. 26.
Marc. 8.

§. 2. *Of the mindfulnes of the presence*
of God.

This also is a most singular remedy,
for who is he, I pray you, vnles he be
quite out of his wittes, that dares and
would offende, when he calls, to minde, that God (that almightie and re-
doubted iudge)seeth euen to the very
bottome of his hart?

In all thy waies thinke on him, and he
will direct thee in thy steppes. Pro. 3. 6.

I will

I will shew thee, o man, what is good, & what our Lord requireth of thee; verely to doe iudgment, and to loue mercie, and to walke solicitous with thy God. Mich. 6. 8.

He hath said in his hart, God hath forgotten, he hath turned away his face not to see foreuer. psal. 10. 11.

Remember God, & thou shalt neuer sinne, saith S. Ignatius Martyr. *epist.6.*

Behould the whole meanes neuer to sinne, if one suppose God to be alwaies nere vnto him. *Clem. Alex. l. 3. pedag. c. 5.*

The remembrance of God, shuts the gate to all sinne. *S. Hierom. l. 7. c. 22.*

Euen as at the arriuing of the Prouost, theeues withdraw them selues from their commō hauntes: euen so at the remembrance of the presence of God, the infamous passions of the soule, are chased away, and it becometh the temple and habitation of the Holie Ghost. But where the memorie of God is not, there doth darknes dominiere with stench, and all kinde

of wickednes is there exercifed . *s.*
Ephrem. l. de virtute tom. 2. c. 10.

Thinkeſt thou that thou art alone,
when thou committeſt fornication?
And remembereſt not that the eyes of
God, doe behould the whole worlde?
All the holy Trinitie is hard by thee,
the Angells his miniſters, the Cherubins and Seraphins, which continual-
lie cry . *Holy, holy, holy, all the earth is*
full of thy maieſtie Thinkeſt thou, that
in the brothel houſe Ieſus Chriſt doth
not behould thee , he who ſaw thee
enter into the ſame ? Thinkeſt thou,
that he ſeeth thee not committing a-
dulterie, he that ſeeth the adulterie
which thou conceiueſt in thy ſoule? *s.*
Amb. in psl. 118. *Serm.* 1. O careleſſe
Chriſtians! o mortall men, how then
liue you!

You offend God, as if God ſaw you
not. What, God, that great God, doth
he not ſee you? He that is aboue you,
beneath you , round about you , yea
euen within you?

GOD

GOD IS EVERY WHERE.

What dooſt thou then (forgetfull of thy God) what dooſt thou?

Hearken in what place ſoeuer you be: *Shall a man be hid in ſecrets, and shall not I ſee him, ſaith our Lord?* Ierem. 23. 24.

Heare this, & tremble for feare, for

GOD SEETH ALL.

What ſaiſt thou, thou who art forgetfull of God? What dooſt thou ſay? What, *he that planted the eare, shall he not heare?* pſl. 93. 9.

I liue, ſaith our Lord, according as you haue ſpoken, I hearing it, ſo will I doe to you. Num. 24. 28.

Take heede then what you ſay, for

GOD VNDERSTANDETH ALL

Alas what thinke you in your hart? What doe you thinke? What, knowe you not then, that at that great day, he wil viſit and examin Hieruſalem with torches? *Sophon. 1.*

Deceiue not your ſelues, it is a point moſt aſſured, that

GOD KNOWETH ALL.

H 6 Yea

Yea euen the most secret thoughtes. What, dare you then offend God in his owne presence?

No Christian, let vs say now, let vs say for euer; rather die, then be damned, rather die, then be defiled, rather die, then to offende before the face of so great, and so good a God. *Dan. 13 28.*

EXAMPLES.

1. The holie scripture, speaking of the old men who coueted carnally the chast Susanna, saith. *And they subuerted their sence, and declined their eyes that they would not see heauen, nor remember iust iudgments. Dan. 13. 9.* And a litle after; *Perplexities are to me on euery side, for if I shall doe this, it is death to me, and if I doe it not, I shall not escape your handes. But it is better for me, without the act, to fall into your handes, then to sinne in the sight of our Lord. v. 22.* O right worthie and generous resolution!

S. Do-

2. S. Dorotheus Abbot, writeth, that at the begining whē Doſithus his diſciple tooke the habit of religion, he gaue this ſentence, worthy to be written in letters of gould. *Let God be neuer out of thy hart, thinke alwaies that God is preſent with thee, and that thou art before his face.* Which Doſithus imprinted ſo deeply in his hart, that he neuer forgot it, no not in his greateſt ſicknes. And by this exerciſe of the preſence of God, he profited ſo well, that of a knight and ſoldiar of the worlde, of one debauched, and vtterly addicted vnto vanities, he became a moſt perfect, and a moſt holy religious perſon, and was ſeene after his death of diuers holy perſonages, moſt glorious and triumphant in heauen amongſt the holy Anchorets *S. Doroth. in his life.*

3. Saint Catharine of Sienna, to keepe her ſelfe alwayes recollected amiddeſt the diſtractions, and occupations which her mother

mother prescribed her , made (according as her heauély spouse had taught her)an oratory of her hart,in the midst wherof she placed her God. O most goodlie and wholsome practise . *Raymond in her life.*

4. Palladius affirmeth to haue learned of a certaine religious man called Diocles,that a deuout person,as soone as he leaueth the remembrance of the presence of God, becomes a beast, or else a diuell. *In hist. lausia. c 98.*

5. An vnmannerly woman , who dwelt hard by the house , where S. Ephrem was one day lodged in Edessa, came and solicited him to lubricitie. The Saint asked her if she were content to come vnto the open market, and that there he would satisfie her demand. What (quoth she) dare we doe this before men ? If we dare not doe this before men(replied the Saint) how dare we to doe it before God, who vnderstandeth all thinges , euen the most secret, and is to iudge vs of
all

all our workes? Thefe wordes touched the woman fo exceeding deeply, that detefting this enterprife, and all her fore-paffed life, from that very houre fhe gaue the farwell to the flefh and the worlde, retyring her felfe, according to the councell of the Saint, into a monaftery, where fhe liued and died moft holily. Bleffed Lord, what change doth thy remembrance make within a hart! Giue it vs, we befeeche thee continually, to the end that this euill neuer arriue vs, as to finne in thy prefece!

§. 3. *Of the remembrance of the moft dolorous paffion of our Lord.*

O Chriftian, canft thou offende thy God and thy Redeemer, when thou remembreft that *he was wounded for our iniquities*, and that *he was broken for our finnes? Ifay 53.5.*

Canft thou well commit any kinde of finne, when thou remembreft thofe lamentable cries of thy Sauiour, all peirced

peirced and wounded vpon a Croſſe.
*O all yee that paſſe by the way, attend and
ſee, if there be ſorrow like to my ſorrow.
Thren.* 1. 12.

If *in the greene wood they doe theſe thinges* (that is to ſay, to him who was
euen iuſtice it ſelfe) *in the drie what
ſhall be done? Luc.* 23. 31.

Who is he ſo irreligious (ſaith S.
Bernard) that remembringe himſelfe
of the paſſon of his Sauiour, is not
touched wih compunction ? Who
ſo proude, that is not humbled?
Who ſo cholericke, that is not appeaſed ; Who ſo voluptuous, that is
not cooled ? Who ſo wicked, that is
not reſtrained ? Who ſo malicious
that doth not pennance ? And this
with great reaſon, ſith the paſſion of
our Lord, hath moued euen the earth
it ſelfe, bruſed the ſtones, and opened
the monuments? *In ſerm. ſeria* 4. *heb.
pænoſæ.*

Acknowledge (ſaith the ſame Saint
in another place) how greuous the
woun-

woundes are, for the which it behoued that the Sōne of God ſhould be wounded, if they had not bene deadly, and to death eternall, neuer had the Sonne of God died for their remedy . *Ser. 3. de natiuit.*

Greater loue then this no man hath that a man yield his life for his friends. Ioan 15. 13. And if loue be not requited but by loue, art thou not more cruell, & more inhuman thē the Tygers, that remembring thee of this exceeding charity of the Sōne of God (who gaue his deareſt life for thee) thou wilt offende him, and crucifie him againe anew? *Heb. 6. 6.*

EXAMPLES.

1. Zenophon writeth, that Cyrus kinge of Perſia, hauinge vpon a day cauſed Tigranes kinge of Armenia (whom together with his wife he helde captiue) to come vnto his table, demanded of him, how much he would giue to ranſome his wife?

I

I should be content (replied Tygranes) to giue for her all that kingdome which thou by force haft taken from me: and yet more. all my blood and my life. Cyrus admiring so great affection, reftored them their realme and their libertie. A while after, Tygranes being in his pallace, demanded of her, what she thought of the beautie of Cyrus? In footh (quoth she) I doe not know what you would fay, nor what Cyrus is; for all the time of our captiuitie, I neuer caft mine eye vpon other, then vpon him, who was ready to giue his blood and his life for the loue of me. O Chriftian, admire and imitate this pagan princeffe. Thou haft before thine eyes, the Sonne of God, who was not only content to giue his life & his blood for thee, but *de facto* hath giuen it: wouldeft thou thē leaue him, to loue a vile and catife creature?

2. Our Lord faid vpon a day vnto S. Gertrude, that a man cafting his eyes vpon the crucifix, ought to imagin, that

that our Lord who is nayled thereon, saith vnto him. Thou seest what I haue endured for thee, to suffer my selfe to be hanged all naked vpon a Crosse &c. and yet notwithstandinge I loue thee so much, that if it were expedient for thy saluation, I would endure for thee alone , all that which I haue endured for the whole worlde . *Lud. Blos. Mo-nil. spirit. c.* 1.

He somtime said the selfe same vnto S. Carpus , as S. Denis of Areopagita reporteth. *Ep. 2. ad. Demophil. & Baron. tom. 1. anno 59.*

3. But he said yet more vnto Saint Bridgit; I loue men (said he vnto her) at this present, euen as much as I did when I died for them : yea if it were possible , I would be ready to dye for euery one in particular , and as many times as there are damned soules in hell. *Ibid.*

4. S. Collecta , reformer of the order of S. Clare, praying to our Lady in the behalfe of sinners, our B. Lady appeared

appeared vnto her, with a platter full
of peeces of flesh, as of an infant newly
slaine, and shewing her the same, said
vnto her. How wilt thou that I pray
for them, who by their sinnes (as much
as lyeth in their power) cut and dis-
member my Sonne into more peeces
then heere thou seest? *Surius tom. 7. ex*
Stephano Iuliaco S. Coletæ contemporaneo.

5. S. Elzear, Count of Arie in Prouence, being asked by his wife Del-
phina, whence it was that he neuer
troubled nor vexed himselfe; answered, that he set before him, the iniuries
done vnto our B. Lord, and that at the
selfe instant, his choler ceased. *Surius*
27. of Sept. c. 23.

See thou now, o Christian, the singular efficacie of this remedie.

§. 4. *Of the memorie of death.*

Who is he that would offend God,
that doth reflect vpon his death? Who
pondereth, that peraduenture he is already

ready arriued to the laſt degree and ſtep of his life , and now at the point to make the laſt leape, vnto happie, or vnhappie eternitie?

It is appointed to men, to die once, ſaith S. Paul vnto the Heb. 9. 27.

I know that thou wilt deliuer me to death (quoth holy Iob) *where a houſe is appointed for euery one that liueth.* Iob. 30. 22. And yet nether know we when, nor how.

Watch yee therfore (ſaith our Lord) *becauſe you know not the day nor the houre.* Mat. 25. 13. *Whether at eueninge, or at midnight, or at the cock crowinge, or in the moringe, leſt cominge vpon a ſodaine he finde you ſleepinge : and that which I ſay to you, I ſay to all, watch.* Marc. 13. 35.

In all thy workes remember thy latter ende , and thou wilt not ſinne for euer. Eccl 7. 40.

Thou art afraid to die ill, and art not afraid to liue ill. Correct thine euil life, for he can neuer dye ill , who hath liued

liued well. *S. Aug. l. de disciplina chri-*
stiana c. 2.

There is nothing which doth more
withhould a man from sinne, then the
memorie of death. *Ibid. l. 2. de Gen.*
cont. Maniche. ser. 3. de Innoc. Cassian
c. 6. col. 10.

He who hath promised pardon
vnto the penitent, hath not promised
to the sinner the day of to morrow.
We must then feare continually this
latter day, which we can neuer fore-
see. *S. Greg. Hom. 10. in euang.*

Fleres, si scires, vnum, tua tempora, men-
    sem,
Rides, cum non sit, forsitan vna dies.
If one monthes certaintie thou hadst to
    liue,
And couldst not haue thy death deferd no
    longer,
Thy eyes would poure forth teares, thy
    hart, would greiue,
For that thou hadst not fallen to penance
    sooner.
Yet now vncertaine of the shortest day,
                            Thou

Thou spendst thy time in dalliance sport
and play.

It is a thinge of great moment,
wheron eternitie doth depend. Eternitie dependeth vpon death : death
vpon life; life vpon an inftant. Choofe
whither thou wilt, if once thou be loft,
it is for all eternitie.

EXAMPLES OF SODAINE
death.

1. The children of Iob feafting together, were fodainly ouer-whelmed
with the fall of a houfe *Iob. 1.*

Isbofeth (*a*) Sifara (*b*) Holofernes
(*c*) loft they not their liues, in the dead
of their fleepe? (a) *2. Reg. 4.* (b) *Iudg.*
4. (c) *Iudith.*

Balthafar making great cheere, receiued the fentence of his death. *Dan.*

Manlius Torquatus in eating a cake.
P. Quintus Scapulus in fupping. De-
cimus Sauferus in dyning. Apeius
Saufeius in fupping off an egge. Fa-
bius

bius Maximus eating of milke, swallowed downe a haire, and died. *Plin. hist. l. 7. c. 53.*

The poet Anacreon, swallowinge downe the stone of a reasin, at a weddinge. Plato.

Foulques Count of Aniou, runinge after a Hare. Cardinal Columnus vice-Roy of Naples, in the time of Charles the fift, talting of Figges, refresht in yce, gaue vp the ghost betwixt the armes of his seruants. *P. Coton in the sermon of death.*

And that foolish Richman in the gospell, who thought him selfe so sure of his health and of his substance, heard he not all vnexpected the sentence of his soddaine death? *Luc.* 12.

Finally, deceiue not thy selfe, for death slayeth in euery place, Aristobulus in the bathe; The Apostata Emperor amidst his armie, Philippes by the Altar, Caligula in a caue vnder ground, Carloman a hunting, Cesar in the senat, Erricus by his mother, Alboinus

by

by his wife , Ariſton by his ſeruants,
Baiazeth by his ſonne, Muſtapha by
his father, Conrad by his brother,and
Cato by him ſelfe.

EXAMPLES OF THOSE
who refrained from ſinne , by the remembrance of death.

1. A certaine brother Conuerſe an
Alman called Leſſard,hauing for many
yeares exerciſed the office of a porter
in his monaſterie,at the laſt debauched
him ſelfe,thinking that (notwithſtanding his nobilitie and decrepid age)he
was ſtill put vnto ſo baſe an office, he
who might be in pleaſures and delightes in the worlde : and ſo reſolued to leaue his monaſterie and his
habit . Now as he was on a night
in this fond fanſie, waytinge for the
breaking of the day to runne his way,
behould a venerable old man which
appeared vnto him , and commanded
him to follow him, the which he did.
They came at the laſt to the gate of the

I   Church,

Church, which opened of its owne
accord; from thence they went into
the church-yard, where they were not
fo foone entred, but all the graues
opened of themfelues. The old man
caufed this religious to draw nere to
the one, and fhewed him the carion
that was therin. Seeft thou (quoth he)
this man? Thou fhalt be like vnto
him within a while, why then wilt
forfake thy cloifter? From thence he
would haue led him to another, but
Laffard had conceiued fuch horror at
the fight of that one, the he befought
the old man to bringe him back vnto
his dortorie, fwearing vnto him, that
from that time forward, he would neuer more thinke of departinge thence,
which he performed. *Vincent de Bau-*
uais in his miroir. Hift. & P. Albertinus in
his treatife of our Angell Gardien c. 6.

O how many fuch repentants would
there be at this prefent day in the
worlde, if only by a ferious reflection
offpirit, they would looke downe in
to

to the sepulcher! *Arise and goe downe into the potters house,* said God our Lord vnto Ieremie (that is, to the church yardes and sepulchers where the pots of earth, that is, bodies are turned into earth by the almightie hande of him that made them) *and there thou shalt heare my words* Ierem. 18. 2.

2. A younge effeminat fellow, who could by no meanes or reason be brought into the right way, was at lenght visited of a good religious man, who at his departing from him, said vnto him. *Vnder thee shall the mothe be strawed, and wormes shall be thy couering.* Isay. 14. 11. and therupon withdrew him selfe. These wordes (though few) yet were not spoken in vaine, for this young man imprinted them so profoundly in his hart, that whatsoeuer he did, he could not thinke of any other thinge. Hence by litle and litle, he had a holy disgust of the worlde, and in the end quite forsooke it, and became religious. *Plautus l. 3. de bono stat. relig. c. 38.*   I 2   3. Theo

3. Theodofius chiefe fuperior of a monaftery, taught his difciples for the firft foundation of a religious life , to haue euer before their eyes , the remembrance of death ; And to this effect commanded them , euery one to make him a graue , the fight wherof fhould reduce to their mindes, that they muft die. *Sur. tom. 1. Ribad. 11. of Ian. ex Metaphraft.*

4. Lord Francis of Borgia Duke of Gandia and vice-Roy of Catalognia: by one only fight of the dead body of the Empreffe Ifabella, wife to Charles the fift, was fo touched, that he refolued from that time to forfake the worlde: and within a while after, hauing geuen order to his affaires, entred into the Societie of Iefus , and therin died the third Generall, leauing to all perfons, great opinion of his fanctitie. *Tom. 1. Hift. of the Societie.*

5. A noble Knight named Rouland, hauing paffed a whole day in feafting and dancing, as he was returned

ned to him selfe, he fell to consider, how al the pleasures of that day were past and vanished, and that all the rest that he could take, would slide away in the same maner: and in the end what shall I haue (said he within him selfe) what will all these vanities auaile me? These thoughtes lasted him the whole night, and made such a breach in his hart, that the morning being come, he went and askt the habit of the Friar Preachers, receiued it, & liued & dyed therin most holily. *Plautus as before.*

6. A certaine Damosell, wholy giuen vnto vanities, refused all the pennances which her Cōfessar proposed vnto her, but at the last she accepted this, as the most easie of all the rest in her opinion, to say within her selfe, as often as she washt her handes; *This flesh shall be eaten vp of wormes:* she performed it, and with such good successe, that she whollie changed her selfe within a while after, and became so virtuous, as she had bene vicious, and as exemplar,

as fhe had bene fcandalous . P. *Coton in his fermon of death.*

7. A monke of Egipt, being vpon the point to fatisfie his fenfuallitie, was hindred by the remembrance of death, as he confeft him felfe to S.Iohn Climacus.

8. Another which had liued very licentioufly and fcandaloufly, fell fick & was reduced to the point of death, yea held for dead. And hauing bene an houre in that eftate, he came to him felfe, and prefently befought his companions to withdraw them felues, and to ftop and damme vp his chamber dore with ftones. The which was done, and fo fhut vp, liued there for twelue yeares, without fpeakinge to any perfon, and eating nothinge but bread and water, hauing his eyes continually fixt vpon the felfe fame place, with aboundance of teares. At laft, when he was to die, his fellowes brake a paffage into his chamber, and praid him to giue then fome wordes or coun-

councell of edification. *Pardon me* (said he vnto them) *for no man can euer sinne, who doth effectually remember him of his death.* S. Iohn Climachus, as an eye witnes, relateth the same, in his booke intituled. *Scala cœli. grad 6.*

9. M. Guido Priest of Niuelle, being Regent at Schonege in Hainault, hauing thorough curiositie, cast his eye a litle too fixedlie vpon a woman, was in such wise tempted, that for the space of three yeares he could doe nothinge but thinke of her, although she was dead. And seing that this tentation was most perillous vnto him, to surmount the same, he went by night, to open the graue of the same woman, & being slidden downe therein, he applied and laid his nostrils vnto the carion, as longe as he was able to suffer the stinke that proceeded thece, but at the last he fel backward as halfedead. Being come to him selfe, he issued thence most victorious, in such sort, that he neuer after felt any prouocation of the flesh.

Tho.

*Tho. de Cantip. affirmeth to haue knowen
this Priest, and writes the historie in his 2.
booke of Ezech. c. 30.*

10. A holy Ermit did almost the like:
for not able to blot out of his imagi-
nation, a woman which was already
dead, he went into her graue to cut a
piece of her flesh, which he applied afterwards vnto his nostrils, as oft as the
remembrance of this woman returned
vnto him, and the stinke which issued
forth of this rotten flesh, rendred him
as many times victorious. *In vitis patrum. p. 2. de fornic. n. 10.*

§. 5. *Of the memorie of Iudgment.*

The memorie of Iudgment, is a most
stronge bridle, to withhould and stay
a man in the course of sinne. For who
(I pray you) is so hardy as to commit
any sinne, who considereth that within a litle while (and perhaps also the
selfe same day) he is to giue an account
of all the thoughtes, wordes & workes
of)

of his whole life, vnto a Iudge infinitly iust, infinitly wise, infinitly powerfull, and receiue from his mouth (according to the good or euil he shall haue done) the definitiue & irreuocable sentence, ether of life, or death eternall?

It is appointed to men to die once, and after this the iudgment. Heb. 9. 27.

We must all be manifest before the iudgment seate of Christ, that euery one may receiue the proper thinges of the body, according as he hath done, ether good or euill. 2. Cor. 5. 10.

I will search Ierusalem with lampes Sophonia 1. 12.

It is horrible to fall into the handes of the liuing God. Heb. 10. 31.

What shall I dee, when God shall rise to iudge? And when he shall aske, what shall I answer him? &c. I haue alwaies feared God: & cap. 9. 28. I feared all my workes, knowing that thou didst not spare the offender.

What can a man imagin more dreadful, more repleat with anxiety, and ve-

hement

hement follicitude, then to be presented at this so terrible tribunall, there to be iudged, and to awaite there vpon a Iudge so exact, and for a sentence so doubtfull ? *S. Bern. Ser. 8. in psal. qui habitat.*

Before sicknes take medicine, and before iudgment examin thy selfe and in the sight of God, thou shalt finde propitiation. Eccl. 18. 19. 20.

Feare the examen of the Iudge, dread him who saith by his propher, in that day I will search-Ierusalem with lampes: he is sharp of eye-sight, he will suffer nothinge to escape. *S. Ber. Ser. in 55. in Cant.*

The iust doe feare whatsoeuer they doe, considering before what Iudge, they must one day infallibly be presented. *S. Greg l. 8. Moral. c. 13.*

O what feare and affrightment will there then be, what teares and groninges ? For if the pillars of heauen doe tremble before him, what then shall sinners doe ? If the iust shall scarcely be be saued, where shall sinners then appeare? Who is he that redouteth not a Iudge infinitly powerfull, infinitly wise, infinitly iust? *Innoc. 3. l. 3. of the contempt of the worlde c. 15.*

Sensuall loue, and the prickinge of lubricitie, shall soone be extinguisht, if one doe set before his eyes the latter iudgment, said S. Anthonie to his Disciples. *S. Athanas. in his life.*

As often as thou feelest thy selfe prouoked forward to any sinne, call to minde the day of iudgment, and thou shalt by this meanes giue a bridle vnto thy soule. *S. Basil. in psl. 35. S. Ambrose also saith the same, ad virg. lap. c. 8. Climachus. grad. 20.*

EXAMPLES.

1. S. Hubertus Bishop of Liege, said to his seruants at the houre of his death, that he greatly feared the iudgement of God, wherat he was to rendre account of all his life. *Sur. 3. of Nouemb.*

I 6   2. S.

2. S. Hilarion likewife , a litle before he rendred vp his bleffed foule,
faid . Goe forth my foule , goe forth,
what dooft thou feare,thou haft ferued
God nighe feauentie yeares, why fea-
reft thou then to goe forth? *S. Hierom*
in his life.

3. S.Arfenius trembling and bitter-
lie weeping a litle before his death,de-
manded by his difciples wherfore he
wept, anfwered. Since the time I haue
bene religious , I neuer was without
this feare. *Sur. ex Metaphraft. c.27. Iuly*
19. If the Saints them felues doe tremble, what fhall the finners doe at that
dreadfull houre?

4. In the yeare 1082. a Doctor of
Paris, reputed of all for a holy man,
being dead , as they read for him the
office of the dead, beingarriued at the
Leffon, *Refponde mihi* , he lifted him
felfe vp out of his coffin in the open
church before all, and faid. *I haue bene*
accufed before the iuft iudgment of God.
This gaue great matter of feare vnto
all

all , and was cauſe that the office was deferred vntill the morrow. Vpon the morrow they began againe, and being come to the ſelfe ſame wordes, he that was dead aroſe againe, and ſaid. *I haue bene iudged , by the iudgment of God.* Theſe wordes were very fearfull, but yet gaue clearly enough to vnderſtand the eſtate of his ſoule: wherfore it was thought good, to defer this office yet once more. it can not be ſpoken how many people ran flockinge on the morrow , to ſo ſtrange a ſpectacle. They ſinge as before, and when they were come to the ſelfe ſame wordes, the dead aroſe againe, and ſaid with a voice , much more lamentable then before . *I am condemned by the iuſt iudgment of God.*

S. Bruno was then amongſt the other ſpectators (a Doctor of Paris, and Canō of Rhemes) who affrighted with ſo horrible a fact, reſolued frō that inſtant, freelie to forſake , all the vanities of the worlde; and to this purpoſe

hauing

hauing found forth fix others of the fame refolution , went together with them, and fhut vp them felues in one of the defert mountaines , which are feated vpon the confines of France and Sauoy, and there gaue begining to the holy order of Char e) houfe monkes. *Franc. Puteus generall of the fame order, vpon the life of S. Bruno. Sur. tom. 5. & Ribad. 6. of Octob.*

Thus the Saintes forfooke all the occafions of finne, at the only memorie of their iudgment, & thou (o Chriftian) remembring thee of a thinge fo horrible , which moft infallibly alfo muft arriue to thee , dareft thou to dwell in the occafions of finne ? See that which followeth after.

§. 6. *Of hell, and of the Eternitie of the accurfed.*

If the feare of death, or fome temporall paine, doth hinder vs ordinarily to doe that , which otherwife we would doe , the apprehenfion of the eui-

euident danger of a death and punish-ment which is eternall, shall it not haue the force to bridle our will, not to consent vnto some sinne?

There is a hell, it is a point we must beleeue, a place designed for all those which die in mortall sinne; where in the companie of the wicked Angells, they are depriued for euer of the sight of God and of all good, and of the ioy-full societie of the Saintes, and plun-ged in a fire vnspeakably actiue, to be bruned therein so long as God shall be God, for euer without end, without truce, without repose.

Be not afraid of them that kill the body, and after this haue no more to doe, but I will shew you whom yee shall feare, feare him, who after he hath killed, hath power to cast into hell. Luc. 12. 4.

Then the king will say (to wit, at the day of iudgmēt)to the waiters, binde his handes and feete, and cast him into the vt-ter darknes, there shall be weepinge and gnashing of teeth. Mat. 22. 13.

Then

Then he shall say to them also that shall be at his left hande, get yee away from me, you cursed into fire euerlasting, which was prepared for the diuell and his Angells. *Mat.* 25. 41.

The seruants of the goodman of the house coming said to him. Sir, didst thou not sow good seede in thy fielde, whence then hath it cocle? Wilt thou that we goe and gather it vp? And he said No, lest perhaps gathering vp the cocle, you may roote vp the wheate also together with it. Suffer both to grow vntill the haruest, and in the time of haruest I will say to the reapers, Gather vp first the cockle, and binde it in bundels to burne, but the wheate gather yee into my barne. *Mat.* 13. 27.

The sinagogue of sinners, is as towe gathered together, and their consumation a flame of fire. The way of sinners is paued with stones, and their end hell and darknes, and paines. *Eccl.* 21. 10,

Which of you can dwel with deuouring fire? Which of you shall dwell with euerlasting heates? *Isay*33. 14.

The

The richeman dyed, and he was buried in hell. Luc. 16.22.

Conſider what an euill it is , to be excluded from the ſweete content-ment of the ſight of God; to be depri-ued of the moſt happie companie of all the Saintes; to be banniſhed from hea-uen, and to die to euerlaſting life ; to be caſt with the diuell and his An-gels , into an eternall fire; where the ſecond death is; where damnation, is exile ; the paine, life; not to feele in this fire , that which doth ligh-ten ; to feele that which doth tor-ment; to ſuffer the horrible crakin-ges of a fierie fornace; to haue the eyes put out with a blind obſcuritie , of the ſmokinge abiſſe ; to be plunged into the bottome of the infernall wa-ues ; to be euerlaſtingiie gnawen with moſt prickinge wormes . To conſider theſe thinges , and manie more , is nothinge elſe, but to bid adieu to all vices , and to refraine all carnall allurements . *Proſp. l.* 3. *de*

But what is it to burne eternallie?
(will you fay vnto me) what doth this
word *Eternall* or *Eternitie* meane?

Eternitie, is a continuation of time
alwaies prefent, or elfe the meafure of
all continuation, faith S. Thomas 1.
p. q. 10. *a.* 6.

It is a circle, wherof *Alwayes* is the
centre, and *Euer* is the circumference.

The meafure of eternitie, is *Alwayes*: as longe as *Alwayes* fhall laft, fo
longe fhall *Eternitie* laft: fo longe as
heauen fhall be heauen, fo longe as
God fhall be God, fo longe fhall the
bleffed be bleffed in heauen, and fo
longe fhall the damned be damned, &
burne for euer, alwayes, and worlde
without end.

Imagin to your felfe a mountaine,
as high and as large as the whole
worlde, and that by the permiffion of
God, a litle Wrenne (the leaft of all the
birdes) fhould come once in euery
hundred thoufand yeares to beare a-
way

way in her bille or breake, as much of this mountaine, as the tenth part of a graine of muſtardſeede, ſo that at euery million of yeares, ſhe ſhould beare away only the quantitie of a graine of muſtardſeed, when ſhould all this mightie mountaine be remoued away? Yet notwithſtanding this ſhould one day be, for albeit ſuch, yet ſhould it be finit in all its parts; And if God ſhould giue this hope vnto the damned, to be deliuered after this litle Wrenne had thus tráſported the whole mountaine, they would be conforted maruellouſlie. But alas, after ſo longe a terme, they ſhall haue as long to burne as they had before. *Dion: ſRickel Charterhouſe Monke in the place intituled; the looking glaſſe of the louers of the worlde.*

What is *Eternitie* (ſaith Adamus Sasbout) who ſhall expres or comprehend, what *Eternitie* is? I thinke a thouſand yeares, I thinke a thouſand millions of yeares, I thinke as many millions of yeares, as all the time contayneth

neth moments, which hath flid and paft away fince the creation of the worlde, and fhall paffe vnto the end: yet neuertheles I haue thought nothing, that approacheth to *Eternitie*. O *Eternitie, Eternitie*, how longe art thou, without bottome, without brimme, without end. *Hom. vpon the firft funday of Lent.*

O heauens ftand aftonifhed, for a pleafure of a moment, men purchafe *eternall* torments! *Eternall*! *Eternall*!

EXAMPLES.

1. A certaine Religious man, demanded vpon a day of another môke named Achilles, whence it came, that being in his celle, he was alwayes wearie and flouthfull? The holy old man made him anfwere, it is becaufe thou haft not yet feene, the repofe which we expect, nor the torments which we feare. For if thou confideredft well and maturely thefe thinges, although thy celle were full of wormes, and that thou wert plunged therin

in to the very neck, thou wouldeſt neuertheles remaine therein very gladly
and content. *In vitis Patrum diſt. 2.*
parag. 103.

2. S. Furſinus patron of Peronne,
hauing ſeene by the permiſſion of God,
in one of his trances, the paines of the
damned, conceiued ſo great a feare,
that in the very depth of winter, and
moſt peircing froſt, at the holy remē-
brance thereof (albeit he had but one
ſimple habit only) ſweat throughout
his whole body, great droppes of
ſweate. *Ven. Beda hiſt. Ang. l. 3. c. 19.*
Alas, what would he haue done, had
he endured them reallie?

3. S. Iohn Climacus, affirmeth to
haue knowen a certaine Conuerſe
(cooke of a monaſterie) who each time
that he approached to his fire, he alwayes wept. And being asked why
he wept, he anſwered. When I ſee
the fire, I alwayes thinke vpon the fire
of hell, and forthwith I melt into teares, for the compaſſion which, I haue
of

4. A certaine Clearke, about the yeare of our Lord 1090. appeared to his companion, saying that he was damned, for that not beleeuing the immortallitie of the soule, he had had no kinde of care to doe good workes. And to giue to vnderstand what kinde of paines he endured, he wipte his forehead with his hande, and let a drop fal vpon the flesh of the other, which peirced it at the same instant, & left a hole therin as big as a hazell nut, together with most terrible paines, and then said vnto him; This fountaine shall be vnto thee a perpetuall memorie of my misery, and a spur vnto thee, to incite thee to leade a better life then I haue liued: and if thou be wise (quoth he) thou will goe render thy selfe religious nere S. Melanius: which being said, he disappeared, returning to his accursed centre, there to burne in all eternitie. The other, for feare lest one day he should follow him, turned back
from

from the way of hell which he had taken vntill that time, and impathed himſelfe in the good and happie way of heauen, making him ſelfe a religious man. *Vincent. ſpec. hiſt. l. 25. c. 89 Math. Paris in hiſt. Ang. in the yeare 1072. in the time of William kinge of England.* What will it profit thee, o mortall man, to haue two or three daies, weekes, monthes, or yeares of contentment, if thou muſt be afterwardes tormented and tortured for all *Eternitie?* That is momentary which delighteth, that eternall which tormenteth.

§. 7. *Of the memorie of heauen, and of the eternitie of the bleſſed.*

O *Iſrael, how great is the houſe of God, and how great is the place of his poſeſſion? It is great, and hath no end, high, and vnmeaſurable .* Baruch 3. 24.

And *he ſhewed me the holie cittie of Hieruſalem (*Apoc. 21. 10.*) The building of the wall thereof, was of Iaſpar. (*v. 18. *the gates, of Saphire and Emraulds (*Tob. 13. 19.*)*

13. 19.) and the streete of the cittie, pure gold (Apoc. 21. 21.) There are nether the coldes of winter, nor the heates of sommer, but an euerlastinge spring-time: nothinge is heard thoroughout all this cittie, but a perpetuall Alleluia. *Tob. 13. 20.* Farwell teares from all those that are there, for they shall neuer weepe more, *for God shall wipe a-way all teares from their eyes, and death shall be no more, nor mourning, nor cry-ing (Apoc. 21. 4.)* They all follow the Lambe, who leadeth them to the liuing waters, and to the fountaines of the water of life. ibid: where they drinke their full draughts of that Angellicall Nectar, which contayneth in it, all the pleasures and contentments that can be wished.

Will you knowe how great this contentment is? *Eye hath not seene, nor eare hath heard, nether hath it ascended into the hart of man, what thinges God hath prepared for them that loue him. I say 64. 4. 1. Cor. 2. 9.*

The

The paſsions of this time, are not con-
digne to the glorie to come, that shall be reuealed in vs. *Rom. 8. 18.*

For that our tribulation, which preſently
is momentary and light, worketh aboue
meaſure exceedingly, an eternall waight
of glorie in vs. *2. Cor. 4. 17.*

S. Peter ſaid vpon a day vnto our
Lord. *Behould we haue left all thinges,
and haue followed thee, what therfore
shall we haue? And Ieſus ſaid to them.
Amen I ſay to you, that you which
haue followed me, in the regeneration,
when the Sonne of man shall ſit in the
ſeate of his maieſtie, you alſo shall ſit
vpon twelue ſeates, iudging the twelue
tribes of Iſraell. And euery one that hath
left houſe, or brethren, or ſiſters, or father,
or mother, or wife, or children, or landes
for my names ſake, shall receiue an hundred fold, and shall poſſeſſe life euerlaſting.*
Mat. 19. 27. &c.

Come yee bleſſed of my father, poſſeſſe
you the kingdome, prepared for you from
the foundation of the worlde: for I was

an

an hungred, and you gaue me to eate: I was a thirst, and you gaue me to drinke. Mat. 25. 34.

For this soueraigne good it was, that all the Saintes haue suffered so much, choosing rather to be afflicted, yea rather to loose their liues after a thousand torments, then to enioy for a litle while the delights of sinne, for they *looked vnto the remuneration.* Heb. 11. 26.

I haue fought a good fight (saith the same Apostle) *I haue consummate my course, I haue kept the faith. Concerninge the rest, there is laid vp for me a crowne of iustice, which our Lord will render to me in that day, a iust iudge: and not only to me, but to them also that loue his cominge.* 2. Tim. 4. 7.

S. Augustine, by the pleasures of this life, coniectured the contentments of the life eternall. If thou doost vs so much good Lord (quoth he) in this prison, what wilt thou doe vs in thy pallace? If there be so much contentment

ment in this day of teares, what wilt thou giue vs in the day of mariage? *Silloq. c. 21.*

These are certaine teſtimonies drawen forth of the booke of God, touching the pleaſures of heauen, and of the life eternall. Now ſo longe as thou art the friend and childe of God by grace, thou art inheritor of all theſe goods. *If ſonnes, heires alſo, heires truly of God, and coheires of Chriſt. Rom. 8. 17.* Wouldeſt thou then expoſe and aduenture at a caſt at dice, or a momentarie pleaſure, all the right thou haſt to an enheritance ſo riche, and ſo delightfull? If thou offend God mortallie, thou looſeſt in an inſtant all this right.

Who ſhall aſcend into the mount of our Lord, who ſhall ſtande in his holie place? the innocent of handes (that is in his workes) *and of cleane hart. pſal. 23. 3.*

There ſhall not enter into it any polluted thinge. Apoc. 21. 27.

Labour the more, that by good workes

K 2   *you*

you may make sure your vocation and e-
lection, &c. for so there shall be ministred
vnto you aboundantly an entrance into the
euerlasting kingdome of our Lord and Sa-
uiour Iesus. 2. Pet. 1. 10.

What lamentations reade we of
the miserable damned, at the consi-
deration of so great a good, as they
haue exchanged and forgone for a fa-
ding pleasure? *Sap.* 5.

EXAMPLES.

1. S. Francis being one day extre-
amlie afflicted with the head-ache,
gaue thankes to God , and asked
strength of him to suffer the same; and
behould he heard a voice which said
vnto him. Francis, if all the earth were
conuerted into gold, the sea, the riuers, and the fountaines into baulme,
the rockes and stones, into pretious
pearles; and further that thou hadst
found a treasure as much more pretious then all this, as gold is more
esti-

eſtimable then the earth, baulme then water, pretious pearles then common ſtones, and that it were giuen thee for this infirmitie, ſhouldſt thou not haue matter to reioyce thee? Alas Lord (ſaid Saint Francis) I am not worthy of ſuch a treaſure. The voice replied vnto him; Know notwithſtading, that this treaſure is, the life eternall which I prepare thee, and this head-ache which thou endu* reſt, is the earneſt. *Tom. 2. Chron. frat. minor. l. 1 c 51.* The glory which I expect (would he ſomtimes ſay) is ſo great, that all paine, all ſicknes, all humiliation, all perſecution, all mor-tification, doth reioyce me.

2. S. Thomas, being asked of his ſiſter (to whom he appeared) what the glory of heaué was: vntil the time that you haue tried it (quoth he) no man is euer able for to tell you. *Rib. in his life.*

3. S. Adrian, being as yet a ſoldiar, of the age of eight and twentie yeares, behoulding the coſtancy of the martirs

K 3 amidſt

amidſt the ſharpeſt of their torments, asked of them, what good they hoped to haue by thoſe torments? who made him anſwer; We hope for thoſe goods *which nether eye hath ſeene, nor eare hath heard, nor yet hath entred into the hart of man.* This anſwere moued him ſo much, that he alſo would be enrolled in the catalogue of the martyrs, and endured conſtantly to haue his members cut aſunder peece by peece, in the ſight of his wife, who likewiſe encouraged him therunto. *Ribad. ypon his life.*

4. Theophilus aduocate, hauinge receiued certaine Roſes and Apples from heauen, which S. Dorothe dying, ſent vnto him by an Angell, found them ſo faire and ſo good, that deſiring to enter in the garden from whence they were gathered, he became Chriſtian, and ſuffered martyrdome. *Ribad. in the life of S. Dorothe virg. and mart.*

5. Sir Thomas Moore Lord Chancelor of England being in priſon, his wife came and importuned him to con-

condeſcend vnto the pleaſure of the Kinge, preſentinge vnto him on the one ſide, her future pouertie, and the miſerable eſtate of all her familie: and on the other part, the honors and riches which kinge Harry had promiſed him, if he would be on his ſide. Sir Thomas demanded of her; How longe (my dearly beloued) ſhall we enioy theſe honors and riches? Very eaſily yet (quoth ſhe) theſe twentie yeares. Then Sir Thomas, all angrie with her, ſaid vnto her; Get thee gone (quoth he) thou fooliſh marchant: what, ſhall I for twentie yeares ·of temporall goodes, looſe all the infinite goods of life eternall? God forbid that I euer make any ſuch market, yea, know that I had rather lie in this priſon as longe as I liue, ſuffer confiſcation of my goodes, all kindes of contumelies, and death it ſelfe, then to expoſe ſo foole-hardily, my felicitie: as indeed he did, for he was put to death for this cauſe.

Sanderus de ſchiſmate Angl.

Would

Would to God we did the same, as often as ouer flesh (like to this womā) incites vs to sinne: and that at the smiting of the clock, yea in all times, we had in our mouth and in our hart, this short sentence.

O glorie eternall, what is it to haue thee, and what is it to loose thee!

THE

The true Christian Catholique,

or

The maner how to liue Christianly,

THE SECOND BOOKE.

THE PROLOGVE.

IT is an error of the heretiques (who vnder the name of a Christian, which they carrie with false markes, and vnder the skin of a sheepe, nourish the hart of a woulfe) that to go to heauen, it is not necessarie to doe good workes. Such an one was Valentinus as S. Ireneus testifieth (*l. 1. c. 1.*) and S. Epiphanius (*l. 1. cont. heref. c. 32.*) And Eunomius and Ætius his Disciple, of whom S. Aug. maketh mention (*l. de heresibus c. 54.*) and in the age last past, Luther, Caluin, Melancthon &c. (*Bellar. tom. 11. controuer. l. 4. c. 20. de iustificatione.*) Yea Luther saith, that faith is nothing worth, vnles it be

K 5   depri-

depriued of all good workes, how litle foeuer. Did any euer heare, more abfurd and pernicious doctrine? Thou art better taught, ô true Chriſtian Catholique (and it is by the fruites alſo of thy good workes, that the ſanctitie of thy ſoule is knowen:)for thou houldeſt with the vniuerſall Church, according to the leſſon, which the holy Ghoſt hath taught her in the ſcripture, and the holy Fathers, that he who intends to goe to heauen, ought to to keepe the comandements of God, & to exerciſe him ſelfe in good workes.

This is that which our Lord ſaid vnto a certaine Doctor in *S. Mat.* 19. 17. *& c.* 7. 22. *Not euery one that ſaith to me, Lord, Lord,* (like as heretiques doe, who haue often in their mouth the name of the Lord, but haue the diuell in their hart) *ſhal enter into the kingdome of heauen, but he that doth the will of my father. Which is in heauen.*

Lord (ſaith Dauid) *who ſhall dwell in thy tabernacle, or who ſhall reſt in thy holie*

lie hil? P*ſal.* 14. 1.

Thou wilt render to euery one according to his workes. P*ſ.* 61. 13. *Mat.* 16. 27.

And if I ſhould haue all faith, ſo that I could remoue mountaines, and haue not charitie, I am nothing. 1. *Cor.* 13. 2.

See the ſentence of S. Peter, in the 1. booke laſt chap. §. 7.

We haue before brought and al-leadged that, whick maketh for the extirpation of vice; And ſith it is not e-nough for a Gardener, to haue rooted vp the naughtie herbes out of his garden vnles he likewiſe ſowe good ſeede therein, and ſet good plantes, I will with Gods aſiſtance in this ſecōd booke, giue aduice vnto the Chriſtiā, who deſires to liue as a good and virtuous Catholique, ought do doe, and ſhew him the meanes proper and eaſie, how to plant in his ſoule ſuch virtues as are moſt neceſſary, for the exerciſe of good workes: follovving the ſelfe ſame order which I did before, to wit, of holie Scripture, holie Fathers, & Examples.

5.

K 6 THE

THE I. CHAPTER.

Of the signe of the Crosse.

THE soldiars of this world accustome, to weare vpon them a scarfe or riban, of the same color of their Ensigne, to giue to vnderstand, vnder what head & banner they beare armes. In like maner the Christian, who is the soldiar of Iesus Christ, and serueth vnder the stâdart & ensigne of the Crosse, hath a custome to giue this signe (*a*) at all times, & in euery houre, imprinting it, ether on his fore-head, on his mouth, or on his breast (*b*) in the morninge at his vp risinge, in the eueninge at his downe lying, at the striking of the clock, in yaninge, both before and after worke, eating, drinking, and in eache necessitie : which from all antiquitie hath bene vsed in the Church (*c*) yea both prefigured and fore-tould by the Prophets (*d*) in the old

old law, and taught and recommended
by our B. Sauiour in the new. *(e)*

(a) *S. Ephrem l. de vera pœnitentia c.*
3. S. Aug. l. de Cat. rud. c. 20. (b) *S. Am-*
broſe de Iſaac & anima c. 8. (c) *Tertul.*
de corona milit. c. 3. (d) *Ezech. 9.* (e)
Mat. 28.

§. 1. *Of the ancient vſe and cuſtome, to*
make the ſigne of the Croſſe, at the be-
gining and ending of our workes: and
how dangerous it is, ether to eate or
drinke, not makinge before hand this
holy ſigne.

The prophet Ezechiel, ſaw vpon a
day ſix men enter into the temple of
Ieruſalem, and heard a voice which
commanded them, to paſſe thorough
the middes of the citty, and to ſtrike or
kill without mercie, al the inhabitants,
except *euery one vpon whom they ſhould*
ſee the ſigne of Thau. Ezech. 9. 5.

S. Iohn in the *Apoc. c. 7. 1.* ſaw four
Angells, who had commandement
from almightie God, to afflict all the
men

men vpon the earth. And as they went
to execute this commandement , *an-*
other Angell came from the rising of the
sunne, hauing the signe of the liuing God,
who turning himselfe towards the o-
thers said . *Hurt not the earth and the*
sea, nor the trees, till we signe the seruants
of our God in their foreheades . And S.
Iohn saith , that the number of those
that were thus signed, were a hundred
fortie four thousand, of euery tribe of
Israell. *Ibid v. 4.*

Our Lord said vnto his Apostles.
Going therfore teache yce all nations, bap-
tising them in the name of the Father, and
of the Sonne, and of the holy Ghost . *Mat.*
28. 19.

Tertullian who liued in the yeare
of our Lord 198. saith , that the true
Christian is accustomed in entring in,
going forth, in putting on his clothes,
at his vprising, at his setting downe at
the table , when candles are lighted,
when he goes to bed , and when he
sets him downe to rest him , in all his
con-

conuersation, and in all his exercises, to make the signe of the Crosse vpon his forehead. If one aske you (quoth he) what the origine is of such like thinges? Answere, tradition hath left them, custome hath confirmed them, and faith hath practised them. *lib. de corona milit. c. 3.*

S. Cyrill catechisinge a Christian, saith as followeth. Be not ashamed to confes the Crucifix, engraue with thy fingars confidently, the signe of the Crosse vpon thy fore-head, & on euery other thinge, vpon thy bread, vpon thy drinke, at thy going out, at thy coming in &c. *Cyrill. Hier. Cat. 13. The same S. Amb saith of Isaac and the soule. c. 8. S. Basill in his booke of the holy Ghost. c. 27. S. Hier. ad Eustoch. de custod. virg. S. Aug. de Cat. rud. c. 20.* Seest thou then (o Christian) that it is not a new thinge to vse this signe?

EX-

EXAMPLES.

1. S. Gregorie the great, writeth in his dialogues, that a certaine religious woman was pofeffed of the diuell, in eating the leafe of a lettice, for not making theron before hande the figne of the Croffe. *L. 1. dialog. c. 4.*

2. Ioannes Niderus, of the order of the Preachers, writeth to haue vnderftood from the mouth of a Doctor in diuinitie, and inquifitor of his order, as an eye witnes, that a religious man of the couent of Boifleduc, was poffeffed alfo of the diuell, tafting but the leafe of a cabbedge, ommitting to make theron the figne of the Croffe. *l. 3. formicarij. c. 1.*

3. S. Bennet, hauing made the figne of the Croffe vpon a pot, wherin fome illwillers of his had put poifon, and prefented it to him, the pot broke in peeces, and all the liquor was fhed a grounde, as if the figne of the Croffe, had bene vnto it the blowe of a ftone.

S.

S. *Greg. l. 2. Dial. 6. 3.*

4. A gentleman of Arras, in the low contries, hauing prepared in his houfe a moft fumptuous banquet for Kinge Cloitarus, and for S. Vaaft, Bifhop of the faid cittie; as the Saint had fet his foote within the place where the banquet was, he made the figne of the Croffe, and behould inftantly all the potts, cuppes, glaffes, and veffells, broke and crackt all in peeces. The Kinge and the afiftants aftonifhed therat, S. Vaaft faid vnto them, that thefe veffells polluted with panims fuperftitions, could not fuffer the figne of the Croffe, which he had made vpon them in entring in. *Doctor du Val in in the life of S. Vaaft 6. of Feb.* Is not this a maruellous virtu of this figne.

5. Ribadeneira in the life of S. Iohn the Euangelift writeth, that a certaine Chriftiã finding him felfe preffed by his creditors, not hauing wher with to cõtent & pay them, all in defpaire, refolued for to kill him felfe, & for this purpofe

pofe had bought of a Iew a poifoned
drinke . But yet before he dranke it,
he made theron the figne of the holy
Croffe, and behould it did him no maner of harme. He returned to the Iew,
and made his complaint: he aftonifhed
thereat , gaue him another yet more
ftronger. But hauing také it in the felfe
fame fafhion as he had the former, he
receiued no kinde of domage therby.
The Iew gaue therof in his prefence
to a dog , and the dog died inftantly.
Then he enquired of the Chriftian,
what he had done before he dranke it.
Who anfwered, that he had done no
other thinge , faue only made vpon it
the figne of the Croffe , accordinge to
the cuftome of all good Chriftiás. The
Iew admiring the virtu of the Chriftiá
ceremonies, went and fought out S.
Iohn Euangelift, recounted vnto him
the fact aforfaid , and caufed him felfe
to be baptifed . Afterwards S. Iohn
made the Chriftian that was thus in
defpaire to come vnto him, bearing a
                                          litle

bundle of hearbes, and hauing made
theron the ſigne of the Croſſe, conuerted it into perfect golde, where with
the miſerable man contented his creditors. Good God what an Antidote,
and what a treaſure is this holy ſigne?

§. 2. That this ſigne is a preſeruatiue a-
gainſt all danger, and particularly againſt
the tentations of the diuel?

S. Cyrill ſaith. Make the Croſſe v-
pon thy fore head, that ſo the deuils
perceiuing the caractar of the kinge, all
affrighted, may take their flight. *Catec.*
4. And in another place he ſaith. This
ſigne is the protection of the faithfull,
and the terror of the diuells. *Catech.13.*
The ſame doth S. Baſil alſo ſay. *lib. de*
Spiritu Sanc. S. Efrem de pœnit. c. 3. & de
armat. ſpirit. c. 2. Origen. hom. 6. in c. 5.
Exod. S. Aug. ad Catech. c. 2. de Simbolo.
S. Paulin natal. 8. S. Felicis.

S. Antonie was wont to ſay, that
the ſigne of the Croſſe, was an vnex-
pugnable rampart againſt the diuels.
Arme

Arme your selues, said he to his disciples, both your selues & your houses with this signe, and the diuells shall vanish away immediatly.

EXAMPLES.

1. S. Gregorie writeth, that a Iew was conuerted to the faith, for hauing being preserued by night from the diuells, within the ruines of an olde temple of Apollo, by the signe of the Crosse, which he had made vpon himselfe, according to the imitation of the Christians; the diuells crying. *An emptie, but, a signed vessel. l.3. dial. c,7.* Now if the signe of the Crosse made by a Iew, had so much force, what shall it haue, being made by a true Christian Catholique?

2. Palladius writeth, that a good old man, hauing espied in the bottome of a well, an ouglie serpent, made the signe of the Crosse vpon the welle, drew of the water, & drāk therof without receiuing any detriment. *Lausiac. c. 2.*   3. Theo-

3. Theodoret in the life of Iulian and S. Martian martyrs, writeth that theſe Saintes only by the ſigne of the Croſſe, ſlew ſundry great and horrible Dragons. The ſame alſo did S. George, *as Metaphraſtes writeth in his life.*

4. Certaine Perſians being ſent to Conſtantinople to the Emperor Mauritius by the kinge Coſroas, were demáded by the ſaid Emperor, why they bore the ſigne of the Croſſe imprinted & grauen vpon their foreheads, ſeeing that according to their owne law, they did no kinde of honor to it? Who anſwered, that this they did, to recall to their minde the benefit receiued by that ſigne, ſaying, that according to the inſtructions which they had learned of the Chriſtiás, in arming themſelues with this ſigne, they had bene deliuered frō the plague. *Niceph. Caliſt. in his hiſtorie.*

5. S. Aug. writeth, that in Carthage, one of the chiefeſt matrons of the citty calied Innocentia, hauing had a cankre vpon her breaſt, was tould of a principall

principall phisitian, that there was no
maner of meanes for to heale her. She
then seeing her selfe vtterly destitute
of humane helpe, resolued to haue recourse vnto God. Hereupon our Lord
said in her sleepe vnto her, that towardes the holy feast of Easter, she should
goe nere to the baptismall fontes, and
that the first baptised mayden or wife
that she should meete, should make the
signe of the Crosse vpon her breast.
She beleeued this councell , which
being done , she found her selfe per-
fectly healed. *Aug. l. 22. ciuit. c.* 8.

6. Tilmanus Bredembachus , recounteth in his conferences , that an
heretique going from Geneua to Lau-
sania , in the companie of a Catholique, the heauens were troubled vpon
a soddaine, with abundāce of thunder-
claps and of lightninge. The Catholique (according to the pious custome
of the Christians) armed and blest him
selfe with the signe of the Crosse ;
which the heretike seeing, asked him
in

in scoffing at him, if he did the same to driue away the flies? But this his blasphemy escaped not without present punishment, for scarcely had he pronounced those wordes, but that the thunder began to redouble its blowes, and stroke him with a bolt, which slew him outright vpon the place, without any hurt in the worlde vnto the Catholique. *l. 7. col. sacr. c. 58.* What say you (o you scoffing heretiques) vnto these maruelles of the Crosse? But behould here more.

7. A certaine Witch, confessing one day vpon the rack, her wicked witchcraft, said that she had bene carried aboue fiftie times by the diuell, to kill the litle sonne of one of her kinred, which was as yet in the cradle, but that she neuer had any power ouer him, for that his mother, before she laid him downe, made alwaies the signe of the Crosse vpon his forehead. *Bartholomeus Spineus master of the sacred palace, quest. de stigibus l. 17. & seq. Martinus Delrio*

Delrio disq. mag. l. 2. q. 10.. Loe what a goodly example this is for you, fathers and mothers.

8. Editha daughter to the Kinge of England, hauing all her life this for a custome, to make vpon all occasions the signe of the Crosse, with her thūbe vpon her forehead, when her body was taken vp, thirteene yeares after her death, S. Dunstan founde, that her eyes, her handes, and her feete being rotten, the thumbe only of the right hande, wher with she was wont to blesse her selfe, still remayned whole and entire. *Surius in her life tom. 5. 16. Sept. e. 4. 5. Pet. de natal. l. 11. c. 70.*

What can be more cleare to proue, that to make the signe of the Crosse, is a thinge marueilouslie aggreable to almightie God?

THE

THE II. CHAPTER.

Of Prayer and Thanksgiuing which a Christian ought to make morning and euening, before, and after meate. And of the inuocation of our B. Lady, of our Angell Gardian, and our other Patrons.

AS the night and sleepe, are not giuen to man, but for the ease and rest of the body, (*a*) for that our enimie the diuell sleepeth not, whilst we sleepe (*b*) ether to strangle vs, if we be in sinne, or to fill vs with dreames and filthie illusions, if we be in grace; And seing that the day is not giuen vs but to worke our saluation (*c*) and yet can do nothing (*d*) say nothing (*e*) thinke (*f*) nor haue any thing, without the asiltace of almighty God, from whom we haue our being, mouing & life (*g*) doth it not follow, that it is more the reason, & altogether necessarie, to haue recourse vnto God in al seasons, espe-

L

especially in the morning, to passe the day profitably, and in the euening, to auoide the dangers of the night ? (*h*) And if an humble acknowledgment, be the meanes to draw and attract new benefits , (*i*) how much ought we to thanke the diuine bountie , which from moment to moment, bestoweth vpon vs so many fauors , giftes , and graces ?

Consider moreouer, that he who will obtaine any fauor of a Kinge , is wonte after he hath presented some request vnto him, to repaire to the Queene, and to such other courtiers as are most &highest in his fauor;iudge the if it be not the part of a wise man , after he hath presented his prayer vnto God, to haue recourse to our B. Lady (*k*) the Queene of Angells and mother of God, to the holy Angells, and (*l*) particularly to him that keepes him (*m*)and next vnto the other Saintes (*n*) but aboue al others,to those of whom one beareth the reliques or their name,

or

or else hath taken them for his espe-
ciall patrons, all which doe loue vs
with a most perfect charitie (o) and
can preuaile exceedinge much with
almightie God (p) as those which are
his courtiars, his domesticalls, and his
fauorits (q)

(a) *S. Bernard ad fratres de monte Dei*
(b) *Mat. 13. 25. 1. Pet. 5. 8.* (c) *Luc. 19. 13.*
(d) *Iuan. 15. 5. Phil. 2. 13.* (e) *1. Cor. 12.*
3. (f) *2. Cor. 3. 5.* (g) *Art 17. 28.* (h)*psal.*
90. 6. (i) *Cassiod. in psal. & in epist.* (k)
Chrisost. Gen. Hom 9. (l) *Ber. in serm.*
in Nat. B. Mariæ (m) *Amb. l. de viduis*
(n) *Heb. 1. 14. Tob. 12. Apoc. 8. 3.* (o)*Iob.*
5. 1. psal. 150. 1. (p)*Ber. ser. 2. de S. Vict.*
(q) *ibid in vigil Pet. & Paul. Apost.* (r)
Damas. l. 4. de orthod. fide c. 16.

§. *1. Of the prayer which a Christian ought*
to make, morning and euening.

It is a thinge vnbeseeming a Christian (who nether sleepeth nor wa-
keth, but for the glorie and seruice of

L 2   al-

almightie God) to employ together with the night, a part alfo of the day in flouthfull fleeping, and to lye a bed without neceffitie, efpecially then, when all creatures (euen the vnreafonable)doe laude and praife their Creator, euery one after his kinde: and that artificers, for the pelfe and goods of this prefent worlde, are bufied about their worke from the breake of the day. How much is one houre worth to him, which liueth not, faue only to negociat his faluation? And what loffe is it, to loofe that which is worth fo much, and neuer can be recouered againe? *Ber. ferm ad fcolares.*

It is enough to fleepe feauen houres, both to yoũg & old, faith the prouerb.

*Loue not fleepe, left pouertie oppreffe thee,*faith the wifman. *Pro. 20. 13.*

S. Bernard faith. Take heede, as much as poffible thou maift, that thou giue not thy felfe wholie to fleepe, left that which ought to ferue for repofe to the wearied body, and for reparation of the

the spirit, serue for the burying of the body, and for the extinction of the spirit. *Ad fratres de monte.*

As soon as thou art awake, make the signe of the Crosse, and say this short prayer (much recommended by S. Iohn Chrisostome, ser. 21. ad pop. Antioch.) *I renounce the diuell, and rely vpon thee o Iesus Christ, who art the way, the truth, & the life:* and by this meanes, thou shalt present and giue thy first thought to almighty God, which the diuel laboureth and casteth how to carry away.

At the houre of risinge, slack not thy selfe, but run before, first into thy house, & there withdraw thy selfe, and there pray (saith the wiseman, *Eccl. 32. 15.*) For feare lest that befall thee, as it did to the Spouse in the Cant. Whilst thou deliberatest to arrise, Iesus Christ thy spouse, doe depart. Can. 5.

In arising and making thee ready, reiect saith S. Bonauéture, al the dreames and thoughts of the night, wherin the deuil endeuoreth to occupy thee, & offer to to God the first fruites of all thy thoughtes, and labor by meditation or by prayer, to excite good thoughtes and affections of deuotion; and this will make thee more prompt and readie to doe good workes, all the day after. *Tract. de interiori Hom. p. 1. c. 4. Clymachus c. 21.*

Recite the Pater, Aue, Credo, Anima Christi, or the soule of Christ &c.

We ought, saith S. Ambrose, euery morning before day, to say, especially the Creede, as the seale & lock of our hart, and as often as we are seased with any feare: for when is it, I pray you, that the soldiar entereth into his tent, or marcheth in battaile, without his watch-word? *S. Amb. l. 3. de Virg. S. Aug. saith the same, tom. 9. l. de simb. ad catechum. c. 1. & l. 2.*

Being apparrelled, fall vpon your knees in your oratorie, or before some picture, and say with hart, and with affection.

I giue thee thankes, o my God, for
all

all the benefits which I haue receiued
of thee, and in particular, for hauing
preſerued me this night from all euill.

I offer vnto thee, my ſoule and bodie to thy ſeruice, with all whatſoeuer I ſhall doe, to thy greater glorie
and honor.

I purpoſe likewiſe, to liue better
then I haue done, and rather to die a
thouſand times, then once to offend
thee mortally. O my God, giue me
the grace, to put in practiſe this my
good purpoſe.

Then addreſſing you to the Queene
of Angells and of Saintes, you ſhalſay.

Holy Marie mother of God, pray
for me. My Angell gardian, pray for
me. My patron Saint N. pray for me.
All the Saintes of heauen, prayfor me.
Pater. Aue, Credo, De profundis.

It is good to confes to our Lord (that is
according to the expoſition of Card.
Bellarmine, it is reaſonable, profitable,
and delectable) *to ſinge to thy name ô
Higheſt, to shew forth thy mercie in the*

L 4 *mor-*

morning, and thy truth in the night. Pſal.
91. 1.

It is now the houre for vs, to riſe from
ſleepe, for now our ſaluation is neerer
then when we beleeued. The night is paſſed, and the day is at hande, let vs therfore
caſt off the workes of darknes, and doe on
the armour of light; As in the day let vs
walke honeſtly, not in banquettinge and
drunkennes, not in chamberinges and im-
pudicities, not in contention and emulation,
but doe yee on our Lord Ieſus Chriſt, and
make not prouiſion for the fleſh in concu-
piſcences. Rom. 13. 11.

Alas who knowes (but only God)
whither that houre wherin thou ari-
ſeſt, ſhall not perhaps be the very laſt
of all thy life? Watch yee therſore, becauſe you know not the day, nor the houre
Mat. 25. 13.

EXAMPLES.

1. Ioannes Niderus writeth, to haue
knowen a gentleman of note, named
Sucher, who whilſt he kept in a caſtle
nighe

nighe the towne of Halle in Germany,
as he grew cold in the seruice of God,
nor frequenting the Sacraments as he
was wonte, becaufe of the quarrells
which he had against thofe of Halle,
went and fild his caftle with a companie of lewed feruants, all trained vp in
warres, and enured to their weapons:
the diuell (difguifed like a foldiar) came
alfo to prefent and offer his feruice to
him. This couetous gentleman, feeing
that this foldiar offred to ferue him
without any wages, he accepted of
him, and made him his horfe-keeper.
The deuil began from that time, to
ferue his mafter with all fidellitie, but
it was obferued after a longe while,
that he neuer went vnto the Church,
conducting his mafter only vnto the
doore, & then returning to his worke.

The gentlemã although debauched,
yet still continued his good cuftome,
now & thē to heare Maffe & wēt not
to bed, nor yet arofe, but frft he made
the figne of the Croffe, and faid fome
L 5 certaine

taine Aue Maries. And hauing bene tould and obseruing him selfe, that his horse-keeper neuer went to Church, he vrged him vpon a day, to tell him freely who he was. The horf-keeper tould him, that he was the deuill, but bid him for all this, not to haue any apprehention, sithe he had still til then found him faithfull, and should still finde him more and more from that time forward. The gentleman was at the firft a litle afraid, not withstanding, moued with couetousnes, resolued to keepe him yet a while.

One night as he slept, behould this diuell horse-keeper, awaked him with a sodaine starting, crying. Master, Master. The gentleman asked what was the matter; Quickly, quickly (quoth the diuell) put on your apparell and your armes, for those of Halle are coming for to take your castle. The gentleman affrighted at these newes, clothed him, and put on his armes with all possible speed, neuertheles not forgetting

getting him selfe to make, the signe of
the Crosse, and to say his prayers he
was wont to say. Being vp, and ready,
he looked forth at all the windoes,
and saw nothinge, whence he perceiued that this was nothing but a false
alarum: and all in cholar, asked of his
deuill, what had moued him, so to
trouble and molest him, in the midst
of his sleepe. The diuell aswered him,
that he had done it for this designe,
thinking that the affrithtment and sodaine haste to get him vp, would haue
made him forgot the making of the
signe of the Crosse, and saying of his
prayers, and by this meanes he would
haue set vpon him. The gentlmā hearing this, was euer after much more
dilligent in this his dutie then he was
before, but he could not for all this be
quit of this deuelish seruant, vntill
such time as he began to frequent the
Sacramēts: for the very first time whe
rin he had recourse vnto them, the diuell vanished quite away, and he neuer

L 6   saw

ſaw him afterwardes. *Niderus l.3. form.*

Loe what diligence the diuel vſeth, to hinder vs to pray in the morning? What virtu the ſigne of the Croſſe hath, the Aue Marie, & the Sacramēts?

If the diuell tempt vs, we haue alſo a good Angell which doth counter-gard vs. *God hath giuen his Angells charge of thee, that they keepe thee in all thy wayes. Pſalm. 90. 11.*

2. S. Raimondus, of the order of the friar Preachers, had an Angell which often times appeared vnto him, and for the moſt part before the belles were rūge to Matins at midnight in the Couents where he was, who a-wakened him, & inuited him to praier.

3. S. Cecily and S. Francis the Romā, and one S. Stilites of Edeſſa, who liued nine and fortie yeares vpō a pillar, had an Angell which ſhewed him ſelfe vn to them viſibly, and conuerſed with them familiarly. *Surius and Ribadeneira. Raderus in virid. ſanct. p. 2. c. 5.*

4. Ioannes Carrera of the ſocietie
of

of Ieſus, from the time that he was a nouice, had a familiar Angel, with whom he diſcourſed very often, and receiued of him, the full reſolution of his doutes: who was wont euery day, about four a clock in the morning, to awake him. And as once (ouercome with ſleepe) he did not ariſe at the Angels waking, he was depriued for certaine dayes of his viſitation, vntill ſuch time as hauing done pennance, he entred againe into his fauour. Notwithſtanding the holy Angell wild him, that from thence forward, he ſhould be more diligent to ariſe earlie. *L. 13. hiſt ſoc. anno 1551.*

If we al haue a particular Angel, who doth accompanie and ſecure vs euery where, is it not reaſon that we ſhould honor him, and often reclayme him? But marke with all, what a hart griefe it is to our good Angell, when he muſt attende nere vnto vs, whilſt we play the truants & ſlouthful ſluggards in our beds!

For

For inuocation of Saintes, see §. 3. following, *sect. 2.*

§. 2. *Of thanksgiuing which we ought to render to God in all times, but particularly after meate and drinke.*

If all benefits require at the lest a God-a-mercie, the Christian, who at euery moment, receiueth so many benefits and fauours of almightie God, can he doe lesse, morning and euening (and somtimes also during the day) then render humble thākes vnto him? The Cocks and Hennes, albeit vnreasonable, neuer drinke, but they lift vp their head and eyes to heauen, as if they would at euery beak-ful, acknowledg and thankfully blesse, God their Creator. O Christian, art not thou worse then the beastes, if so often fed and refreshed by the liberall hande of this our Lord, thou vouchsafest not once to lift thine eyes towards heauen, to giue and rendar thankes vnto him?

him? If a man condemned to perpetuall imprisonment, were euery day
fed deliciously, by one which would
let him down from aboue both meate
and drinke, should he not be a very
beast, if he daigned not to lift vp his
head, to see and acknowledge that
good person, which should doe so
great a good vnto him? Alas, we
are all prisoners, as longe as we liue in
this valley of teares, our good God
notwithstanding, moued with mercie
and compassion, causeth to fall vpon
vs from heauen, an infinite number of
good thinges: he clotheth vs, giueth
vs both to eate and to drinke, there
is no moment nor yet minute, wherin
he doth not poure into vs of his fauors, both for our body and our soule.
Yet how many are there, notwithstanding, which not at euery houre, nor
yet in euery day, daigne so much as to
lift vp their head towards heauen, to
acknowledg him?

Our Lord gaue vpon a day to vnderstand,

derftand, how greeuoufly he tooke it,
that hauing healed ten Leapers, there
was but one of them which returned
to thanke him. *Luc.* 17.

I haue brought vp children and exalted
them, but they haue defpifed me, faith our
Lord by his prophet; *Ifay* 1. 2. 3.

In al thinges giue thankes, for this is the
will of God in Chrift Iefus 1. *Thef.* 5. 18.

When thou haft eaten and art full, thou
maift bleffe the Lord thy God. Deutro. 8.
10. *Although thou eate twice a day, yet*
take alwaies thy meate with giuing of
thankes. S. Ephrem adhort. 1.

What may we (faith S. Aug) thinke,
fpeake, or write better, then *Deo gra-*
tias, thankes be to God! Nothing can
be pronounced more briefly, heard
more willinglie, nor practifed more
profitably. *Aug. ad Marcellinum ep.* 5.

EXAMPLES.

Father Martinus Delrio, in his treatife of Magick, writeth, that three
                                   lewed

lewed companions in a certaine place
of Flanders, eaſhe he, with his eache
ſhe, after they had ſet at table till midnight was paſt, the one of them ſaid.
We haue eate and drunke, it is now
time to giue God thankes. As for me,
replied another, I giue thankes vnto
the diuell, for he it is whom we doe
ſerue. Theſe wordes were entertayned of all with great laughter, but
not of God; for as they lay by their
ſtrumpets, behould how on a ſodaine, the chamber doore opened of
it ſelfe with a great noiſe, and a
man of a high pitch, in the habit
of a hunter, horribly frightfull, black
of face, and his eyes ſparkling, entred in, and two ſeruants after
him, who carried a countenance
and inſtruments, as if they were
Cookes.

Hauing walked awhile vp and
downe the chamber, he turned him towards the beds wherin theſe whores
and knaues were lodged, and ſaid.
Where

Where is he, that not longe since gaue
me thankes, I come to requite him
for his kindnes? And as none made
anfwere, he him felfe approached to
the bed where this blafphemer was,
more dead then aliue, rooke him by
the armes, & puld him forth vpon the
floore, then commanded his two Cookes, to put him vpon the fpit, and to
rofte him; The which was done as inftantly, for he was put vpon the fpit,
and after rofted like a quarter of mut-
ton, fo that the others from their beddes, felt the odor and the fmell.

After that he was all rofted, this
great diuell thus difguifed, addreft
him to thofe others who remayned in
their beddes. You(quoth he)haue merited as much as he, but God hath not
giuen me power, faue only vpon him
who gaue me thankes:amend your felues, or elfe you alfo fhall fhortly be
myne: which hauing faid, he difap-
peared. Where I leaue you to thinke,
whither the refidue of that night feemed

med longe vnto them, yea, or no, and
in what a tranſe they paſſed the ſame.

The day being come, they lept out
of their beds, and (a thing moſt fearfull) ſaw their companion all roſted,
and ſtarke dead. Ah good God, what
a horrible ſpectacle, and what an example for them, and for vs, beloued
Reader? *Delrio diſq. magic. l. 3. p. 1. q. 7.*

§. 3. *Of prayer, examen of conſcience, and*
Inuocation of Saintes, which a Chri-
ſtian ought to make before he
ſleepe.

Reaſon willes, that the childe acknowledg his father, ſaluting him at
his vpriſing, and before he goe to bed
to reconcile him ſelfe vnto him, and
to aske him bleſſing. The ſoldiar con-
uinced of enormous crimes, and for
the ſame in danger of his life, ſhould
he not merit to be hanged without
mercie, if he might haue preſently pardon for his faultes, by caſting him ſelfe
only

only with true repentance at the feete
of his captaine, and yet fhould difdai-
gne to doe it? Now fo it is, that God
the Creator, is our father (*a*) yea our
Head and foueraigne Emperor, as we
haue faid herebefore (*b*)what then doe
they deferue who daigne not to acknowledg him, laying them felues
downe in their beddes, like very beaftes, without thanking him for the benefits receiued the fame day? without
demanding his bleffing to efcape the
dangers of the night? and that which
is yet more to be weighed , without
making any reuiew of their life paft,
and asking him forgiuenes for the
faultes committed in the day? In the
meane while death (perhaps)is at their
beds feete, who the fame night is to let
fly his dart and arrowe at them, and to
fende them from their bed, to hell, and
from their foft boulter, to a burning
furnace of fire and of eternall flames.
Hapned it not fo to Holofernes? (*c*)
Sifara? (*d*) the rich glutton? (*e*) to the
                              flouth-

flouthfull feruant in the gofpell? (f) &
to a thoufand others, who laying the
downe like vnto thefe, and falling a
fleepe in perfect health, haue bene
found ftone dead on the morrow morninge? (a) *Malach. 1. 6. Mat. 5. 6. 23.*
Rom. 8. 15. & 16. (b) *l. 1. c. 1.* (c) *Iudith*
13. (d) *Iudg. 4.* (e) *Luc. 16.* (f) *Luc. 12.*

Watch yee therfore, faith our Lord,
that is to fay, ftande vpon your garde,
put your felues in good eftate) *for you*
know not when the Lord of the houfe co-
meth, at euening, or at midnight, or at the
cock crowing, left coming vpon a fodaine,
he finde you fleepinge (that is to fay, in
finne, without care, without folicitu-
de for the faluation of your foule:) *and*
that which I fay to you, I fay to all, watch.
Marc. 13. 35,

§. 1. Of the examen of our conſcience.

The examen of our confcience con-
fifteth in three pointes.

1. To

1. To thanke God for all benefits receiued, and particularly of that day.

2. To search and seeke forth diligently, all the thoughtes, wordes, and workes of that day, in the selfe same maner as if one should confes himself.

3. To excite an act of Contrition, with a firme purpose of amendment, and to be confest with the first occasion. (*See the act of Contrition pag. 265.*)

Next to recommend him selfe to the good protection of almighty God, of our B. Ladie, his Angell gardian, and of his patrons.

This practise is maruellous profitable, for by an act of true contrition, all sinnes are forgiuen (albeit we remaine obliged to confes them to the priest) in so much that, if a person hauing committed a great number of mortall sinnes, after he shall haue excited in him such an act of contrition, should come to die sodainly, not hauing the meanes for to confes them, he should be assured of his saluation; as contrariwise,

wiſe, not hauing made this act, he ſhould be damned infallibly.

See you the importance? Marke now what the holy ſcripture, and holy fathers ſay.

In the 4. pſal. 5. *The thinges that you ſay in your hartes, be yee ſorry for* (that is to ſay, for euill thoughtes, and with much more reaſon for euill workes) *in your chambers.* That is to ſay, aske God forgiuenes in going to bed.

Which S. Chriſoſtome explicating, ſaith. What meaneth this, *The thinges that you ſay in your hartes? &c.* that is to ſay, after ſupper when you goe to bed, being alone, in peace and ſilence, iudge your conſcience, and demand an account of your ſelfe: ſeeke forth all the bad actions of the day, and hauing ſet them before you, take vengance of them, and put them to death by a holy compunction.

And *in the 76. pſal. v. 6. I thought vpon old dayes, and the eternall yeares. I had in minde, and I meditated in the night* With

with my hart, and I was exercised, and I swept my spirit : that is to say, examining my conscience, and cleanfing it by a holy forrow, as S. Aug. expoundeth it? And the fame that holy Dauid did, the fame did kinge Ezechias, as is to be found in *Ifay, 38. 15.*

S. Anthonie was wont to recommend it ferioufly to his Difciples. *Athanaf. in his life*, as alfo S. Cyprian *fer. de paff. Chrifti.* S. Bafil. *fer. commonit. ad monach. fer. de Afcen. & fer. de inftit. monach.*

The marchants of the worlde (faith S. Efrem) are accuftomed, to calculate euery day, the gayne or loffe betyded to them in their traffique : and you, euery euening, confider in what termes your traffique ftandeth, examine what you haue done that day ; and in the morninge, that which you haue done during the night. *Ser. Afcet. de vita relig. See S. Chrifoft, Hom. 43. in Mat. S. Greg. Hom. 4. in Ezech. & 35. moral. in Iob. c. 6. & 7. S. Iohn Climach*
grad.

grad. 4. S. Doroth. de vita recte & piè insiit. c. 11. S. Bernard ad fratres de monte Dei. S. Benet. c. 4. of his rule. instru. 48. according to the explication of Trithemius l. 1. comment in hanc. reg. S. Bon. in opusc. de purit. consc. c. 12. & alibi. Tho. a Kemp. l. 1. de Imit. Christi c. 19. & l. 2. de discipl. claust. c. 9. & discipl. mon. c. 11.

The Act of Contrition put in practise.

An excellent praier, which euery Christian ought to haue by hart.

MY Lord Iesus Christ, *true God, and true man,* who art my Creator and my Redeemer, I am sorry from my very hart, for that I haue offended thee, and this for that thou art my God, and for that I loue thee aboue all thinges; And I purpose firmely neuer more to offend thee, and to withdraw my selfe far off from all occasions of sinne. I purpose also to confes me, and to fulfill the pennance which shall be imposed me; Moreouer, I offer vnto thee in satisfaction

M *of*

of all my sinnes, my life, my labours, and all the good workes which I shall euer doe. And as I humbly aske pardon of my sinnes, so I hope in thy goodnes and infinite mercy, that thou wilt forgeue them all, thorough the merits of thy most pretious blood, death, and passion, and giue me the grace for to amend me, and to perseuer in good estate vnto the end, Amen.

EXAMPLES OF CON-
trition.

1. Thomas of Cantimpre, somtimes Suffragan to the Archbishop of Cambray, writeth, that a wicked man, after he had violated his owne daughter, came to the reuerend Archbishop of Sens, to confes him selfe vnto him of his sinne, and hauinge declared it with many teares and true remorce of soule, he demanded if he might hope for pardon at Gods handes. Yes (quoth the Archbishop) if you be ready to fulfill the pennance which I shall giue you. All whatsoeuer your Lord-
ship

ſhip ſhal pleaſe (anſwered the penitent) although I ſhould endure a thouſand deathes. I enioyne you only (quoth the Archbiſhop) ſeauen yeares of pennance. What is that, replied the penitent? Albeit I ſhould doe pennance vntill the ending of the worlde, yet ſhall I not ſatisfie ſufficientlie. Goe, ſaid the Archbiſhop, I will that thou faſt only three daies with bread and water. Here the poore man began to weepe, beſeeching him to impoſe vpon him a pennance anſwerable to his crime. The Archbiſhop ſeeing him ſo truly contrite, ſaid vnto him finally. I ordaine that thou only ſay one *Pater noſter*, aſſuring thee that thy ſinne is forgiuen thee. Which the penitét hearing, he entred in to ſo great compunction, that hauinge caſt forth a deepe ſighe, he fell downe ſtarke dead vpon the place. The Archbiſhop aſſured ſince in his ſermon, that this man by reaſon of his great contrition, went ſtraight to heauen, without paſſinge

M 2   thorough

thorough Purgatorie. *Tract. de vniuerso lib. 2. c. 51. p. 7.*

2. Iacobus of Vitry Cardinall, writeth the like, of a maiden (who had sinned with her owne father, and afterwardes cut his throate, and poisoned her mother) who died at her confessars feete, thorough the vehemencie of her contrition : and he assured that it was needles to pray for her, for that she was alreadie saued . *Iul. Mazaim, repartes it of the said Cardinall vpon the 50. psal. p. 1. discourse 10.*

3. A great sinner died also of very sorrow, at the feete of S. Vincent Ferrier, and appearing to him said, that he was in glorie, without passing at all thorough Purgatorie, God being satisfied with his sorrow, for the full expiation of his sinnes. *Ribad in his life 5. of Aprill.*

4. S. Gregorie also writeth, that a religious man bewaylinge his sinne, heard a voice which said vnto him, that his contrition had blotted it out. *Hom. 34.*   Seing

Seing then that contrition is of ſuch moſt ſingular force, is it not wiſdome often to excite acts thereof, but eſpecially, before we goe to bed, or fall a ſleepe, to the end to put our ſelues in full aſſurance by this meanes?

EXAMPLES.

§. 2. *Of the Inuocation of Saintes.*

1. S. Edmond, Archbiſhop of Canterburie in England, from the time that he ſtudied in Paris, was wonte to ſay euery day in honor of our Lady and of S. Iohn Euangeliſt, the praier which beginnes. *O intemerata*, And chancing once to forget him ſelfe, S. Iohn appeared vnto him in the night with a feruler, make ſhew that he would ſtrike him. Notwithſtandinge he appeaſed him ſelfe and withheld his hande already lifted vp, gently admoniſhinge him, no more to ommit it. *Surius & Ribad. in his life the 16. of Nouemb.*

2. The ſelfe ſame Saint, experienced

M 3

rienced at another time, how dangerous it is to goe to bed, not hauinge first said his prayers. For hauing ommitted them vpon a certaine hollieday, behould how at the breaking of the day, the diuell appeared vnto him in a horrible forme, who seasing both his handes, hindred him so, that he could not make the signe of the Crosse. But the virtuous Saint, seeing that he could not make it, nether by deed, nor yet by worde, he made it in his hart and in spirit, and forthwith the diuell fell downe vpon the pauement betwixt the bedsted and the wall; Which S. Edmond seeing, he lept vpon his bellie, and tooke him fast by the throate, and coniured him in the virtu of the passion of Iesus Christ, and of his pretious blood, to tell vnto him by what meanes he was most easily ouercome? By these meanes (quoth the diuell) which thou hast euen now named to me.

3. The deuout Thomas a Kempis canon

canon regular, being yet a younge ſcholler at Dauentrie, was wont dailie to offer vp a certaine number of prayers, in the honor of our Lady, to whō he carried a ſingular affection : but as youth is light and inconſtant, he grew by litle and litle to be ſo luke-warme, that he began to be, firſt one day without ſaying them, then two, then four, and at the laſt, he left them off for all together.

But behould, one night in the dead of his ſleepe, he thought he was in the halle (of Maiſter Florence his teacher) full of ſchollars: amongſt whom, as he harkned as he thought with great greedines vnto the word of God, which the religious men of that order expounded vnto them, heauen did open vpon a ſodaine, and in a faire and moſt bright cloude, the queene of Angells deſcended into this halle, with a ſweet and ſmiling countenance, and in a habit very ſumptuous : then ſhe embraced them all with great demonſtration

M 4   and

and fignes of loue. This good Thomas
thought with him felfe that his turne
alfo would come at the laft, but he was
foully deceiued herein, for hauinge
embraced all the others, fhe turned
to him, and looking vpon him with a
difcontented eye, faid vnto him. It is
in vaine that thou expecteft this my
kindnes (light and incoftant that thou
art) who thorough an accurfed and
wretched flouth, haft left to pay me
that number of prayers, thou was accuftomed. Where are thofe deuotiõs
wher-with thou feruedft me? Where
are thofe fighes and thofe louing dar-
tinges? There is now no more loue in
in thee, and yet thou awaiteft (auda-
cious that thou art) to be cherifhed &
made much of by me. Hence (quoth
fhe) get thee gone from me, for thou
art vnworthy of my embracinges, and
fhalt fo be, as longe as thou ommitteft
to offer vnto me thy accuftomed prayers: which hauing faid, it feemed vnto
him, that fhe afcended againe vpp to
hea-

heauen, and diſappeared.

Thomas awaking after this viſion, remaynéd maruellouſly perplext and ſorrie: he examined his conſcience, & founde to haue fayled for ſome weekes paſt, in his exerciſe of deuotion; wher-vpon he preſently aroſe, fell vpon his knees, and humbly asking God forgi-uenes and his mother, made a firme purpoſe, neuer more to ommit thoſe prayers, for any occaſion whatſoeuer: which he afterwards obſerued faith-fully euen till his death. *ſpecul. exempl. diſt. 10. §. 7.*

4. A certaine Dominican, had for a time kept this good and god-lie cuſtome, neuer to goe vnto his bed, but firſt to offer vp ſome prayers in the honor of S. Barbara, and by this meanes, had often bene preſerued from ſundry perills. At the laſt, he vtterly left it; And behould vpon a night, Sainte Barbara appeared to him, ſaying vnto him, that as he had left her, ſo ſhee likewiſe would

leaue

leaue him, nor would no longer doe
him the fauors , which he had well
founde and proued vnto that present.

He related this vision to his bretheren, but yet for all this, did not amend
him . Wherupon forsaken of the succour of this Saint, he debauched him
selfe by litle and litle, in such sort, that
at the last he cast his habit vpon the
hedge, and left his religion . After he
had wandred abroade here and there,
he came to Nuremberg, where he fell
sick , and was forced to lodge in the
common hospitall . Father Conradus
(one of his order) hauing knowledge
therof, sent vnto him the habit by some
of his religious, and prayed him to returne againe vnto them, but he swore
with an othe, that he would not. They
returned back, and forthwith he fell
into an ague , and so died miserably.
Ioan Niderus S. Theol. Doct. ord. pred. for-
micatorij l. 2. c. 4.

5. About Erklentz in low Germanie, a young man was wont to say
euery

euery day certaine prayers, and some-
times to faſt, in the honor of S. Barbara, that ſhe ſhould obtaine for him
that he might not die without confeſſion and communion. It chanced that
he was taken priſoner, and there remayned the ſpace of twelue whole
daies, without ſo much as eatinge or
drinking, by the prayers and interceſ-
ſion of S. Barbara, vntill ſuch time as
he had receiued thoſe Sacraments, and
preſently after he deceaſed. *Ibid. l. 4.
c. 2.*

6. Another at Gorcome in Hol-
lande, was all burnt by a ſodaine fire
which tooke in the houſe, and nothing
remayning whole, ſaue only the tongue and the eyes, was taken forth of
the flames by S. Barbara whom he had
inuoked, to the end he might not die
without Confeſſion & Communion:
and being confeſſed, and communicated, dyed in the yeare of our Lord.
1548. *Surius 8. of December. Et Bredembachus l. 4. c. 1.*

Loe

Loe then, is not this enough to proue, that it is good to recommend our selues vnto the Saintes, and that it is dangerous to goe to bed, not hauing first implored their asistance?

§. 4. *Of holie water, wherewith a Christian ought to sprinkle himselfe, at his going in, or coming out of his bed and chamber.*

Holie water is of great virtu, and of singular efficacie, by reason of the prayers which holy Church vseth at the benediction & hollowing thereof. For she prayeth, that God vouchsafe to giue the virtu of his blessing vpon it, to driue away the diuills and other diseases, all immondicities and dangers, all corrupted or pestifferous ayres, and other snares of the malignant spirit, and that all which may trouble the health or peace of the inhabitauts, may be expelled by the aspersion of this water. This loe, is the reason, why we ought to sprincle our selues

ſelues often there with, but principallie when as we riſe and goe to bed,
enter in, or goe out of our chamber, or
houſe : for we haue euery where the
diuell, who followeth and purſueth
vs euen to death.

EXAMPLES.

2. With holy water, S. Hilarion
diſſolued the enchantments of a carter
that was a gentile. *S. Hieron in Hilarion.*

2. With holy water, S. Marcellus biſhop of Apamia, put both to
feare and flight, the very diuells,
who would haue hindred to burne
the temple of an idole. *Theod. hiſt
l. 8. c. 21.*

3. With this water, S. Macarius,
draue away the illuſions of the diuells
and magicians. *Pallad. in lauſiac. c. 6.*

4. With this water, S. German bishop of Antiſiodore, appeaſed the ſea,
which the diuells troubled . *Venerable
Bede, de geſt. Aug. l. 1. c. 17.*

5. But behould here one of a freſher
date,

date. In the yeare 1609. at Limoges in Guienna, a Baker that had good store of customers, was much enuyed of an old witche, which entring into his house, charmed the ouen and the dowe, mumbling out certaine barbarous wordes and vnknowen. She was forthwith taken with the fact, but they did naught, saue only laugh a litle therat; vntill that on the morrow morning, the Baker coming to looke vpon his past, which he had made readie the day before, founde that it was all spoiled and plainly stunke. The like happened vnto him the day followinge, and the third day also, so that he founde him selfe in great necessitie, and so perplexed, that wanting meanes to pay his creditors, and forced to goe beg his bread, he was vpon the point to forsake his house, and to goe like a vagabond about the contrie.

But before he put in practise his designe, he went and recounted his affliction to a father of the Societie of
Iesus,

Iesus, who counselled him to confes
him selfe with al his familie, and made
him to promise, to doe the like from
that time forward, once a monthe. After that they were all confest, he gaue
to ether of them an Agnus Dei, and a
litle botle full of holy water, enioining
the Baker to sprinckle his paste there
with euery day.

He did as he was wild, and at the
first sprinckling (a strange case) he saw
issue forth of his dowe, a stinkinge va-
por, which caused a trembling thorough all his bodie, but blessing him
selfe with the signe of the Crosse, it
vanished away, and he found his dow
or past all changed, and the loaues wel
come. He continued the same a whole
yeare with the like successe, but at the
last quite neglected this good custome,
to sprincle his paste with holy water:
and behould presently, the aforesaid
witch-craft began againe, and for a
month together he found his paste all
corrupted, al black and so stinking, that
none

none durſt come nere vnto it, nor would the very dogges ſo much as eate it. Wherupon he ſprinckled it againe, and behould he was preſentlie ſeazed with ſo great a feare, that it was needfull to cary him to his bed; but this paſt within a while, & on the morrow he found his dowe both faire and good, and his batch of bread came paſſing well. *Taken out of the hiſtorie of the colledge of Limoges, of the Soc. of Ieſus, anno 1609.*

§. 5. *Of Agnus Deies.*

It is an auncient cuſtome in the Churche, to beare or weare an Agnus Dei hanged or tyed about our neck; for Cardinall Baronius makes mention in the yeare of our Lord 58. and ſaith, that this was practiſed, to counterpoint the ſuperſtition of the panims, who were wont to carry hangd about their necks, certaine ticquers or lotteries, wherin there was a hart printed, againſt the enchantments of ſorcerers, wher-

whereof Varron alſo maketh mention. The holy Church hath conſecrated certaine images of wex with holy chriſme, imprinting theron the figure of a Lambe repreſenting Ieſus Chriſt our Lord, and this is the cauſe why we call them Agnus Deies; to the end that Chriſtians bearing them about them, may be countergarded againſt the diuels, & againſt witchcraftes, the plague, thunder, lightning, and other dangers. Theſe are the thinges which the Pope asketh of God, at ſuch time as he doth hallow them, who only hath this power, and doth it not but only once in ſeauen yeares.

EXAMPLES.

1. At Drepano in Sicilie, the yeare of our Lord 1585. the diuell hauing tormented a maide for ſundry monthes, together with thoſe of the ſame familie, a father of our companie, cauſed her to hange an Agnus Dei about her neck. The deuill,

not

not able to endure it, threatned her to
wreste her neck in two, if she tooke it
not off; but by the councell of the said
father being resolute, the diuell was
confounded, and forced to leaue both
her, with all her familie, in rest and
peace. *Out of the historie of the Societie
anno 1585. Father Martin Delrio to 3. disq.
mag. l. 6. c. 2. sect. 3. q. 3.*

  2. In the confines of Treues, the
same yeare as aforsaid, a childe of eight
yeares old, which had bene led sundry
times to the assemblie of witches, was
taken and brought vnto the Archbishop, who sent for a father of the Societie to instruct him in matters of
faith. The father hauing catechised the
childe, hunge an Agnus Dei about his
neck. The night following, the diuell
appeared vnto him, sharply reproo-
uing him, to haue suffered him selfe to
be seduced by the father, and commanded him to take off that Agnus. The
childe did as the diuell commanded,
and presently was carried by a Buck to
                                      the

the dances, and afterwardes brought
back againe. Thus much is the power
which the diuell hath of those, who
are disfurnished and destitute of this
holy armour. *Mart. Delrio. 6. disq. mag.*
c. 2. ser. 3. q. 3. tom. 3.

3. The yeare followinge, another
boy somwhat elder, was brought before the same Archbishop, for the like
subiect, who assured him, that one of
theirs, had accesse vnto his chamber,
to giue vnto him a poisoned drinke,
because he had left in going to bed, an
Agnus Dei vpon the table, forgetting
to weare it about his neck : and that
if the glasse had bene greater, he had
bene dispatcht. Then the Archbishop
remembred him selfe, indeed to haue
bene one night without his Agnus
Dei, and that in the morning of the
same night, he found him selfe stricken with a troublesome disease, which
lasted him for some dayes after. This
boy going afterwards to the Prouost
of the citie of Treues; and you Sir also
(quoth

(quoth he) were in great danger, for certaine witches haue bene twice attempting to betwich you, but yet they could not, becaufe you beare (I know not what) hallowed about you. It was alfo an *Agnus Dei*. *Father Martin Delrio aboue.*

4. Not far from the citie of Arima in Iaponia, in a place called Iamada, a young youth of the age of fifteene yeares, was very often tormented with the malignant fpirit. An oncle of his, Bonze (for fo they call the religious panims of Iaponia) laboured to deliuer him, by his prayers and panim ceremonies, addreffed to Chami and Fotoqui their falfe gods, but all in vaine. Which the youth feeing, he went and complayned to a certaine Chriftian woman. She confiding in her holy faith, puld forth her *Agnus Dei*, and put it about the neck of this boy. Inftantly the diuell moued, cried, and kept a greuous ftur, and at the laft was conftrayned to diflodge. *Father Lewis*

Leᵭis Froez , *in the hiſtory of the So-cietie of the colledge of Arima anno* 1595.

What thinke you now (ô Chri-ſtians) of Agnus Deies? Is it not worth the while, to carry them about you both night and day?

§. 6. *Of the Reliques of Saintes.*

Beſides Agnus Deis , many beare about them ſome reliques of Sain-tes , which alſo ſerue them for ar-mour againſt the diuells, and for ef-fectuall meanes to obtaine fauours and bleſſinges of almightie God . For the councell of Nice in the 7. act , cal-leth the reliques of Saints , health-ſome fountaines, which diſtill into vs, the graces and giftes of almightie God . And S. Baſill ſaith , that who ſo toucheth the bones of the holie Martyrs , by reaſon of the grace which reſideth in the bodies, beco-mes partaker of their ſanctification . *Hom. in pſal.* 115.

The bodies only of Saints (ſaith
S.

S. Greg. Nazianzen) haue the same power which the holy foules haue, be it that they be touched with our hāds, or that they be honored : yea , the droppes only of their blood, and the very leaft fignes of their paſſion, haue the fame power that their bodies haue. *Orat. 1. in Iulian about the midſt.*

S. Iohn Chrifoſtome faith, that the diuells are not able to endure the ſhadow, nor yet the garments of the holy martyrs . *Lib. cont. gent. de vita S. Babylæ Ant. epiſ. & Mart.* Theſame S. Ambroſe writeth, *ſer. 93. Nat. 55. Martÿ, Nazarÿ, & Celſi.*

EXAMPLES.

1. How many perils did the Iſraelites efcape, for the fpace of fortie yeares in the defert? The fcripture noting, that they carried with them, the holie bodie of Iofeph and of the other holy patriarkes. *Exod. 13.*

2. The Emperor Theodofius, marching

ching in battaile, was wont to carrie in
steede of a casket, the litle cloake and
hoode of S. Senuphius Monke; and for
his launce, the staffe of the same Saint:
esteeminge that those holie reliques,
would countergard him a great deale
better, then all other sortes of armour
whatsoeuer. *Acta Cyri & Ioannis apud
Metaphrast 31. Similia habet Glicas 4. p.
annalium*.

3. A certaine Ermit of the desert of
Sennaar, as the cheife of al those which
were carried by Araches, to Auenir
Kinge of the Indes, bore about his
neck a litle purse made of haire, full
of reliques of the holie fathers of the
desert. *S. Iohn Damascen in the life of
Barlaam and Iosaphat. c. 2 2.*

4. S. Antonie wore vpon the feastes of Easter and Whitsontide, the
garment of S. Paul, the first Hermite:
wherof S. Hierom speakinge, who
wrote his life, he saith at the end therof. If God would giue if it me, I had
rather haue the robe of S. Paul with
his

his garments, then all the purple of kinges, with their kingdomes.

5. S. Thomas of Aquin, was neuer without reliques of S. Agnes, which he had in a Reliquarie, faſtned about his neck. *Ribad in his life.7.of March.*

6. S. Bernard bore ſo great affection to the reliques of S. Thaddeus Apoſtle, which he receiued in the laſt yeare of his life from Ieruſalem, that not contented to haue honored them, and borne them about him during his life, he commanded that they ſhould be layd vpon his body in his tombe, after his death. *Guliel.Abbas ſub fine l.3. c. 2. vitæ eius.*

From all this which hath bene ſaid, who ſeeth not, that it is good to carry about vs, both night and day, ſome reliques of Saintes? And what, I pray, you, can the diuells doe, againſt a Chriſtian, which layes him downe armed with a good conſcience, by the excited act of contrition, fenced with the weapons of holy water, *Agnus Dei,*

Dei, and reliques of Saints? And marke in this place, that euen as our holie mother the Church, concludeth eache cannonicall houre with the prayer for the departed . *Et fidelium anima &c.* euen ſo oughteſt thou to finiſh thy daies iorney, recommendinge to God the ſame ſoules, ſaying for their refreshinge, one *Deprofundis* , or one *Pater* and *Aue.* See for this purpoſe the 8. §. of the 6. Chapter of this booke.

Loe in few wordes, that which we muſt doe morning and euening. Let vs now ſee that which we ought to practiſe during the day.

THE III. CHAPTER.

Of the three Theologicall virtues , Faith, Hope, and Charitie.

IT is not enough to carry the exterior markes & ſignes of a Chriſtian ſoldiar, who ſo expecteth recompence from his captaine, for all thoſe which

N   ſhall

shall say Lord, Lord, shall not for all
this enter into the kingdome of heauen Mat. 7. but the interior must also
be answerable to the exterior. The interior signes of a true Christian, are
the virtues, whereof the chiefe and
most necessary of all other are, Faith,
Hope, and Charitie, as the Apostle
saith. 1. *Cor. 13. and S. Aug.l.2.Retract.
c. 63. & Enrichid. c.2. & 3.*

§. 1. *Of faith.*

Faith, is a gift of God, and a light,
whereby a man being enlightned, beleeueth and holdeth firmlie, all whatsoeuer God hath reuealed to vs, and is
proposed to vs to beleeue, by our holy mother the Catholique Church.
Canis. de fide & simbolo.

This virtu is the basis and foundation of all the others, without the
which we cānot approache vnto God,
nor obtaine his grace. *Heb. 11.6.*

To shew that one hath a true faith,
he must beleeue *simplie*, without en-
quiring

quiring curiouſlie, how this or that can be done, ſubmitting and captiuating his iudgment, to all that which the Church propoſeth. One muſt beleeue *firmely*, without ſufferinge him ſelfe to be ſhaken, for any kinde of oppoſition or contrarietie whatſoeuer. *Freelie*, and holding vpp his head, without leauing or ommittinge any thinge, of that which toucheth the profeſſion of his faith, for any reſpect or humane conſideration.

EXAMPLES.

1. Such an one was S. Paul, who in the 8. of the Romans ſaith v. 38. *I am ſure, that nether death, nor life, nor Angells, nor Principallities, nor Powers, nether thinges preſent, nor thinges to come, nether might, nor height, nor depth, nor other creature, ſhall be able to ſeperate vs from the charitie of God, which is in Chriſt Ieſus our Lord.* Whence had he this aſſurance (ſaith S. Ierom)

but

but from the firmitie of his faith? *In cap. 1. epist. ad Galat.*

2. Surius in the life of S. Hughe bishop of Lincolne, writeth, that a certaine Priest of a scandalous life, vpon a day saying Masse, when he was come to the breaking of the B. Hoste, he saw the blood runne downe, whéce being touched inwardly, he amended his life, & published the fact to euery one. It came to passe, that S. Hughe, passing by the village where this Priest dwelt, not to see this miraculous blood but to discourse with him of spirituall thinges (for this priest had at that present the bruit and fame of a holy mã) after sundry discourses, the Priest began to speake of this stupendious miracle, and besought S. Hughe to goe as far as the Church, for to see that miraculous blood, which was there reserued vnto that present: but the holye Bishop would not goe. And as his followers did likewise presse and importune him, he said that those who
will

will ſhew ſome ſignes of their infide-
litie, may goe: but to vs who firmelie
beleeue, that the body and blood of
Ieſus Chriſt, is truly vnder the Sacra-
mental ſpecies, what doe theſe ſignes
and miracles profit? And then alleadged that worthie ſentence of our Sauiour. *Bleſſed are they that haue not ſeene,
and haue beleeued. Iohn 20. 29.*

3. See the like anſwere of S. Lewis
kinge of France, in Ribadeniera, in the
diſcourſe vpon the feaſt of the moſt
holy Sacrament.

4. S. Bernard writing to Pope Innocentius, againſt the heretique Peter
Abailard, ſaith. If our faith be doutfull
(as this heretique ſaid) ſhall not our
Hope alſo be in vaine? All the martyrs then were great fooles, to ſuffer
ſo great torments, for thinges doutfull and vncertaine? No, no, our
faith is founded vpon the truth &c.
Epiſt. 190.

Seeing that from the Eaſte vnto
the Weſt(ſaith Lactantius Firmianus)
N 3   the

the diuine faith is receiued, and that
euery sex, age, and nation, are found,
who serue God vnanimously, and
that we see in all, one selfe same patience; one selfe same contempt of
death; we ought to knowe, that there
is great reason for this law, sith it is de-
fended vnto death, for the ground and
soliditie of this religion, sith iniuries
and torments can not ouerthrowe it,
but rather from day to day, doe make it
stronger. *lib.* 5. *c* 13.

Of Popes only, there are found
twentie seauen, who chose rather to
loose their life, then their faith. And
in the Church of Rome only, there
haue bene aboue three hundred thousand Christians, who to maintaine the
faith, haue endured death; wherof a
hundred and eightie thousand are buried in the Churchyard of S. Calistus.
Tho. Bozius de signis eccle. l. 20. Now if
in one cittie alone so many are founde,
how many are there in the whole
worlde?

Where

Where are the eleuen thouſand virgins? where thoſe twentie thouſand,
which in the time of Diocletian, were
all burnt for the faith, in one church?
Niceph. l. 7. hiſt. eccl. c. 6.

All ages haue furniſhed vs with
theſe braue ſoldiars and Amazõs, who
to defend their faith promiſed to Ieſus Chriſt their Captaine, haue giuen
their liues.

5. In Iaponia in our age, the yeare
1613. eight perſons were burnt aliue
men, women, and children, in the
cittie of Arima for the Catholique
faith, and were accompanied with
more then twentie thouſand Chriſtians in white robes, and with their
Beades in their handes: and ſeauen &
twentie beheaded in another place.
The yeare 1614. two brethren, with
another Chriſtian, were likewiſe burnt
aliue, and their ſiſter beheaded. Others
had their noſes, and their thumbes cut
off, and the toppes of their handes and
fcete, and were marked with a hot

iron vpon their foreheades. And the yeare 1618. other fiftie endured death also for the same cause.

6. The yeare 1612. at Cocura in the same Iaponia, as the Prince persecuted the Christians, a Neophite demanded of a litle childe of foure yeares olde, saying. If the Tyrant would kill thee, wouldest thou forsake the faith? No Sir, said the infant. What then, quoth the Christian, will you be a martyr? I forsooth, said he, and my father and mother, and I with them, shall all be martyrs. But perhaps you knowe not, replied the Christian, what it is to be a martyr. Yea but I doe, yea but I doe, answered the childe, it is to haue our heads cut off for the faith of Iesus Christ. I marry, but yet when this shall happen, you will cry a pace, quoth the Neophite; Quite contrary, I will reioyce (replied the childe) and with a cheerfull countenance, will I present my head vnto the hangman. These answeres made the Christian to
stand

stand aſtoniſhed, and ceaſed not to giue
thankes to God, for hauing put into ſo
litle a body, a ſoule ſo manly and ſo
generous.

7. Another childe of ſix yeares old,
vnderſtanding of the Gouernor, that
he cauſed twentie Croſſes to come
from the cittie of Sanga, to crucifie the
Chriſtians, anſwered. O how glad I
am of ſo good newes, for I hope, that
there will alſo come a litle one for me.
Goe Chriſtians, goe to ſchoole to theſe
litle children, you who at euery leaſt
occaſion, turne your backes to almightie God.

8. In the ſame Iaponia, and the
ſame yeare aforſaid, nere vnto Nan-
gaſachi, an olde man a Chriſtian, very
ſimple, and of litle vnderſtandinge,
who could neuer learne other prayer
then *Ieſus Maria*, the which he had continually in his mouth, fell ſick: his
friédes who were pagás, endeuored to
make him forſake his faith, but he ſaid
vnto thé. I am very ſorry that being a

N 5   Chri-

Chriſtian, I am ſo ignorant in heauen-
lie thinges: but yet knowe you, that
if I knew for certaine, that I were to
be condemned by God to euerlaſting
fire, I would not for al this forſake the
Chriſtian faith;for I had rather be tormented in hell being a Chriſtian, then
(if it were ſo poſſible) to be in heaué,
and be a Gétile. O excellent anſwere!
All this hitherto, is taken out of the hi-
ſtorie of Iaponia , ſent to our reuerend
father Generall.

§. 2. *Of Ignorance in thinges of faith, how*
    dangerous it is, and which the points
    are, that neceſſarily are to be knowen.

It is not enough to haue habituall
faith, which we haue receiued in holy
Baptiſme, but moreouer (being come
to age and vnderſtanding) we muſt excite actes thereof:but how can we doe
it , if we know not in particular what
we ought to beleeue? There is then, a
ſtrict obligation to learne the principall pointes of our faith: which is the
                                  cauſe

cauſe alſo, that God doth threaten ſo oft, & with ſuch efficacie, thoſe which are ignorant.

Poure out thy wrath vpon the Gentiles, that haue not knowen thee. pſal. 68. 6. If the Gentiles and Pagans, merit to be chaſticed of almighty God for their ignoráce, what may the Chriſtiás merit?

If any man know not, he ſhall not be knowen, 1. *Cor.* 14. 38. *that is, ſhall be reproued, as S. Aug. explicateth.*

Be thou taught Ieruſalem, leſt perhaps my ſoule depart from thee, leſt perhaps I make thee a deſert lande, not habitable. Ier. 6. 8.

What is it then that we muſt know neceſſarily? The vnitie of God, and Trinitie of perſons, and the miſterie of the Incarnation and paſſion of Ieſus Chriſt, for ſo our Lord him ſelfe ſaith in S. Iohn. 17. 3. And we muſt likewiſe haue the knowledge of hell and heauen. *Heb.* 11. 6.

Now all theſe pointes are contayned in the Creed which the Apoſtles

N 6   haue

haue compofed , as a fommarie of all
that we are to beleeue. It is neceffarie
then that it be learned : and this it is
which both S. Aug. and S. Ambrofe
recommend fo much. *Aug. l. 1. de fimb.*
ad Catech. tom. 9. & ferm. 181. de tem-
pore. Amb. l. 3. de Virg.

We muft likewife know the commandements of God. *Marc. 10. 18. &*
19. of the Church, and the Sacraméts,
at laft thofe which we purpofe to receiue . Good God, how many are
there to be founde, who from their
tender youth , knowe exactly that
which concerneth their ttade & pro-
feffion : and yet know not at thirtie or fortie yeares of age, nether the
commandements of God , nor their
beliefe ? Yee fathers and mothers,
you fhall render an account to God,
to haue fo great a care to inftruct your
children in that which doth concerne
the body , and to be fo careleffe of
their foule, to fende them to fchoole,
and to the Catechifmes.

The

The time, the time wil come (ſaith
Saint Iohn Chriſoſtome) that we ſhall
be chaſticed for our ignorances. The
Iewes are ignorant, but their ignoraunce, deſerues not pardon. The
Greekes are ignorant, but they haue
no iuſt excuſe. If thou be ignorant
of that which can not be knowen,
thou ſhalt not be blamed at al : but if
thou knowe not that which both is
poſſible and eaſie to learne, thou ſhalt
be chaſticed rigorouſlie. *Homil. 26.*
in epiſt. ad Rom.

EXAMPLES.

1. What miſeries were they, which
the people of the Iewes did not endure, in the time of their captiuitie?
All which arriued vnto thē by reaſon
of their ignoraunce, and of their great
careleſnes, to learne thinges belon-
ging to faith. *Therfore is my people led*
away captiue (ſaith the prophet) *be-*
cauſe they had not knowledge &c.
Ther-

Therfore hath hell dilated his soule, and opened his mouth without any limite, and their strong ones, and their people, and their high and glorious ones, shall descend into it. Isay 5. 13. O how easie is it for the diuell, to captiuate and enter into a soule, which knowes in a maner nothing concerninge God? Hence doe heresies, witcheries, and sorceries proceede.

2. Iulian the Apostata, did neuer so great domage to the Church, as then when he forbid all the Christians by edict, to instruct youth, ordaining that the Gentiles alone should haue the authoritie & credit to keepe schooles. *Ammianns l. 22. 23. Eunap. in Muson. Ambros. epist. ad Valent. Imp. Hier. in Chron. Baron. Annal. eccl. tom. 4. anno Christi 362.*

He knew full well (wicked that he was) that as ignorance in matters of faith and religion, is the springe and nurcerie of all euills, Christians not being instructed in the pointes of their
faith,

faith, would be eafily drawen to the worſhip of the falſe Gods, and to panim ſuperſtitions.

§. 3. *Of Hope.*

Vpon this foundation of Faith, Hope is builded, which is a virtu, infuſed diuinely into the ſoule, by which we expect from God with certaine confidence, the goods of ſaluation, & of euerlaſting life. *Caniſ. c. 2. de ſpe & orat. Dom. q. 1.*

We haue acceſſe thorough Ieſus Chriſt, and thorough faith, into this grace. Wherin we ſtande and glorie, in the hope of the glorie of the ſonnes of God. And not only this, but alſo we glorie in tribulations, knowing that tribulation worketh patience; and patience, probation; and probation, hope; and hope confoundeth not; becauſe the charitie of God is poured forth in our hartes. Rom. 5. 1. &c.

The grace of God our Sauiour hath appeared to all men, inſtructing vs, that denying impietie and worldly deſires, we liue ſoberly

soberly and iustly, and godly in this world,
expecting the bleßed hope and aduent of
the glorie of the great God, and our Sa-
uiour Iesus Christ. 1. Tit. 2. 13.

　This is the confidence which we haue
towards him , that whatsoeuer we shall
aske according to his will, he heareth
vs. 1. Iohn. 5. 14.

This virtu , is the staffe of all the
pilgrimes of this life, which doth sup-
port them and strengthen them, in the
deepest of their afflictions.

EXAMPLES.

Iob hauing whollie lost his children,
goods, honor, and health , and assaulted with all the diseases that might be
imagined, and that al together (by the
entermise of the diuell) were encam-
ped like a companie of armed men
within his body, laid vpon a dunghill,
and vtterly forsaken of humane helpe,
comforted him selfe neuertheles in
the hope that he had of the resurrec-
tion,

tion, and life eternall. *I know* (quoth he) *that my redcemer liueth, and in the laſt day I ſhall riſe out of the earth, and I ſhall be compaſſed againe with my skinne, and in my fleſh I ſhall ſee God: this my hope is laid vp in my boſome.* Iob. 19. 25. And in another place he ſaid. *Although he ſhall kill me, I ſhall truſt in him.* Iob. 13. 15.

2. The Prophet Ieremie ſaid, ſpeaking to God; *Thou art my hope, in the day of affliction.* Ierem. 17. 17.

3. The Apoſtle S. Peter (*a*) S. Maurus diſciple of S. Benet (*b*) S. Raymondus of Rochefort (*c*) thorough only confidence in God, walked with all aſſurance vpon the waters. (a) *Mat.* 14. (b) *S. Greg. dial.* 2. *c.* 7. (c) *Surius* 1. *tom.* 6. *Ian. Ribad.*

§. 4. *Of diſtruſt of our ſelues: and how we muſt neuer begin, nor vndertake any thinge, but firſt to recommend the ſame to God.*

Curſed be the man, that truſteth in man,

man, and maketh flesh his arme : for he shall be as litle bushes in the desert, and shall not see when good shall come, but he shal dwell in drynes in the desert, and in a lande of saltnes, and not habitable. Ierem. 17. 5.

Woe vnto renegate children, *saith our Lord, that you would take councell, and not of me: and would begin a webbe, and not by my spirit.* Isay. 30. 1. What else is it, to begin a webbe, and yet without the spirit of God, but to begin some worke, without recommending it first to God?

Vnles our Lord build the house, they haue laboured in vaine that build it. psal. 126. 1. That is to say, without God, one can doe nothinge, as him selfe affirmeth in *S.* Iohn 15. 5. And the Apostles hauing laboured all night longe without our Lord, they tooke nothinge. Luc. 5. 5. but as soone as they had cast their net vpon his worde, they had a great and happy draught.

For this it is that S. Paul so much recom-

recommendeth, that all whatſoeuer
we doe, we would doe it in the name
of God. *Col.* 3. *17. & 1. Cor.* 10. 31.

Dauid compareth himſelfe to a litle childe, newly weaned pſal. 130.
2. Euen then as a litle infant, newly taken from the dugges, can not goe a
ſtep, if his mother guide him not by
the arme, and as ſoone as ſhe lets him
ſtand alone without houlding, he ex-
tendeth his armes, and cryeth with
teares after his mother: euen ſo wee
(for we are a great deale, yea infinite
leſſe before God) neuer ought to goe,
nor to doe ought whatſoeuer, but to
holde God by the hande, and as ſoone
as we feele our ſelues in any diſtreſſe,
to implore, more then euer, his aſiſtance, ſaying with Dauid. *O God intend
vnto my helpe, Lord make haſte to helpe
me. Pſal.* 69. 1.

EXAMPLES.

1. I thought (ſaid S. Aug.) that I was
ſome body of my ſelfe, and I ſaw not
that

that thou art he who didſt cōduct me,
vntill ſuch time as thou retyredſt thy
ſelfe a litle from me and thus forthwith I fell . Then I ſaw & knew that
thy hande gouerned me, & that to be
fallen, came from me, and to be riſen a-
gaine, came from thee. *Soliloque c. 15.*

2. S. Dominique nether did , nor
euer vndertooke ought , without hauing firſt recommended him ſelfe to
God, and to our Ladie, by the intercef-
ſion of whom, he ſaid he alwayes obtained what he would of her Sonne.
Sur tom. 4. & Ribad. 4. Auguſt.

3. Albeit S. Francis had triumphed
ouer his fleſh , and quenched the flames of ſenſual fire, and that it was reuealed to brother Leo his companiō,
that S. Francis was numbred in heauē
in the number of thoſe , which were
true virgins both in ſoule & body, yet
was he neuertheles maruellouſly retired & ſtrange amonge women, hauing
his eye ſo modeſt when he ſpake vnto
them, that he hardly knew ſo much as
anie

anie one by ſight. For he was wonte to ſay, that by occaſions the ſtronge became weake, and the weake was vanquiſhed: & that to conuerſe familiarly in the cōpanie of women, or women with mē, without being burned or ſowhat ſinged, was as harde as to walke vpon hoate coales, or to beare fire in ones boſome, without being hurte. He further added, that he who is hardy, is not crafty, and that the diuel ſo that he finde wheron to take hould (although it be but at a bare haire) will make thereupon a terrible warre. *Ribad. 4. of Octob.*

4. Our holy Father Ignatius, ſo much diſtruſted his owne ſelfe, that in al his affaires, he neuer reſolued ought, albeit he knew all reaſons probable, without firſt recōmending it to God. *Ribad. in his life.*

5. The ſixt of Nouember, together with the four crowned martyrs, the Church celebrateth the feaſte of fiue other martyrs, Claudius, Nicoſtratus, Sim-

Simphorianus, Caftorus, and Simpli-
cianus, which were moft excellent
grauers and Chriftians, except Simpli-
cianus who was a panim; who feeing
that the workes of marble & of other
riche ftuffes of his companions, were
founde fo perfect and compleate, and
that in labouring of them, all thinges
fucceeded as they defired, where to
the contrarie he fpoyled a number of
tooles about his art; he demanded of
Simphorianus (who was the chiefeft
of the reft) whence this proceeded?
Who anfwered him, that alwayes in
taking any inftrument to worke with
all, they called vpon the name of Iefus
Chrift their God: and inftructed him
fo well, that thorough the grace and
goodnes of our Lord, he was conuerted and baptifed, and after martyred
in their companie. *Ribad. 6. of Nouebr.*

So true it is, which our Lord faid to
his Difciples, fo many ages paft. *He
that abideth in me, and I in him, the fame
bringeth much fruite: for without me you
can*

can doe nothinge. Ioan. 15. 5.

§. 5. *Of Charitie, and particularly of that which we owe vnto God.*

Charitie is a virtu diuinely infuſed, by the which we loue God for him ſelfe, and our neighbour for God. *Caniſ. cap. 3. de charitate & decal. q. 2. ex S. Aug. l. 3. de doctrina Chriſt. c. 10.*

A certaine lawier, asked of our Lord vpon a day. *Maſter, which is the greateſt commandement in the law? Mat. 25. 35.* Or according to S. Luke. *c. 10. 25. By dooing of what thinge shall I poſſes life e-uerlaſtinge?* Our Lord made anſwere. *Thou shalt loue thy Lord the God with thy whole hart, and with thy whole ſoule, and with all thy ſtreꝛght, and with all thy minde, and thy neighbour as thy ſelfe.* Vpon which paſſage S. Bernard faith. The reaſon to loue God, is God him ſelfe, the maner and the meaſure to loue God, is to loue him without mea-ſure: God muſt be loued for him ſelfe, and that for two reaſons. Firſt, becauſe we

we can loue nothing more iuſtly . Secondly , becauſe we can loue nothing
more profitable. God deſerueth to be
loued for him ſelfe, yea euen of an Infidell, for although he know not Ieſus
Chriſt, yet Ieſus Chriſt knoweth him.
This is the cauſe why euen a Panim is
inexcuſable , if he loue not God with
his whole hart, with his whole ſoule,
and with all his ſtrenght: for the iuſtice
and the reaſon which is in him , cry,
that we ought to loue him aboue all,
whoſe dettor we know our ſelues to
be in all. *Tract. de diligendo Deo.*

With how much more reaſon ough-
teſt thou to loue him (o Chriſtian)
who illuminated with the light of
faith, haſt more particular knowledge
of his bountie?

All the other virtues are meerly nothing without this, for. *If I ſpeake with
the tongues of men and of Angels, & haue
not charity, I am become as ſounaing braſ-
ſe, or a tinkling cymball. And if I ſhould
haue prophecie , and knew all miſteries,*
and

and all knowledge; and if I ſhould haue all faith, ſo that I could remoue mountaines, and haue not charitie, I am nothinge. And if I ſhould diſtribute all my goodes to be meate for the poore, and if I ſhould deliuer my body ſo that I burne, and haue not charitie, it doth profit me nothinge. 1. Cor. 13. 1.

Will you haue a certaine proofe of the loue of God? *If you loue me* (ſaith our Lord to his Apoſtles) *keepe my commandements.* Ioan. 14. 15.

This is the charitie of God (ſaith S. Iohn) *that we keepe his commandements, and his commandements are not heauie.* 1. Ioan. 5. 3.

How dooſt thou loue him, whoſe commandement thou hateſt? Who is he that will ſay; I loue the Emperor, but I hate his lawes? *S. Aug. tract. 9. in ep. Ioan.* The proofe of loue, is the performance of the worke, and the keeping of the commandements of God. *S. Greg. Hom. 30. in Euang.*

O   *The*

The properties of the loue of God.

The firſt propertie of the loue of God, is gladly to be with God, and not to be auerted frõ him, but with griefe.

So the eſpouſe loued her ſpouſe in the Canticles, ſaying. *I founde him who my ſoule loueth, I helde him, nether will I let him goe. Can. 3. 4.*

2. To be inſatiable, and neuer to become wearie to doe any thing for the loue of God ; for this cauſe it is, that the Holy Ghoſt compareth charitie vnto death, to the graue, to hell, and vnto fire, who neuer ſay, it is enough. *Prou. 30. 15. Cant. 8. 6.*

3. To haue a ſimple and vpright intention, addreſſing all his thoughtes, wordes, and workes only to God.

That (ſaith S. Bernard) is called true ſimplicitie, which hath a wil perfectlie conuerted to God alone , and which with Dauid deſireth but one thinge alone, that is to ſay, to pleaſe God.

God. *S.Bernard ad fratres de monte Dei.*
The espoule saith in the Canticles.
In our gates, all fruites, the new and the
old, my beloued, I haue kept for thee.Cant.
7.13. By the fruites of the yeare passed,
are to be vnderstood, the workes of
nature, as to eate, to drinke, to sleepe,
and the like. By the new, the workes
of grace, or supernaturall, as all the
workes of virtu are: as if she said, I offer vnto thee all my workes, good, indifferent, supernaturall, and naturall,
without any sort or manner of reser-
uation.

4. To be inuincible, that is to say,
neuer to suffer him selfe to be beaten
downe, for any kinde of difficultie.
Who shall seperate vs (saith the Apostle) *from the charitie of God which is in*
Christ Iesus our Lord? Rom.8.35.

5. To thinke allwayes vpon God,
and by the creatures, as by so many
steppes, to ascend and lift vp him selfe
allwayes to him. *Come my beloued*
(saith the spouse) *let vs goe forth into*
O 2 *the*

*the fielde, my beloued to me, and I to him,
that I may behould thee, as thou behouldest
me. Cant. 7. 10.*

EXAMPLES.

1. S. Marie Magdalen ſo greatly
loued our Lord after her conuerſion,
that ſhe could in no wiſe be ſeparated
from him, following him euen in his
paſſion, amidſt the preſſe of ſoldiars
and people vnto the mount of Caluarie, and there alſo ſtanding nere
vnto him, vntill ſuch time as he was
dead and buried. And what greater
proofe of her loue could be giue, then
the teſtimonie of our Lord him ſelfe,
who ſaith (defendinge her againſt Simon the Phariſie) *Many ſinnes are forgiuen her, becauſe ſhe loued much. Luc. 7. 44.*

2. *Who then ſhall ſeparat vs from the
charitie of Chriſt? Tribulation, or diſtres,
or famine, or nakednes, or danger, or
perſecution, or the ſworde? But in all
theſe thinges we ouercome, becauſe of him
that hath loued vs: for I am ſure, that ne-*
ther

ther death, nor life, nor *Angells*, nor *Principallities*, nor *Powers*, nether thinges present, nor thinges to come, nether might, nor height, nor depth, nor other creature, shall be able to separate vs from the charitie of God, which is in Christ Iesus Lord. *Rom* 8. 35.

3. S. *Peter* beinge asked by our Lord if he loued him, bouldly answered him three feuerall times. *Thou knowest Lord that I loue thee. Ioan. 21. 15. 16. 17.*

4. S. *Ignatius* bifhop and Martir, was fo enflamed with this burninge charitie, that he faid (writing to the Romans when he was led prifoner to Rome there to be executed.) I make it knowen to all the Churches, that I die for Iefus Chrift, with exceeding ioy, vnles you trouble me. I befeeche you, let not your affection, be domageable to me, let me be torne in pieces by the wilde beaftes, that fo they may fend me foone to God. I am the corne and graine of God,

O 3   and

and ſhall be ground betwixt their teeth, ſo to be made the wheate & delicious bread of Ieſus Chriſt. And a litle after he ſaith. Let fire, croſſe, beaſtes come, let all my members be cut in peeces, bruſed and ground, let the death of this miſerable body, and all the torments of the diuell come vpon me, ſo that I may come, and be vnited with Ieſus Chriſt. *Epiſt. ad Rom. Hier. in Ignat. Ribad. 1. of Feb.* After his death, his body being opened, the name of Ieſus was found engrauen in his hart.

5. S. Bonauenture writeth of Saint Francis, that he conſidered God in euerie thinge, making of all the creatures a ladder, to aſcend to him, who is to be deſired aboue all thinges. *In his life cap. 9.*

6. S. Iacopon, of the order of Saint Francis, being all alone in a certaine garden, ran as a man beſides him ſelfe, embracing the firſt tree that there he founde, crying. *O ſweete Ieſus, ô my*
ꝑell

well beloued Ieſus! &c. Raderus in vita ſanct. p. 2. c. 3.

7. Our Lord vpon a day comman-ded S. Gertrude, that ſhe ſhould offer him more eſpecially, then ſhe had yet done vntill that time, all her actions, as all the letters which ſhe wrote, the meate ſhe eate, the wordes, the ſteps, the reſpirations, and beatinges of her hart, all in the vnion of the life and naturall actions of his Sonne. She did ſo, and by meanes of this exerciſe, ſhe arriued vnto ſo great perfection, that our Lord ſpeaking of her to S. Mech-tildis (a religious woman of the ſame monaſterie) ſaid. *There is no place vpon the earth (after the moſt B. Sacrament) wherein I abide more particularly, then in the hart of B. Gertrude. Lud. Bloſ. in mo-nil. ſpir.*

8. The bleſſed father S. Xauerius, ſeeing in the night by diuine reue-uelation (in an hoſpitall in Rome) all the paines and afflictions which he was to ſuffer in the Indes, cryed out to

O 4　　　God

God. *Yet more , yet more , (o Lord) yet
more. Ribad. in the abridgment of his life:*
and *Horatius Turselinus* : so greatly de-
sirous was he, to endure and suffer for
the loue of God.

If these examples doe not suffice,
reade the liues of the B. Saintes , and
you shall finde no man nor woman
Sainte, which were not enflamed with
this loue.

§. 6. *Of Charitie towards our neigh-*
bour .

After that our Lord had deliuered
the first commandement of charitie,
he said . *And the second is like to this;*
Thou shalt loue thy neighbour as thy selfe:
on these two commandements , dependeth
the whole law and the prophets . Mat.
22. 37.

If *any man shall say , that I loue God,*
and hateth his brother, he is a lyer. For he
that loueth not his brother whom he seeth,
God, whom he seeth not, how can he loue?
I. ep. c. 4. 20.

Be-)

Before all thinges, haue mutuall cha-
ritie continually among your selues. 1.Pet.
4. 8.

The maner how to loue our neighbour, is comprehended in these few
wordes. *According as you will that men*
doe to you, doe you also to them in like ma-
ner. Luc. 6. 31. And contrary-wise.
That which thou hatest to be done by thee
to another, see thou doe it not to another at
any time. Tob. 4. 16.

The properties of this charitie, are
set downe by S. Paul. 1. *Cor.* 13. *4.*
Charitie, is patient, is benigne; charitie
ennieth not, dealeth not peruersly, is not
pufſed vp, is not ambitious, seeketh not her
owne, is not prouoked to anger, thinketh
not euill, reioyceth not vpon iniquitie, but
reioyceth with the truth, suffereth all
thinges, beleeueth all thinges, hopeth all
thinges, beareth all thinges.

We are all bretheren *(Mat.* 23. 8.)
members of the same body (1. *Cor.* 12.
27.) created for the same end, to enioy the celestiall enheritance (1. *Pet.*
O 5   1.4.)

1. 4.) What should let vs then to loue one another?

Blessed is he (saith S. Aug.) whom thou louest, o Lord, his friend in thee, and his enimie for thee: For he alone loseth no friende, who loueth all his friendes in him , who can not be lost. *Confes.l.4.c.9.*

Euen as (saith S. Dorotheus) two lines drawen from the circumference after the centre, the nerer they approache vnto the centre, the nerer are they one to the other : euen so the nerer that we approache vnto God , who is our centre, the nerer also are we by affection, one to another. *In the 6.discourse, not to iudge our neighbour.* The same doth S. Bonauenture say. *In stimulo amoris p. 2. c. 7.*

EXAMPLES.

1. Our Lord hath so exceedingly loued vs, that he hath giuen his very life for vs. He could not possibly giue
a grea-

a greater proofe of his loue, as him selfe saith in S. Iohn. *cap.* 15.

2. The first Christians, loued one another so entirely, that S.Luke saith. *The multitude of beleeuers had one hart, and one soule. Act. 4. 32.*

And Tertulian, who liued about that time writeth, that the Infidells seing the Christians so to loue, as to dye one for another said . *Behould how they loue together?*

3. Moyses so loued his people,that seeing God would punish them for their sinnes, he said. *Lord pardon them, or blot me out of the booke of life. Exod. 32.*

4. *I wished my selfe* (said S. Paul) *to be an anathema from Christ, for my bretheren. Rom. 9.3.*

5. S. Serapion became a slaue to certaine tumblers and players, to the end to haue some meanes to discourse with them,and to conuert them to the faith : which he effected.*Theod.in hist. sanct.pat.c. 83.& Marulus l.3.c.2.*

O 6 6.S.

6. Paulinus bishop of Nola, did as much, to deliuer the sonne of a poore widdow, forth of captiuitie. *S, Greg. l. 3. dial. c. 1.*

7. S. Leo Abbot, to redeeme certaine of his monkes that were captiues, gaue a good somme of mony to the barbarous people which detained them, and praid them to accept him in their place: as they did, and within a while after, they cut off his head. *Sophon. prat. spirit. c.* 112. *& Baron. tom. 7. anno* 586.

8. S. Sanctulus of the prouince of Nursie, hauing accesse vnto the prison where a Deacon was detained, caused him to get out secretly, and he remayned in his place. And when afterwards those of Lubardy would haue behedded him, he cald vpon S. Iohn, and the hangmans armes instantly became benumd. Which the Barbariãs seeing & admiring, they gaue him life and libertie, and to all the other captiues also. *S. Greg. dial. l. 3. c. 37.*

O great

O great & renowned Saintes, who after the example of our Lord, haue poſtpoſed their owne liues, to their neighbours! And thou (o Chriſtian) for a litle point of good or honor, wilt enter into proceſſe & quarrels againſt thy neighbour? O how far is this to giue thy life for him!

Let vs now come to the ſeauen virtues, contrarye to the capitall ſinnes, ommitting the others, leſt we be too tedious.

THE IV. CHAPTER.

Of the ſeauen virtues contrary to the capitall ſinnes.

GOod the Creator, cōmanded the prophet Ieremie, at the very beginning of his miſſiō, to goe thorough the realmes, *to pluck vp, deſtroy, waſt, and diſſipate, and to build and plant.* Ieremie 1. 10. to wit, to take from ſoules, by the force of his wordes,
and

and examples, sinnes and vices, and to
plant virtues in their places.

This is the whole endeuour of a
good Christian; which we labour to
perswade in these two bookes. In the
first I haue laid downe the meanes to
take away sinnes, amongst others the
seauen capitall, which are as the fountaine and roote of all the rest. I will
now (God willing) open the way, to
plant virtues in their places, and nam-
lie those, which are also by contrarie,
as the springe and fountaine of all the
others.

§. I. Of the virtu of Humilitie.

Humilitie (according to S. Bernard)
is a virtu, by the which a man doth
villifie or despice him selfe, by a true
and perfect knowledge of him selfe.
Lib. de grad. Humil.

This virtu is so noble, that the Sonne of God him selfe would teache the
same, both by wordes, and by examples. *Learne of me* (saith he) *because I*
                                    am

am meeke and humble of hart, and you shall finde rest to your soules. Mat. 11.29. And *in cap.* 5. 3. he placeth the poore of spirit (euen of this life) in the ranck and number of the blessed: and by the poore of spirit, S. Aug. vnderstandeth the humble. *De sancta virginit.c.232.*

Humilitie, is called by the holy fathers, the firme foundation of a spirituall buildinge (*a*) the head (*b*) the mother (*c*) the mistris (*d*) and the treasure (*e*) most assured of all virtues. (a) *Cassian Collat.* 15. *c.* 7. (b) *Ambros. in Psal.* 118. *ser.* 20. (c) *Greg. l.*23 *mor.c.*13. (d) *ibid. & Cassian.* (e) *Basil. in const. mon.c.* 17.

The swathing clothes and cloutes of our B. Sauiour, are more pretious then all purples: & the manger much more glorious then all the golden throanes of Kinges: the pouertie of Iesus Christ, is much more riche, then all the treasures and store-houses in the world : for what is there more riche and pretious, then humilitie, wher-

wher with the kingdome of heauen it selfe is bought and purchased? *S. Ber. fer. 4. in vig. nat. Dom .* And in the 2. *fer.* of the Afcenfion, he faith, that humility is the marke of the predeftinate.

What fhall we fay of the neceffitie therof ? That which Truth him felfe hath pronounced of it . *Amen I fay to you, vnles you become as litle children, you shall not enter into the kingdome of heauen. Mat. 18. 3.*

Perfeuer (my deareft) faith S. Bernard, in the difcipline which you haue vndertaken, to the end that by humilitie, you may afcend vnto fublimitie, for fhe is the way, nor is there any other . He that walketh by any other way, he rather falleth, then afcendeth, for it is humilitie alone which exalteth, it is humility alone which leadeth and conducteth vnto life . *Ser. 2. de Afcenfione.*

Her profit is great, for fhe it is who procureth vs acceffe to the fecret cabinet, and efpeciall graces of the kinge
of

of heauen, and makes vs to participate
of all his treaſures : behould the
proofes .

The *prayer of him that humbleth him*
ſelfe , ſhall penetrate the cloudes . Eccl.
35. 18.

The *prayers of the humble , haue euer*
bene agreeable vnto thee , ſaid the chaſte
Iudith. *c.* 16. *God reſiſteth the proude, and*
giueth grace to the humble . Iac. 4. 6. 1.
Pet. 5. 5. Will you that I comprehend
all in one worde? *He that humbleth him*
ſelfe , ſhall be exalted . ſaith our Lord.
Luc. 14. 11.

To attaine to the top of this virtu,
S. Anſelme giueth ſeauen degrees or
ſtepps . 1. To acknowledge ones ſelfe
contemptible, or worthie to be deſpi-
ced. 2. To reioyce therat . 3. Freely to
confes it. 4 To perſuade it to others.
5. To ſuffer patiently that the ſame be
ſaid to him ſelfe. 6. To ſuffer him ſelfe
to be treated contemptibly. 7. To take
contentment & pleaſure in it. *De ſimi-*
litud. c. 10. *ad.* 18.

E X-

EXAMPLES.

1. The Sonne of God, is the true miroir and patterne of al humilitie (for which cause he said, *learne of me for I am humble.*) For who saw, or euer shall see the like humilitie as that, of God incarnate? God a litle infant? God in a stable, in a manger, betwixt an Asse and an Oxe? Who was euer more abased then God circumcised? God, baptised? God amongst sinners, seruing them, wasting their feete, wiping them, and kissing them? God subiect and obedient vnto a poore carpenter, and to the base hangmen? God nourishing his seruants with his flesh, and giuing them his blood to drinke? God bound, howted, mocked, bespitted, cudgelled, buffeted, trampled vnder feete, whipped, crowned with thornes, bearing his crosse, nayled, hunge and dying on a gibbet betwixt two theeues?

Be-

Behould the humilitie of the Sonne of God, *who* (as the Apoſtle ſaith) *humbled himſelfe, made obedient vnto death, euen the death of the croſſe: for the which thinge God hath alſo exalted him, and hath giuen him a name which is aboue all names, that in the name of Ieſus euery knee bow, of the celeſtialls, terreſtrialls, and infernalls.* Phil. 2. 8. Behould Chriſtian and imitate this goodly example.

2. The firſt in humilitie, after the Sonne of God, is his moſt holy and immaculat mother, who albeit endued with all the graces which a pure creature could poſſibly haue, yet was troubled at the praiſes of the Angell, called her ſelfe the handmaide of God; and hauing conceiued the Sonne of God, went inſtantly to ſerue her coſin Elizabeth. What humble patience had ſhe in her humiliations, not finding an Inne to lodge in; when ſhe was at the point of her lying downe, conſtrained to withdraw her into a ſtable, and to bring forth at midnight,
in

in winter time, both her creature and
her Creator, and to lay him vpon a
litle ftraw, in a maunger, betwixt
beaftes? Moreouer, what patience,
to beare him in hafte into Egipt a-
mongft Idolaters? To fee him taken,
bound, whipt, hunge, and dying on
the Croffe?

It is no maruell then, if cafting our
eyes vpon thefe two fo beautifull mi-
rors, fo many Saints of all ages, fexes,
and conditions, haue humbled them
felues? If one S. Gregorie Pope (*a*)
and S. Lewis (*b*) kinge of France,
efteemed them felues honored to ferue
the poore. If a S. Helen Empreffe (*c*)
tooke fome time fo great contentment, to giue water to poore virgins
when they went to dinner; if fhe ferued in the platters, filed forth drinke,
and fet her on her knees before them.
If one S. Heduuige (*d*) Dutches of Po-
lonia, befides the feruices aboue faid,
kiffed (when no body was aware therof) the very printes and fteppes where
the

the poore had paſſed . B. Father Ignatius (e) being generall of the companie
of Ieſus , exerciſed him ſelfe with ſo
great contentment in the moſt humble and baſeſt offices, euen to the playing the ſcullian, to wipe the pots, rub
the ſtoue-houſe, ſcoure the platters,
carrie wood, kindle fire, draw water,
ſerue in meate, and other like ſeruices.
If infinite others , notwithſtandinge
their eſtate and greatnes , haue abaſed
them ſelues in all ſortes of humiliation, they knew full well, that the honor and glorie of good ſoldiars, is, to
follow their captaine , as nere as they
can (a) *Ioan. Diac. in eius vita* (b.) *Ribad.*
25. of Aug. (c) *Rufin. li. c. 8. Socrates l.*
1. c. 13. Theod. l. 1. c 18. Sozom. li 2. c.
1. Baron anno 316. (d) *Surius tom. 5.16.*
Octob. (e) *Ribad. l. 3. of his life.*

§. 2. *Of Liberallitie.*
Liberallitie is a virtu, which mode-
rateth the loue of riches, and maketh
a man facile and prompt to employ
them

them and fpend them, when reafon iudgeth it expedient. *S. Tho. 2. q. 117. art. 1.2.3. ex Arift. l.4 Ethic.l.1.*

Liberalitie is a great virtu, faith S. Hierom, and a royall way, from hence he declineth on the right hande, who fo is fcarce, nether giuing to others, nor yet to him felfe that which is neceffarie: and on the left hande he, who eateth and confumeth his meanes amongft ftrumpets, and faith. Let vs eate and drinke, for to morrow we muft dye, *lib. 16. in Ifay.*

Heare how Saint Iohn Chrifoftome fpeaketh. Euen as the daughters of fuch as are riche and noble, are wont to weare fome iewell about their neck for an ornament, without euer putting it off, becaufe it is a figne of their nobilitie: euen fo muft we clothe and adorne our felues in all times with bountifulnes, to declare that we are the children of him who is mercifull, and caufeth his funne to fhine vpon the good & bad. *Chrifoft. Hom. 1. vel in præfat.*

præfat. in ep. ad Phillip. See hereafter
of this virtu. *Chap. 7. §. 2. 3. & 4.*

§. 3. Of Chaſtitie.

Chaſtitie is a virtu neceſſarie to e-
uery Chriſtian that pretendeth to come to heauen, which doth repugne to
the ſinne of Luxurie, & giues a bridle
to concupiſcence. The Apoſtle calls it
ſanctification. 1. Theſ. *4. 3.* and *holines,
without which, no man ſhall ſee God. Heb.
12. 14.*

Now, there are three ſortes of cha-
ſtities; The firſt is, of virgins. The ſecond, of widowes. The third, of married folkes. Iſidor. Peluſian. compareth virginall chaſtitie to the ſunne,
that of widdowes to the Moone, that
of married folkes to the ſtarres. *epiſt.
391.* S. Ierom expounding the parable
of the ſeede. *Mat. 13.* attributeth the
hundred-fould fruit, to virginitie, the
ſixtie fould, to viduitie, and the thirtie fould to mariage. The ſame S. Aug.
ſaith. *de virgin. c. 44. & venerable Bede.*

I would

I would all men to be as my selfe (saith the Apostle) 1. Cor. 7. 7. *but euery one hath a proper gift of God, one so, and an other so*. But I *say to the vnmarried and to widdowes, it is good for them if they so abide as I also, but if they doe not conteine them selues, let them marrie, for it is better to marry, then to be burnt*. And a litle lower. v. 25. *And as concerning virgins, a commandement of our Lord I haue not, but councell I giue, as hauinge obtained mercie of our Lord to be faithfull. I thinke therfore that this is good for the present necessity. Art thou tied to a wife? Seeke not to be loosed. Art thou loose fro a wife. Seeke not a wife.* And v. 32. *He that is without a wife, is carefull for the thinges that pertaine to our Lord, how he may please God: but he that is with a wife, is carefull for the thinges that pertaine to the worlde, how he may please his wife, and he is deuided. And the woman vnmarried and the virgin, thinketh on the thinges that pertaine to our Lord, that she may be holy both in body and in spirit : but she that is*

mar-

maried, thinketh on the thinges that per-taine to the worlde, how she may please her husband. And he concludeth in the end. v. 38. *He that ioyneth his virgin in matrimonie, doth well: and he that ioyneth not, doth better. A woman, if her husband sleepe, she is at libertie, let her marrie to whom she will, only in our Lord: but more blessed shall she be, if she so remaine, according to my councell; and I thinke that I also haue the spirit of God.*

O how beautifull is the chast generation with glorie, for the memorie therof is immortal! Sap. 4.

All waight is not worthie a continent soule. Eccl. 26. 20. that is to say, there are no riches nor treasures, which can be compared to a chast soule.

I praise mariages (saith S. Ierom) but in as much as they engendre virgins. I gather the Rose, from amongst the thornes, the gold from the earth, the pearle frō the shell. *epist. ad Eustoch.*

S. Ciprian speaking to virgins, saith. You haue already begun to be, that
P which

which we shall be hereafter, you haue euen from this life , the glorie of refurrection, paffing by the world, without the thoughtes of the world; when as you perfeuer chafte and virgins, you are equall to Angells. *Cyp. de hab. virg.*

O chaftitie (exclaimes S. Ephrem) which reioyceft the hart , and giueft winges to the foule to fly to heauen! O chaftitie, which dooft diminifh paffions, and deliuereft the foule from all vnquietnes! O chaftitie, which giueft light to the iuft, and darknes to the diuell ! O chaftitie, fpirituall chariot, which carieft vs to thinges fublime and celeftiall! O chaftitie, who like a fweet fmelling Rofe amidft the foule, replenifheft it with all good odor! *Tom. 1. fer. de caft.*

Humane bodies , refemble glaffes, which cannot be borne one with another touching together, without encurring danger to be broken ; And vnto fruites , which albeit found and

well

well seasoned, yet receiue detriment by touching one another; Water it selfe, how fresh soeuer it be with in a vessell, yet being touched by any terrestriall creature, can not longe keepe its freshnes. A chast soule, must be like the spouse in the sacred Canticles, hauing her handes distilling mirrhe, a liquour preseruing from corruption: her lippes are bound vp with a vermillian riband (a marke of the shamfastnes of her wordes:) her eyes, are of Doues, by reason of their puritie and simplicitie: her nose is like the Cedars of Libanus, a wood incorruptible.

EXAMPLES.

Of the puritie of our Lord Iesus Christ, and of his most holie mother, it is now no neede to speake, then which nothing can be imagined more noble or better; Let vs therfore speake of some Saints, both of the olde, and new law.

P 2   How

1. How exceeding chaſt was the patient Iob, who ſaid. *I haue made a couenant with myne eyes, that I would not ſo much as thinke of a virgin.* Iob. 31. 1.

2. The patriark Ioſeph, being ſundry times ſolicited vnto lubricitie in the verie flower of his age, by the wife of Putephar his Lady and miſtris, conſtatly refuſed her, for feare of offeding God. And at the laſt, as ſhe inſtantly vrged him vpō a day, he fled frō her, leauing his cloke behinde him. *Gen.* 39.

3. *For that thou baſt loued chaſtitie, and after thy husband not knowen any other, therfore alſo the hande of our Lord hath ſtrenghtned thee, and therfore ſhalt thou be bleſſed foreuer.* Iudith 15. 11.

4. Godfrie of Bullen in the conqueſt of Hieruſalem, being enquired of by the Turkes (after diuers notable exploites and ſtratagemes which he had done) whence it was that his hand was ſo mightie, anſwered. Becauſe he had neuer bene ſtained with any vnchaſt or diſhoneſt touch. *Tb. Sallius c. 8.*

Of

Of his ſpirituall practiſe.

5. Suſanna, ſeeing her ſelfe reduced to ſo hard a caſe, as ether to dye, or to conſent to the wicked concupiſcence of the two old men, choſe rather to dy, then to defile by ſo filthy an act, the puritie of her body and ſoule. *Dan. 3.*

6. S. Potamiana, an Egiptian virgin, being requeſted ſundry times by her maſter, to yeld aſſent to the act of vncleanes, did alwaies deny him conſtantly; & being deliuered by him into the handes of the Prefect of Alexandria, and threatned to be throwen into a cauldron full of boylinge pitche, vnles ſhe condeſcended to her maſters pleaſure, ſhe ſtil withſtood him, and choſe rather to be plunged by litle & litle in this ſcaulding cauldron, and ſee al her fleſh boyled to peeces: vntil ſuch time as after the tormēts of an houre, being put therinto vp to the neck, ſhe rendred vp her ſoule into the hādes of her celeſtial ſpouſe, thē for ſo ſhort a pleaſure, to looſe the pretious treaſure of

her pu-

pudicitie. This historie hath bene declared by S. Antonie, to one Isidorus, and he recounted it afterwards to Palladius, who reporteth it *in his Lusiac. c. 1. Card. Baron. tom. 3. anno. 310.*

7. S. Euphrasia led to the stewes, seeing that she could not escape the handes of a younge lecher, she said vnto him, that if he would leaue her honor vntouched, she would bestowe an ointment vpon him, wherwith being annointed, he should neuer be hurt: wherupon she praied him to make proofe in her. He was content, and when she had caused her neck to be rubbed with wax melted in oyle, she said vnto him, that he should strike with his sword with all the might that he was able. He did so, and at the first blow, smote off her head. *Niceph. l. 7. hist. ecclef. c. 13. Baron. to. 3. anno 309.*

8. Casimirus, sonne to Casimirus kinge of Polognia, being in danger of death, according to the iudgment and opinion of the best phisitians, vnles

les he gaue him ſelfe to the pleaſures
of the fleſh, choſe rather to die, then
in ſo dooing, to looſe the flower of
his virginitie. *Cromerus l. 29. Ret. Pó-
lon.* And *Politianus writeth that the like
hapned to Michael Vernius Poet, of the
age of eightene yeares.*

9. S. Macrina virgin, ſiſter to S:Ba-
ſil and S. Gregorie of Nice, being often requeſted by her mother, to put
into the Chirugians handes, a ſore
breſt which ſhe had, which threatned
an incurable cancker, if it were not
lanced in due time: ſhe was ſo chaſt
and ſo ſhamfaſt, that her diſeaſe ſeemed
nothing vnto her, in reſpect of expo-
ſing to the eyes and handes of men,
ſome part of her body. She went then
into her oratorie, and there beſought
God with trickling teares, that he
would heale her, without diſcouering
her fleſh to the ſight of men. This
done, ſhe went and lookt forth her
mother, and beſought her to make the
ſigne of the Croſſe vpon her diſeaſe;

which

which she did, and therupon was healed inftantly. *Ribad. in her life, the 19. of Iuly.*

10. S. Anthonie being enforced vpon a day to ftrip him felfe naked to paffe the flood of Lyeus, befought Theodorus his companion, to remoue him felfe a far off from him; and being vpon the point to vnclothe him felfe: he was afhamed of him felfe : which thing was fo gratefull vnto God , that he paffed him ouer miraculoufly on the other fide, without the puttinge off his clothes. *S. Athanafius in his life.*

11. S. Nympha of Palermo in Sicilia, hauing preferred virginitie before mariage, receiued of her good Angell, a crowne made of Lillies and of Rofes. *Baron. in Martirolog.*

See the liues of S. Agnes, S. Agatha, S. Cecilie, S. Vrfula, S. Dorothe and others in Ribadeneira.

12. S. Iulian hauing induced her husband Bafilliffes the firft night of her

mariage, to keepe with her, his virginitie, a most sweet odor dispersed it selfe thoroughout the chamber, and a resplendant light appeared to them, and two quires, one of Saintes, wherin our Lord presided, the other of virgins, wherin our Lady presided. The quire of Saintes began to singe. *Thou hast ouercome Iulian, thou hast ouercome:* That of virgins, *Blessed be Basillisses, who hath followed such holie councell, and despising the vaine pleasures of the worlde, hath made him selfe worthie of euerlastinge life*. This done, two men clothed in white, tooke them by the handes and ioyned them together : then a venerable old man presented them a booke, wherin he reade vnto them these wordes ensuinge, the which were written in letters of golde.

Who so desiring to serue God, shall contemne the deceitfull delights of the world, as thou hast done, ô Iulian, shall be written in the number of those, who haue not
defiled

defiled them selues with women. And Ba-
fillißes, because of the intention which he
hath to remaine a virgin, he shall be put
into the booke of virgins, wherof Marie
the mother of virgins, holdeth the first
place. See their liues, in the flowers of
the liues of Saintes, by father Ribad. 9. of
Iulie, taken out of Metaphrastes.

§. 4. Of Charitie.

Abstinence is a virtu, which bri-
dleth the disordinat pleasures and desires of meates, and prescribeth a due
moderation vnto eating. By disordered
desires, are to be vnderstood those,
which draw and allure a person to that
which is vnlawfull, as to eate meates
forbidden, or in time and place not
conuenient, or in too great quantitie,
or in an vndecent maner, or elfe for
that these desires be too importunat,
hauing no other thought but of the
guttes, and the bellie.

By due moderation is vnderstood,
that which is agreeable to the health
of

of the body, and to the functions of
the soule. For which cause it was that
S. Aug. said . Thou hast taught me,
O Lord, that I approach vnto meates,
no otherwise then I would doe vnto
phisick. *l. 10. Confes. c. 31.*

Sobrietie (according as it is taken
in *Eccles. c. 51. Titus. 2. 1. Pet. 1.*) is a
virtu, which doth duly moderate, the
affection and vse of drinking which
may make drunke . This virtu, as also
the precedent, is the mother of health,
in that she taketh away, and hindreth
all the cause of sicknesses, which is
ouermuch fulnes, and cruditie or raw-
nes . For it is a maxime receiued of
all Phisitians ; *None shall be seazed on
by maladies, who is carefull not to fall
into crudities .* But it is much better to
heare the same from the spirit of God.
*Be not greedie in all feasting, and poure
not out thy selfe vpon all meate, for in many
meates there shall be infirmitie. Because of
surfet, many haue died, but he that is abstinent, shall adde life. Eccl. 37. 32.*

P 6   Adde

Adde hereunto, that this virtu maketh the body liuely, & expeditious, to al its motions and its functions.

But what shall I say of the vtilities the soule receiueth therby? It both conserueth and augmenteth memorie, sharpneth the wit, & rendreth it more capable to receiue diuine inspirations, & contemplatiõs. *Whom shall he teach knowledge? And whom shall he make to vnderstand the thinge heard?* (saith the prophet) *them that are weaned from the mylke, that are plucked away from the breasts.* Isay 28. 9. That is to say, to those that withdraw themselues from the delightes and pleasures of the bellie . Hence it proceedeth, that the abstinent and sober, doe better discouer the snares of the diuell, and are more stronge for to resiste him . For which cause S. Peter said . *Be sober and watche, because your aduersarie the diuel, as a roaring lion goeth about , seeking whom he may deuoure.* 1. Pet. 5. 8.

EXAM-

EXAMPLES.

1. All the first men which were from the creation of the world, vntil the deluge, the space of a thousand six hūdred yeares, abstained both from wine, and from flesh: whence it was that they liued to nine hundred yeares old. *Theodoret. Chrisost. Hieron. in Gen.*

2. Venerable Bede, entring into religion at seauen yeares old, by reason of his great abstinence, liued therein vntill the age of nintie two. S. Hilarion till eightie four. S. Paphnutius, and S. Macarius, vntill nintie. Saint Iames hermit, till a hundred and four. Saint Antonie, till a hundred and fiue. Saint Simeon Stillites, till a hundred and nine, whereof he passed eightie one, vpon a pillar, exposed to the sunne and windes, S. Paul the first heremit, vntil a hundred and fifteene, wherof he liued a hūdred in the desert. S. Arsenius, and S. Romualdus liued

a hun-

a hundred and twentie. *S. Hier. in vita*
Hilarionis & Pauli.Athanasius in Antonio.
Cassianus collat.3. c. 1. Theodoret in Iu-
liano . De ceteris vide Lessium in suo Hy-
giastico fol. 60.

3. Some yeares past, the Suffragan
of the bishop of Bamberg, visiting his
dioces , penetrated as far as into Tu-
ring, where he gaue the Sacrament of
Confirmation (which since a hundred
yeares, had not bene giuen out of the
citties of this Bishoprick) to six thousand persons; amongst which, aboue
the number of two hundred, had past
aboue a hundred yeares : so that the
children were a hundred yeares olde,
the nephues seauentie, & so of the rest,
vnto the fourth regeneration. *Extrac-*
ted out of the annales of our Societie. And
I my selfe aboue four yeares past, spake
at Teux in Franchimont with a poore
contriman, who was aboue a hundred
and twentie yeares old , and was yet
lustie : and this by reason of the sobrietie which he had obserued in his
liuing.

4. Io-

4. Iosephus writeth, that the Esse-nois, liued for the most part, to a hun-dred yeares old, by meanes of the sim-plicitie of their foode, and the good gouerment which they obserued, for (saith he) there is giuen to eache one, nothing else but bread and pottage. *Lib. 2. de bello Iudaico.*

5. From this abstinence and sobrie-tie, it proceeded, that all the Saints a-forsaid, were euermore in vigor of spirit, spending both the daies and nights in holy prayer and contempla-tion, with such contentment, that it seemed vnto them, euen already to tast the delightes of the blessed: as a-mongst others, S. Anthonie and S. Arsenius, who from the setting of the sunne, to the rising therof, remayned in prayers without so much as once mouing them: angrie that the sunne, (beating with her beames vpon their eyes) disturbed them from their pray-ers, so able were they, and contented for to pray. *Athanas. Ribad. 19. of Iuly.*

6. To

6. To conclude this matter, it will not be from the purpose, to set downe in this place, what Tertulian writeth as an eye witnes, of the sobrietie and abstinence of the first Christians. They neuer (saith he) set them downe to table, but first they make their praiers to God. They eate as much, as those doe, that rise a hungred. They drinke as much, as is meet for those that are chast and modest. They fill them selues, as those who remember, that they are to pray vnto God in the night. They talke together, as those that know that God doth heare them. After meate, they washe their mouth and handes, and after discourse turne by turne, vpon some point of holy scripture, and by this meanes it is one knowes, how much they haue drunke. They arise from the table, not to enter into debates and quarrells, not to talke of lasciuiousnes and knauerie, but of that which is both honest and modest

deſt , *vt qui non tam cœnam cœnaue-rint , quam diſciplinam* , as thoſe who had not ſo much fed of a ſupper , as of diſcipline , ſo that a man would iudge , that they rather came from ſome leſſon, then from the table . *Tertul. c. 39. Apologet* . O admirable ſo-brietie of theſe firſt Chriſtians, from which how far off are we at this preſent !

§. 6. Of the virtu of Patience.

Patience is a virtu, wherby we en-dure voluntarily , and with tranquil-litie , the euils which doe happen to vs, ſent from God, from the diuell, or from men, as ſickneſſes , loſſe of goo-des , of children , of parents &c; in-iuries, ſadneſſes , ſcruples , and other afflictions of ſpirit : and this for the hope we haue of better goodes.

There are ſix degrees of patience. 1. To receiue the iniurie or the e-uill, without any reſiſtance . 2. Not to reuenge it . 3. To beare no ha-tred

tred to the partie , from whome the
euill doth proceede. 4. To loue him.
5. To doe good vnto him. 6. To pray
to God for him.

*All that shall be applied to thee, receiue;
and in sorrow , sustaine; and in thy humiliation haue patience* (faith the wifeman) *for gold and siluer, are tried in the
fire, but acceptable men; in the fornace of
humiliation.* And v. 16. *Woe be to them,
that haue lost patience.*

*He that is patient , is gouerned with
much wisdome, but he that is impatient,
exalteth his follie.* Pro. 14. 29.

*My sonne, cast not away the discipline
of our Lord , nether doe thou faint when
thou art chasticed of him : for whom our
Lord loueth he chasticeth, and as a father
in the sonne, he pleaseth himselfe.* Pro. 3.
11. The same doth the Apostle say.
Heb. 12. 17. and S. Iohn in the Apoc.
3. 19.

The most effectuall motiues which
one can giue, to excite and aduance
him selfe to this holy virtu, are.

1. To

1. To confider the patience of God the Creator, who giues fo many good thinges vnto finners, and indures, fo gently all their iniuries ; *who maketh his funne to rife vpon good and bad , and rayneth vpon iuft and iniuft,* as our Lord faith in *S. Mat. 5. 45.* Which point Tertullian deduceth elegantly *lib. de patientia:* and S. Cyprian, *lib. de bono patientiæ.*

2. To confider the patience which our Lord Iefus Chrift had during his whole life, in whom God (as Tertullian fpeaketh) hath placed his fpirit with all patience, *who when he was re-uiled did not reuile, when he fuffered he threatned not, not but deliuered him felfe to him that iudged him vniuftly.* 1. *Pet.* 2. 25.

3. To confider all the Saintes of the old Teftament , as Abell, Abraham, Ifaac, Iacob, Iofeph, Moyfes, Dauid, Tobie, Iob, what is it they haue not endured? Now, if in that rude worlde, before the doctrine and examples of Iefus Chrift , all thefe holy Saintes haue

haue bene ſo patient in their aduerſities, what ought we to be (ſaith Tertullian) in the light of the goſpell, in
the ſchoole of Ieſus Chriſt, in this a-
bundance of grace, amongſt the infinit examples of the Saintes of the new
teſtament?

4. To conſider the great vtilities
of this virtu. 1. It ſatisfieth for ſinnes,
redeeming by a litle paine, the moſt
horrible torments of the other life.
It is eaſie to ſuffer the loſſe of ten
crownes, when one knowes that by
this meanes, one redeemeth the confiſcation of then thouſand. 2. It aideth,
confirmeth, and perfecteth all virtues.
Eſteeme it, my bretheren, al ioy, when you
ſhall fall into diuers tentations (ſaith S.
Iames) *knowing that the probation of*
your faith worketh patience, and let
patience haue a perfect worke. Iac. 1.
2. 3. It maketh vs alſo to merit euerlaſting life. 2. Cor. 4. 17.

And our Lord ſaith. *Bleſſed are*
they that ſuffer perſecution for iuſtice,
for

for theirs is the kingdome of heauen.
Blessed are you when they shall reuile
you and persecute you, and speake all
that naught is against you, vntruly,
for my sake, be glad and reioyce, for
your reward is verie great in heauen.
Mat. 5. 10.

EXAMPLES.

1. Iob, one of the greatest Princes of all the east, being spoiled by the deuill of all his goodes, afflicted with al sorts of diseases that might befall vnto a man, and this thoroughout all the members of his body, and for the space of many yeares despiced of all men, yea euen assaulted by his owne wife, who prouoked him to deny God: hauing no other lodging then a dunghil, and for all sortes of moueables, an il-fauored piece of a broken pot, to scrape his soares, and to cleanse the filth that issued out of them: notwithstanding all these afflictions,

he

he neuer changed nor loſt his courage, no not ſo much as of ſpeeche or of viſage , but ſinging cherefully theſe wordes, ſo full of reſignation to the will of God. *As it hath pleaſed our Lord, ſo is it done.* Iob. 1. 22.

2. Tobias falling a ſleepe againſt a wall, a Swallow let fall her dunge vpon his eyes, which made him blinde at the ſame inſtant . God permitted this affliction to happen to him (ſaith the holy ſcripture) *that an example might be giuen to poſteritie of his patiēce, as alſo of holie Iob. For Wheras he feared God alwayes from his infancie, and kept his commandements, he grudged not againſt God, for that the plague of blindnes had chanced to him, but continued immoueable in the feare of God, giuing thankes to God all the dayes of his life.* Tob. 2. 12. And after the Angel Raphael had healed him, he ſaid vnto him. *Becauſe thou waſt acceptable to God, it was neceſſary that tentation ſhould proue thee.* Tob. 12. 13.

3. S.

3. S. Serulus a beggar, lying paralitique his whole life at a gate of Rome, at eache new accesse of dolor, alwaies rendred thankes and praise to almightie God ; for which cause he deserued at his death, to be visited and recreated with the musick of Angells. *S. Greg. Pope writeth it in his Dialogues l. 4. c. 14. & Hom. 15. in Euang.*

4. S. Galle daughter to Simachus Consull of Rome, being left a widdow in the flower of her age, had all her body couered ouer with an infamous scale : and the Phisitians assuring her that she should soone die, yea that a beard would growe out at her chinne like to a man, vnles she married her selfe againe, she chose rather to endure both the sicknes and death, then to marry againe the second time. At last, as she drewe by litle and litle vnto her death, hauinge one of her breastes all full of soares, and that S. Peter appeared vnto her, she asked not of him to be healed, but only if her
sinnes

finnes were forgiuen her : and vnder-
standing that they were, she died with
most exceeding consolation *S. Greg. l.*
4. dial. c. 13.

5. The Emperor Mauritius , hauing bene the cause of the massacre, of
sundry of his captiue subiects , which
he might haue set free for a smale matter , besought of God to haue his punishment in this life, and wrote to all
the Patriarkes and Monkes of the easte,
to the end they should offer vp to God
their praiers for this effect. God granted him his demand, for he saw all his
children put to death before his eyes,
he saying no other thinge , saue only
that verse of the psalme. 118. *Thou art*
iust o Lord, and thy iudgment is right: and
within a while after, he him selfe had
his head cut off. *Niceph. l. 18. hist. c.*
38. *and Card. Baron. anno. 602.*

6. S. Liduuine natiue of Holland,
from the age of fifteene yeares, to fifty
three , was neuer without sicknesses
and diseases . And first hauing an
Apo-

Apoſtume broken within her body, was afterwards ſmitten with the pal-ſie, and fire of S. Anthonie, had al her members rotten and full of holes. Out of her breaſts, wormes iſſued by whole hundreds, which eate and gnawed all her body ; She had her head afflicted with moſt ſharp paines, her fore-head open, her chinne cleft, one eye out, and the other not able to behould the light; caſt commonly blood out at her mouth, eyes, noſe, and eares ; had the ſquinzie in her throate, the tooth-ache, agues, ſingle, double, triple, quadruple, and the dropſie : and beſi-des all theſe euills, ſhe was accuſed of witcherie . Now what feeling could ſhe haue amongſt ſo many and ſuch afflictions? notwithſtanding, ſhe ſaid no other thinge, but . O my ſweete Lord, augment my paines . Wretch that I am, alas, what is it that I endure? Alas how litle is it in compariſon of that which thou endureſt for me ? *Surius to. 7. 14. of Aprill. See the example*

Q   *of*

of Saint Frauncis here before lib. 1. *c.* 7.
§. 7. *example* 1.

7. S. Nichola or Coleda, hauing
craued of our Lord, to make her partaker of his paines, for the space of fiftie yeares was neuer without sicknesses and most greeuous dolours, which
allwayes redoubled vpon solemne
feastes. And as they that looked vnto
her, wept at the very sight of her torments, she in smyling wise said vnto
them. Wherfore weepe yee, my good
sisters? that which I suffer, deserues not
so much as to be thought of. If God
haue sent it me, alas, should I be so
perfidious, as to quarrell against the
bountie of my sweet Lord, who hath
so great a care of his poore seruat? And
as she ommitted not for all her paine
to come and goe, to doe some seruice
vnto God, some saying vnto her; You
will die by the way. So that (quoth
she) we die betwixt the armes of good
Iesus, what forces it (my poore sisters)
whither we die in the fieldes or in the
cittie

cittie vpon the pauement , or vpon a matteras? We cannot fall amisse, falling betwixt the handes of God. *Surius 6. of March ex Stephano Iuliaco. See Binet in ses consolations des malades e. 7. §. 4.*

8. S. Spiridion being called by the Emperor Constance as he entred the pallace, a courtiar seeing him poorely apparelled, gaue him a box vpon the eare; the Saint presented him the other. Which touched in such sort the hart of this arrogant person, that he cast him selfe before his feete, and asked him forgiuenes. *Surius 24. of December.*

9. S. Romuald, of the house of the Dukes of Rauenna, being often strucken with a pole by Marinus the Hermit, when he hapned to misse in saying his psaulter, replied not a word, vntill such time as after certaine daies, seeing that by this meanes he lost the hearing of one eare, he said vnto him, that if he thought good, he should frō

Q 2   thence

thence forth ſtrike him vpon the right
ſide, becauſe he had loſt the hearing of
the left, by reaſon of the blowes that
he had giuen him. Marinus was ex-
treamly amazed at this patience, and
was the cauſe that he euer afterwards
reſpected him ſo much the more. *The*
B. Card. Damian in his life, & Ribad.
7. of Feb.

10. Our Lord ſaid vpon a day to
the B. mother Tereſa of Ieſus; Beleeue my daughter, that he that is moſt
beloued of my Father, is he to whom
he giueth the greateſt troubles. Behould and conſider my woundes, neuer will thy euills be equall to my paines. This ſo encouraged her, that ſhe
had no other deſire but to ſuffer, ſo
that being buffeted, ſpit on, and trode
vnder foote, ſhe fell a laughing: being
calumniated in all that poſſible might
be ſaid, ſhe ſet not by it. Yea, ſhe
prayed to God, that ſhe might neuer
be without paines, as ſhe was not.
And after ſhe had bene once tormented

ted for the ſpace of fiue houres by the
deuill, with great dolors and interior
and exterior troubles, ſo that ſhe
thought that ſhe was able to endure
no more; ſhe notwithſtanding, ceaſed
not to craue patience of our Lord,
offring her ſelfe according to her cuſtome, that if he would make vſe therof, that then this paine might laſt her
till the day of iudgment: and this was
her ordinarie prayer. My Lord be it to
dye, or to endure, I for my ſelfe aske
naught elſe of thee.

11. Bleſſed Father Zauerius, endured much in the Indies, but it was nothing in regard of that which he deſi-
ered to endure: for amidſt his greateſt
paines, he praied to God to giue him
greater. And when vpon a day, our
Lord had ſhewed him the croſſe and
torments by the which he was to
paſſe, he began to cry. Yet more, yet
more (o Lord) yet more. *Ribad. in the
abridgment of his life.*

12. S. Iohn Gualbertus hauing

pardoned from his hart the murdering of his brother, as he praied a while after before a crucifix, our Lord who was nayled theron, enclined his head downe vnto him. *Blaſ. Mediolan. general. ord. val. vmbroſæ circa annum 1040. & Baron. tom. 11. anno. 1051.*

13. An Engliſh gentilman, hauing likewiſe pardoned him who had kild his father, as he praid before a Crucifix, the Kinge (who was preſent) perceiued that at eache genuflexion which he made, the Crucifix bowed its head vnto him. *Math. Pariſ. hiſt. Anglic. anno 1090.* Thou confirmeſt (o Lord) by this miracle, the truth of thy doctrine, vttered ſo many ages paſt. *Forgiue, and it ſhall be forgiuen you. Luc. 6. Mat. 6.*

14. Our Lord ſaid vpon a time vnto S. Gertrude, that euen as the ringe which is giuen at a making ſure, is a ſigne of the faith which the parties promiſe one to another: euen ſo patience in corporall and ſpiritual aduerſities

ſities, endured for the loue of God, is a ſigne of diuine election, and of the mariage of the ſoule with almightie God. *Bloſ. l. de conſol. puſillam.*

He ſaid the ſame, to the B. Mother Tereſa; Thou knoweſt full wel (quoth he vnto her) the mariage there is bet-wixt thee and me, and that by this meanes, all that I haue is thyne. I giue thee then, all the ſorrowes and paines which I haue ſuffered. *In the booke a-forſaid cap.* 10.

Length of time can nether be yrk-ſome nor tedious vpon this ſubiect, there being nothinge more profitable and neceſſarie for vs, as S. Paul ſaith, *Heb.* 10. 36.

§. 7. *Of ſpirituall diligence.*

That which I haue alleadged here-tofore againſt Slouth and Idlenes, ſuffi-ceth to excite vs to the loue of this virtu: yet to the end to ſay ſomwhat, more directly and particularly.

We muſt conſider, that this life is

giuen

giuen vs for no other end, but to negociat our saluation, for which cause
it is, that our Lord compareth vs to
labourers, sent to the vyniard there to
worke, who are to receiue our wages,
answerable to our labour. *Mat. 20. 8.
& 16. 27. The Sonne of man shall come
in the glorie of his Father, with his Angells, and then will hee render to euerie
man according to his workes.* The same
also S. Paul saith. *1. Cor. 3. 8. Euery
one shall receiue his owne reward, according to his owne labor.* And S. Iohn in
the last of the Apocalips 12. and in the
Galat. 6. 9. *Doing good, let vs not faile,
for in due time we shall reape not fay-
ling: therfore while we haue time, let vs
worke.*

We shall haue no more glorie in
heauen, then we haue acquired merits in our life. If the Saints could
be sorrie, nothing would so much
peirce their hart, as to haue let the
time to passe so vnprofitably, which
was giuen them for the gayning of
their

their glorie .

Our Lord compareth him ſelfe vnto a maiſter , who going to tra-uell into a far contrie, gaue to eache one of his ſeruants , certaine tal-lents to trafique with all : who at his returne , was to call them to account for the diligence or negli-gence , loſſe or gayne , which they had made in their trafique, and ac-cordingly to giue them recompence. What ioy hath a Chriſtian at the houre of his death , who hauinge carried him ſelfe like a good ſer-uant, may truly ſay . *Lord thou didſt deliuer me two talents , behould I haue gayned other two* . And to heare his Maſter ſay . *Well fare thee , good and faithfull ſeruant , becauſe thou haſt bene faithfull ouer a few thinges , I will place thee ouer many thinges , en-ter in to the ioy of thy Lord* . *Mat.* 25. 22.

How much more courageous ough-teſt thou to be in the field of God (ſaith

S. Aug.) sith thou hast the promise of
the truth, which can nether fayle,
nor deceiue? And what is it which
is promised to thee? Gold or siluer,
which men doe loue so excessiue-
lye? Or enheritances, for which men
doe melt gold? Or gardens, houses, or
heardes of beastes? No this is not the
recōpence for which God doth encou-
rage vs for to trauaile. What is it then?
Life eternall. *Aug. tract. 3. in ep. Ioan.*

S. Gregorie of Nazianzen, compares our life, to a faire or market, the
day wherof being expired, one findes
no more to sell of that which he desi-
red. *In sentent.*

Behould the industrie of sundrie
tradesmen, who moyle and toile from
the breake of day vnto midnight, and
this with ioy and songes of myrthe,
only to gaine a litle bread: and thou (o
Christian) to gaine the bread of Angells, heauen it selfe, and life eternall,
wilt thou refuse the labor and diligence of a few daies?

EXAM-

EXAMPLES.

1. In the monasterie of Arnsberge of the order of the Premonstrenses, a certaine English monke called Richard, to fly idlenes, spent the time which he had free, to write forth the bookes of the monasterie, hoping that for this paine & diligence, God would one day recompence him. Twentie yeares after his death, his graue being opened, his whole body was turnd to ashes, excepting only his right hande, which was still as fresh and as whole, as if at that instant it had bene cut or pluckt from the liuing body. This arme is yet kept vnto this day in the same monasterie. *Casarius l. 12. c. 47.*

2. S. Bernard seing vpon a day one of the bretheren of his couent labouring in the field with great feruor, and aboue his forces, said vnto him in the presence of all the other religious, who laboured as well as he. Follow on my brother, I assure thee, that

thou

thou shalt haue no other purgatorie after this life. *Thom. à Cantipr. lib. 2. ap. cap. 5.*

3. S. Marcian Anchoret, meeting with a hunter, was demanded of him, what he did in that desert? But the Saint demanded likewise of him, what he did there? The hunter answered, that he hunted there after Hares and Deeres. And I (said S. Marcian) hunt here after my God, nor will neuer giue ouer this goodly chace, vntill I take him, and embrace him. *Theodor. in Philotheo.* Blessed is he who emploies his time and labour in such a chase See more vpon this matter. c. 6. the Examples of the 7. §.

THE V. CHAPTER.

Of the holy sacrifice of the Masse.

THe Masse is a sacrifice (a) wherin the body and blood of Iesus-Christ, is consecrated and offered vp to God,

God, with sundrie ceremonies, prayers and sacred wordes, instituted by
our Lord him selfe , as touching the
substance , in his last supper (*b*) and as
concerning the rest, by the B. Apostles,
and principallie by Saint Peter, Saint
Iames , and by their successors. (*c*)
(a) *Iustin. in dial. cum Tryph. Basil. ser.*
2. de baptis. c. 2. Tertullian. de orat. Aug.
ep. 23. & lib. 20. cont. Faust. c. 21. (b)
Luc. 22. Iren. l. 4. c. 32. Cypr. ep. 63.
Aug. l. 10. de ciuit. c. 20. & alibi sepe.
Conc. Trident. sess. 2. c. 1. (c) *Conc.*
Trid. ibid. cap. 5.

§. 1. *Of the fruites and vtilities of* *the Masse.*

By meanes of this Sacrifice we redre
thankes vnto God, for all the benefits
we haue receiued of his infinit boutie:
& as we are infinitly bound & obliged
vnto him, so is there nothing by the
which we can better satisfie him, then
to offer vnto him the immaculat hoste
of his B. Sonne , which of it selfe is
of in-

of infinit value and merit . Nether are
they Priefts only , which may make
this offringe , but all thofe likewife
who afift at Maffe.

Moreouer, by meanes of this facrifice,there is obtained and applied vnto
vs, all that which our Lord hath pur-
chafed for vs by his death and paffion
(a) And what other thinge is the holy
Maffe , but the felfe fame reprefenta-
tion of the paffion of our Lord? (b) (a)
Greg. Naz. orat. 1. in Iulian. Greg. mag.
Hom. 37. in euang. (b) *Luc. 22. Chrifoft.*
Hom. 17. in ep. ad Heb. Aug. fer. 4. de
Innoc. See the Catechifme of Bellarmin.

There are yet many more vtilities.

1. By the facrifice of the maffe, we
fatisfie for our finnes:and venial finnes
are forgiuen vs. *Cyp, Bafil. Chrifoft.*
Ambrof. citati a Canifio Hic.

2. We receiue grace, to refolue to
confeffe our mortall finnes, how e-
norme or in how great number foeuer
they be : and not to fall againe into
them .

								3. We

3. We receiue sundry graces and helpes, to resist the malignant spirit, and ro surmount the difficulties of this life. *Aug. l. 22. de ciuit.*

4. We asist the soules detayned in Purgatorie. *Greg. l. 4. dial. c. 57. Ioan. Damas. ser. de defunct. Aug. l. de cura pro mortuis & alij.*

5. Our Lord is wont also to impart a great deale of prosperitie to the temporall goods of those, who deuoutly asist or serue at Masse. *Chrysost. hom. 77. in Ioan. & hom. 18. in Act. Apost.* O what fruites and vtilities are these for those, who daily asist at the holy Masse!

§. 2. Of the reuerence and attention we ought to haue, during the sacrifice of the Masse.

Where the Kinge is, there is the court; we haue already said, that the Masse is no other thinge, then the sacrifice of the pretious body and blood of the Sonne of God, which is offered vp to God him selfe. Here then is
pre-

prefent the Kinge of Kinges, yea all
the moft holy Trinitie, together with
the whole celeftiall court: what attention then and modeftie ought we to
bring with vs vnto the fame?

Hearken how S. Iohn Chrifoftome
fpeaketh . The lambe of God is offered vp, the Seraphins afift therat, cou-
uering them felues with their winges , all the Angells intercede for
thee with the Prieft, the fpirituall fire
defcends from heauen, blood is draw-
en forth of the fide of the immaculat
Lambe, and put into the Chalice for
thy purification ; and thou haft nether fhame nor refpect, nor endeuo-
reft not to make thy God propitious
to thee. The weeke hath 168. houres,
and God hath retayned but one only
for his feruice, and yet thou employeft
this, in fecular and ridiculous affaires.
Serm. de Euch. & Hom. 36. vpon the firft
of the Corinthians . The Church is
nether a Barbers nor Apoticharies
fhop, but the place of Angells and
                                    Archan-

Archangells, the court of God, heauen it selfe. *So S. Chrisostom.*

EXAMPLES.

1. The same holy Doctor saith, that a certaine deuout person, saw one day as Masse was said, a great multitude of Angells in shining garments about the Altar, with their heades enclined. *Lib. 6 de Sacerdot.* Which the same S. Chrisostom was wont also to see, as B. Nilus Abbat writeth. *Epist. ad Anastas. & Baron. tom. 5. annal. anno 407.* Other holy persons haue had the like visions, as is to be seene in *Sophron. prat. spirit. cap. 199. And in Cyril Ermite in the life of S. Euthymius.* The Angells, for lack of asistants, haue some times them selues serued Masse: as amongst others, S. Oswald bishop of Vigorina. *Sur. 16. of Octob.* To Saint Gregorie Pope. *Ioan. Diaconus in his Life.* To brother Iohn of Parma, a Frauncifcan Friar, after

after he had discharged him selfe of his Generalls-ships. *Chron. Fratr. Minor. tom. 2. l. 1. c. 57.* Hence you see, what honor it is to asist at Masse, and what attention and reuerence is required therto, sith the Angells them selues asist and serue therat.

2. S. Ambrose writeth after Valerius the great, that whilst Alexander the mghitie Kinge of Macedony sacrificed, one of his pages let fall at vnawares, a burning coale into his sleeue betwixt his shirt and his flesh, and albeit that his flesh burnt, yet he shewed no maner of signe, nor cast so much as one only sighe, for feare he should disturb the sacrifice. Learne o virgin (saith S. Ambrose) with what modestie thou oughtest to asist at the Sacrifice of thy God. *lib. 3. de virgin.*

3. S. Iohn the Almes-giuer, Patriarch of Alexandria, had a custome to cause those to goe forth of the Church, whom he saw to talke or tatle during Masse. *Sur. tom. 1. fol. 569.*
4. The

4. The kinge of Porca in the Indies, being yet but a young man (the yeare 1605.) had nine hundred Pagodes or Idoles, to eache of which, he exhibited euery day, a particular reuerence and adoration, and offered vp a present vnto them: entring into the place where they were, at six a clock in the morning, and remayning there vntill twelue, during which time, he gaue no audience to any person. O what confusion is this for Christians, who scarclie once in eight daies, deuote so much as one houre, to the onely true God which they adore? *P. Petrus Iarric l. 6. hist. Ind. orient. c. 10.*

5. The father in law of the kinge of Congo being baptised, as vpon a day he heard Masse, there were some of his pages (Princes children) who playd the fooles during the same, and and made a noize at the entrie of the chappell. He, iudging it a haynous cryme, not to bringe such attention and reuerence as was conuenient for
so

fo dreadfull a facrifice, commanded
that his pages fhould inftantly be put
to death. And de facto they had bene
executed, if the Portugalls (takinge
compaffion on the tender age of thefe
young nobles) had not begged and obtained their pardon. *The fame author in
the 2. tome of the hiftorie of the orientall
Indies, anno 1484.*

§. 3. *Of the vtilities of the Maffe proued by
examples, with fome remarkable pu-
nifhments of thofe who haue defpiced
the fame.*

1. S. Thomas of Aquin, after he
had faid Maffe, was wont to heare another wherat he ferued: wherin (as he
confeft to S. Bonauenture) he receiued
more light and more knowledge, then
he had done in all his ftudies. *Aut.
Sennen. Ribad.*

2. S. Monica made fo great account
of the Maffe, that coming to die, fhe
requefted no other thinge of her fonne

ne S. Auguſtin and his brother , then to remember her when they ſhould ſtande at the holie Altar (wherat ſhe had not her ſelfe omitted to aſiſt one only day) which he performed . *Aug. Conſ. l. 9. c. 11. & c. 13.* Inſpire (o Lord) (ſaith he) inſpire my bretheren thy ſeruants who ſhall reade theſe thinges, to remember thy ſeruant Monica at the Altar , and her husband Patricius .

3. Ferdinandus Antolinus , being vpon the point to giue battaile to the Sarazens , would firſt before hand heare Maſſe . And whilſt he was buſied in this good office, the battaile was begun , and his Angèll Gardian tooke his place, mounted vpon Ferdinandus horſe, eache one thinking that it was he, & with ſo good ſucceſſe,that the victorie was attributed to him ; And there was afterwards founde in his armour and his horſe , the markes and woundes, which it ſeemed he had receiued who fought in his place.

Ioan.

Ioan. Vaseus in Chron. Hispan. anno. 941.
Simile refert Casarius l. 7. mirac. c. 39.

4. The like hapned to Paschalis
Viuas, a great knight of the troupe of
Don Garcias Ferdinandes Count of
Castile , in the battaile which was
fought againſt Almancor kinge of
Cordoua. For as he heard Maſſe in S.
Martius Church , he was ſeene to
fight , kill the Standar bearer, and
beare away the victorie. *Ioan. Oſorius*
ex hiſt. Hiſpanic. tom. 4. conc. de Sacri-
ficio Miſſæ.

5. Andreas Dacq being in Hieruſalem , would not goe with his companions , vnles he firſt had heard Maiſe.
And behould at his coming forth of
the Church, a horſman preſented him
ſelfe vnto him, who inuited him to get
vp behinde him vpon his horſe: wher
being got vp , he fell aſleepe , and at
his waking, he found him ſelfe the
ſelfe ſame day in his contrie, iuſt at the
gate of his owne houſe. *Thom. a Can-*
tip. l. 2. ap. c. 40. §. 3. And addeth, that
                                    the

the horseman in bidding him God
bay, said vnto him; That this benefit
had bene granted him of almightie
God, for the deuotion that he had to
heare Masse.

6. Cæsarius relateth the like *lib.* 10.
of his miracles c.2. See you the old prouerb is proued true ? *To heare Masse,*
doth neuer hinder.

7. In Alexandria in the time of S.
Iohn the Almes-giuer, there were
two Shoomakers, the one whereof
(charged with children, and also with
his father and mother whom he was
to nourish) hearing Masse euery day,
became riche : the other hauing no
childe at all, and neglecting Masse,
was alwayes poore, notwithstanding
he laboured night and day. *Surius in*
vita S. Ioan. eleemos. tom. 1. *fol.* 570.

8. For the fruites which redounde
to the soules in Purgatorie, there needes no more but to consider that which
Cardinall Baronius writeth, of one
from whom the chaynes and bandes
fell

fell off in prifon, euery time that his brother caufed Maffe to be faid for him, thinking he had bene flaine in the war. *Tom. 8. annal. anno 679.* Giuing fufficiently to vnderftand, that had he bene in Purgatory, he had bene deliuered. The like accident is recounted by S. Gregorie *hom. 37. in euang. & l. 4. dial. c. 57.*

See the life of S. Malachias written by **S.** Bernard; with a multitude of other goodly examples, in the flowers of the liues of Saints by father Ribadeniera, in the difcourfe of the commemoration of the faithfull departed.

9. In Styria, a gentleman becoming defperat, and being tempted to hange him felfe, receiued counfell of a good religious man, euery day to heare Maffe: the which he did, giuing wages for this purpofe vnto a Chaplaine, who faid Maffe vnto him in his caftle, and by this meanes, was deliuered of his tentation. Now it came to paffe vpon a day, that his Chaplaine went
to

to a place neere by, to helpe and pleaſure a friend of his; The gentleman
ſeeing him ſelfe to be fruſtrated of
his only redreſſe, went to ſeeke his
Chaplaine, thinking to heare Maſſe
where he was, but he was tould in the
way by one of the village, that the
Maſſe was already ſaid, and inſtantly
his former tentation tooke him a-
gaine; which made him ſo ſorrie, that
he preſently fell downe at the feete of
the contrie man as in a ſound; Who
ſeeing him make ſo great account of
the Maſſe, asked him if he were contented to giue him his cloake, and he
would yeld to him all the merit of that
Maſſe which he had heard. He answered yea, that he was well content;
But being departed the one from the
other, behould the gentlemans tentation tooke hould of the villager, and
that ſo vehemently, that not able to
ſurmount it, he hunge him ſelfe
with his cloake, which the ſelfe
ſame gentleman ſaw at his returne.

R

Aeneas Syluius, *who being afterwardes created Pope*, *was called Pius the second*, *in the historie of Bohemia*. *Pettus Massias c. 22. p. 3.* Iudge by this, what ought to be the value and efficacie of the Masse.

10. S. Anthonie Archbishop of Florence writeth, that two younge youthes, being gone vpon a holly day to shoote at birdes (one of which had heard Masse, the other not) a storme arose vpon a sodaine, with great lightninges and store of thunder, and a voice was heard which said; *strike him, strike him*: and presently the thunderbolt fell, and stroke him that had not heard Masse. The other all affrighted, ran to the place he had resolued to goe to, and behould the voice rebounded againe; *strike him, strike him*. And as he expected nothing but death, another voice was heard, which said; *I can not, because he hath heard to day. Verbum caro factum est*: giueing hereby to vnderstand, that God forbad to kill him,

be-

cauſe he had heard that day a whole
Maſſe. *2. p. Chron. tit. 9. c. 10. §. 2.*

11. At Serrelionne in the Indies,
two young men going a fiſhing vpon
a Sonday, as they were on the ſea, one
of them heard it ringe to the laſt Maſſe,
and knowing that he had not as yet
heard Maſſe, he exhorted his companion to goe with him to heare the
ſame, and therupon went out of the
boate. I will not goe (quoth the other)
vnles I haue firſt taken ſomwhat. He
had no ſooner ſpoke theſe wordes, but
a vehement eddy ſodainly aroſe which
turned all vpſide downe, and ſent the
boate vnto the bottome, in the ſight
of the other, who learned by his example, what account one ought to
make of the Maſſe. *Taken forth of the
letters of Father Emanuel Aluares, ſent
from the Indies into Portugal. anno 1610.*

THE VI. CHAPTER.

*Of Confession, or of the Sacrament
of Pennance.*

PEnnance is a Sacrament, wherin
priestly absolution is giuen of all
sinnes, to him who hath entirely confest them, and detested them . *Canis.
Trid. sess. 14. c. 1. & can. 1. Item. sess. 6. c.
14. & can. 29. Florent & Constant. sess. 15.*

The holie fathers call it, the second
table after shipwrack , in as much as
those who haue once escaped the shipwrack of sinne by Baptisme , if since
they be fallē into sinnes, how greuous
and enormous soeuer they be , may a-
gaine escape by the Sacrament of Pennance, and arriue safely at the harbour
of grace , and friendship of God . *S.
Pacian epist. 1. ad Symp. Hier. in c.
3. Isay. & ep. 8. ad Demetriad. Amb.
ad virg. laps. cap. 8. Trid. ses. 6. cap.
14. & ses. 14. can. 2. Tertul. de pœnit.
Ezech.*

Ezech. 18. & 33.

Penance hath three partes (*a*) Contrition, Confeſſion, and Satisfaction: becauſe as S. Chriſoſt. (*b*) ſaith) God will that we reconcile our ſelues vnto him, by the ſame meanes, that we haue diſgraced our ſelues, to wit, by hart, by word, and by worke. In hart by Contrition, in word by Confeſſion, in worke by Satisfaction. (a) *Conc. Flor. & Trid. ſeſ. 14. can. 3. & can. 4.* (b) *Chriſoſt. ſer. de pœnit.*

§. 1. *Of Contrition.*

Contrition (the firſt part of Penance) is a ſorrow of the ſoule, and a deteſtation of ſinnes committed with a firme purpoſe to commit them no more. *Caniſ. Trid. ſeſ. 14. can. 4. Florent.*

I will recount to thee all my yeares, in the bitterneſ of my ſoule. Iſay 38. 16. quoth the good kinge Ezechias.

A Sacrifice to God, is an afflicted ſpirit, a contrit and humble hart, o God, thou wilt not deſpice. Pſal 50. 19.

Rent

Rent your harts, and not your garments.
Ioel. 2. 13.

To obtaine this contrition, it is necessarie for a man well and exactly to
examine his conscience, and next to
consider the enormitie of his sinnes,
by the points set downe heretofore. *l.
1. c. 2. See the act of Contrition in this 2
booke c. 2. §. 3. sect. 1.*

Sect. 1. EXAMPLES FOR THE *first part of Contrition.*

The holy scripture doth furnish vs
with most goodly examples for this
first part.

1. Of kinge Ezechias. Isay. 38.
2. Of kinge Dauid. 2. Reg. 12. 13.
3. Of Marie Magdalen. Luc. 7.
4. Of S. Peter. Mat. 26. Marc. 14. Luc. 22.
5. Of the good thiefe. Luc. 23.
6. Of S. Thomas Apostle. Ioan. 20.
7. See before two goodly ones. l. 2. c. 2. §. 3. Sect. 1. The one of a maide

Ex-

Example 2. 1.

8. The other of the Emperor Theodosius. l. 1. c. 6. §. 6.

9. Of Henry 2. kinge of England, in the
flowers of the liues of Saintes by
Father Ribadeniera in the life of
S. Thomas of Canterburie 29. of
December.

10. Of Othon the 3. Emperor, in the
same booke, in the life of S. Romuald Feb. 7.

Sect. 2. of the second part of Contrition.

This is a point much to be noted,
because it is greatly to be feared, that
many do amisse and fayle in this point,
by reason wherof their Confessions
are voide.

It is, a firme purpose, no more to
commit the said sinnes : to fly the occasions of falling into them: to satisfie
those, from whom one hath taken
away ether goods or honor; for as S.
Aug. saith. *ep. 54. ad Macedon.* The
    R 4   theft

theft is not forgiuen, vnles the thinge
ftolen be reftored, or at the leaft that
one haue the will to reftore it. And that
which is faid of theft, is alfo to be vnderftood of ones good name taken a-
way by detraction.

EXAMPLES.

1. Father Iohn Lodinus, a great diuine of the Societie of Iefus teaching
at Paris, related to a father of the fame
focietie (who fince preached the fame
at Bruxells before their moft excellent
Higneſſes) to haue knowen a gentleman in Italie, who for that he was a
vfurer, and coming to Confeſſion,
would not leaue his finfull vfuries,
could not be abfolued, nether of his
Curat, nor of the fathers of the Societie: wherupon he went at the laft, and
found forth a certaine Religious man,
who taxing the other of fcrupulofitie,
without any difficultie, gaue him ab-
folution as oft as he prefented himfelfe
vnto him, and by this meanes wonne
the

the fauor of this gentleman, and was
almoſt day by day at his table. Vpon
a night they hauing well ſupped and
made good cheere together, the Religious man being retired into his monaſterie, this gentleman died ſodainly.
And at the ſame time that he lay labouring for life, two diuells in the
ſhape of ſeruing men, knockt at the
gate of the monanaſterie, asked for
this Religious, & led him to the houſe
of the ſick. As they were come to the
market place, the Religious man eſpied
the gentleman in his furred gowne,
walking in the moone light, and ſup-
poſing him ſelf to be deceiued, entring
into choler with him ſelfe, the gentleman ſaid vnto him, that he had indeed
beene ſick, and that he was dead and
damned for his vſuries, & for his pro-
phaning of the Sacraments. And becauſe, he inſteed of reprehēding him as
he was boūd, had ſupported him in his
ſinne, that it was but reaſon that he
ſhould be alſo puniſhed with the like
R 5   paine. This

This said, the two dissembled seruants, caught betwixt their clutches,
the one the gentleman, the other, the
Religious, and were neuer seene since
that day. His companion remayned a-
lone halfe deàd, who went and related the whole to the other Religious
of his order. See you by this most horrible exãple, that it is not enough for
one to confes his sinnes, vnles he haue
a will also, neuer more to committ
them, and to restore the goods which
one hath stolen?

§. 2. *Of Confession.*

Confession, the second part of Penance, is a secret accusation of all the
sinnes which one remembreth, after
he hath duly examined him selfe,
made to a Priest to haue absolution.
Canisius.

We must carefully marke and consider all the circumstances.

I sayd, *an Accusation*; becaufe it is
not to confes, whè one excuseth or di-
miniſ-

miniſheth his ſinnes; or when one ſay-
eth nothing, vnles he be asked.

I ſayd, *Secret*, to diſtinguiſh it from
publique, which was ſomtimes made
in times paſt: and to ſignifie, that one
ought to tell his ſinnes in ſuch ſort,
that none may heare them but the
Prieſt.

Of all; for if you remember a hun-
dréd mortall ſinnes, and doe confes
but nintie nine, your confeſſion is
voide, and you commit in doing this,
another moſt greeuous ſinne of ſacriledge.

What ſinne can be more horrible,
then to ſet on his knees before the
kinge, and to make ſhew to aske him
forgiuenes, and to deſire to enter a-
gaine into his amitie hauing offended
him greuouſlie, not withſtanding at
the ſelfe ſame time that his pardon is
pronounced, to raiſe him ſelfe vpp a-
gainſt the Kinge, tread him vnder his
feete, and to ſtab his poynard into his
throate? Thou dooſt this (o ſinner)

when

when thou concealeſt any mortall ſinne in thy Confeſſion.

How much more thinke you doth he deſerue worſe puniſhments, which hath trodden the Sonne of God vnder foote, and eſteemed the blood of the Teſtament polluted, wherin he is ſanctified, and hath done contumelie to the ſpirit of grace? *Heb.* 10. 29. S. Amb. and Theophilaﬅ, explicat this ſentéce, of thoſe who approache vnworthely to the Sacraments.

What auayleth it the ſick, ſtabbed with diuers mortall woundes, to diſcouer to the phiſitian one or two, if he conceale the others ? The confeſſar is a ſpiritual phiſitian (*a*) who can heale thee infallibly, prouided that thou diſcouer thee as thou oughteſt.

That which is not diſcouered (ſaith S. Ierom) the phiſitian can not cure. *In c.* 10. *Eccl.* (a) *Conſil. Lateran. can.* 21. *Wormatien. c.* 25. *Orig. Hom.* 1. *& 2. in Pſal.* 37. *Trid. ſeſſ.* 14. 6. 5.

He is alſo a Iudge (*b*) He cannot then

then abſolue the criminall penitent,
vnles he haue full and perfect knowledge of his crimes. (b) *Aug.l.20.de ciu.*
c. 9. Greg. Hom.26. in Euang. Chriſoſt. l.
3.. de ſacerd. & hom. 5. de verb. Iſay.
Hieron. ad Heſiod. ep. 1.

There is no part of the body ſo
ſhamfull , which one diſcouereth not
to ſaue life:and ſhall the ſinner dout to
diſcouer the ſpirituall ſicknes of his
ſoule,for his euerlaſting health?

I haue ſaid, *of his ſinnes* ; to giue to
vnderſtand, that one muſt not reueale
the ſinnes of another.

Note further, that they muſt be
tould in particular, and not in general,
which is a fault too too frequent and
ordinarie in many perſons.

To the prieſt; for it is to the Prieſt, &
to no other,that God hath giué power
to pardon ſinnes. *Ioan.20. 23.*

EXAMPLES.

1. A holy father ſaw vpon a certaine day, the diuell make his circuit
to

to all the feates of confeſſion : and asking him what he did there, he replied,
that he reſtored to the penitents that
which he had taken from them. And
being asked, what it was. I tooke
(quoth he) all ſhame from them at the
time they ſinned, that ſo they might
ſinne ſo much the more freely : and
now I reſtore it vnto them againe, to
the end they may not confes them. *In
vitis patrum.*

2. A Lady in Italy reputed for holie, appeared to her daughter in forme
of a roſted Sow, ſaying that ſhe was
damned, for hauing concealed in Confeſſion a carnall ſinne which ſhe had
committed with her husband. *Seraph.
Raz. in hortulo exempl. tit. 1. de conf. c.
3. & Gabr. Inchino chanon. Reg. Lateran.*

3. An other concealing in confeſſion a ſinne of the fleſh; ſeemed to caſt
out, & to take in toades at his mouth;
and after his death, appeared to his
confeſſar horribly tormented, ſaying,
that he was daned, for that he had concealed

cealed his ſinne . Adding, that people
went to hell by all ſortes of ſinnes, but
women principally by four: by the ſinne of the fleſh , by vaine ornaments,
by witchcraft , and by ſhame for to
confes them . *Io. Iunior in ſcala cœli.*
Gulielmus Pepin 1. ſup. Confiteor c. 13.

4. At Itate a cittie of the orientall
Indies, the yeare 1590. a chriſtian maiden called Catharin, giueing and aban-
doning her ſelfe ſecretly to the filthines of the fleſh, neuer confeſt her ſelfe
at all. Falling ſick, a father of the Societie went to ſee her, and endeuored
to induce her to a good confeſſion; She
confeſt her ſelfe nine times , but all-
waies cōcealing her ſinnes of the fleſh.
And as the other ſeruants of the houſe
fell a talking with her , ſhe ſaid vnto
them , that euery time her ghoſtly father was nere vnto her, a Black a More
appeared vnto her by her beds ſide,
who ſaid vnto her , that ſhe ſhould
take good heede not to confes all her
ſinnes, ſaying that they were but petty
faults:

faults: and that on the other side, S. Mary Magdalen exhorted her to confes them. The seruants hearing these her speeches, called back the father, but he profited nothing, so that she dyed in that estate. After her death, she appeared to one of the seruants all in fire, saying that she was damned, for hauing confessed none but litle sinnes, and concealed the great; adding that she was forced to tell them this, for their example. An Angel appeared also at the same time, who willed the seruant to harkne vnto her, and to related the whole vnto the rest. *Taken forth of the historie of the Indes, written by F. Iacques Samitiego superior of the mission of the Itatins anno 1590. P. Thyreus de loco infest. p.1.c.1 fuse narrat pat. Delrio in suis disq. mag.*

5. At Arone in Lombardie, the yeare 1595. and litle maide but six yeares old, dyed, crying out that certaine Black a Mores, went about to throw her into a boyling cauldron, and finally

nally she said. Deuil cary me away, deuill carry me away, and in saying this,
she gaue vp her soule vnto the diuels.
Her parents knew by her no other
thinge, but that she was of a quick
spirit, had bene seene to play too libe-
rally with litle youthes, and that she
neuer had bene at holie confession.
Taken out of the historie of the Societie
anno 1595.

§. 3. *Of frequent Confession, and how dā-*
gerous it is for to delay it.

If thou hadst swallowed poison, &
that thou knewest it, wouldst thou tar-
ry to seeke after phisick and after the
phisitian, til the poison were dispersed
thoroughout all thy body?

If thou wert taken of the enimie, &
mightest instatly be deliuered, wouldst
thou tarrie till some one had tyed thee
with more chaines, & put thee into a
deeper dungeon? As long as a man is
in mortall sinne, he meriteth nothing by his good workes, he doth not
par-

participat of the merits of our Lord,
nor of his Church : he is depriued of
the particular asistances of almightie
God, and of his Angell Gardien; And
that which yet is worst of all, he is
hunge by a thrid ouer the welle of the
infernall pit; and who knowes, whither this thrid shall not perhaps be
cut a sunder before to morrow? Why
then in an affaire of such importance,
and wherein is treated of thine eternall saluation , doost thou defer the
time vntill to morrow (wherof thou
art vncertaine) to doe that , which
thou maist now doe assuredly?

Slack not to be conuerted to our Lord,
and differ not frō day to day, for his wrath
shall come sodainly. Eccl. 5.8.

Sonne hast thou sinned? doe so no more,
but for the old also, pray that they may be
forgiuen thee. Eccl. 21. 1.

Doost thou contemne the riches of his
goodnes, and patience , and longanimitie,
not knowing that the benignitie of God
bringeth thee to peunance? But according
                                        to

to thy hardnes and impenitent hart, thou heapest to thy selfe wrath, in the day of wrath. Rom. 2. 4.

He that hath promised the penitent pardon, hath not promised the sinner the day of to morrow. *S. Greg. Hom. 10. in Euang.*

He that doth penance, and reconcileth himselfe at the end of his life, that he departs this life with assurance, I am not assured. I say not that such an one is damned, nor yet say I, that he shall be saued. Wilt thou be deliuered from this dout? Wilt thou auoide that which is vncertaine? Doe penance whilst yet thou art in perfect health, & whilst thou canst as yet sinne: for if thou wilt doe penance when thou cast sinne no more, sinne leaueth thee, but thou hast not left sinne. *S. Aug. lib. 50. Homil.*

EXAMPLES.

1. Chrysaurius, a riche man, hauing passed all his life in pleasures,
seeing

seeing him selfe reduced to the point of death , and compassed about with diuells, ready to carry him to hell, turned him towards heauen , crying out. *Inducias vel vsque mane, inducias vel vsque mane.* Truce only till to morrow, truce only til to morrow:& with these wordes gaue vp the ghost. *S. Gre. Hom. 12. in Euang. & l. 4. dial. c. 38.*

2. A Courtiar of Coenredus kinge of England, admonished by the kinge him selfe to be confessed in his sicknes, refused to doe it, saying that he would not be confessed then , but when he was well recouered and able to goe broad, saw, being nere his death, the diuells, who shewed him all his sinnes written in a huge booke , and the Angells who gaue place vnto them: he saying, that two deuils were entred into his bodie, the one by his head the other by his feete, to deuoure his soule; and so dyed at the same time. *Venerable Bede , lib. 5. hist. Ang. c. 14. anno 704.*

3. An

3. An other deferring his repentance after the like maner, ſaw a litle before his death, his place in hell, neere vnto Caiphas. *The ſame author cap. 15.*

4. At Squira a cittie of the Philippine iſles, an Indian woman, feeling her ſelfe moued of God to make a Confeſſion of her whole life (and that for many dayes together) ſhe imparted the ſame vnto her parents, who gaue her councell to defer it. A litle after ſhe fell ſick; a Prieſt was called, but he could not heare her, for he found her dumbe to euery thinge, ſaue in theſe wordes which ſhe repeted oftentimes, ſtretching forth her handes towardes her parents. *Take hence theſe Catts, what make they here? Ah wretch that I am, behould the blackmores who will carry me away.* They prayd for her, but all in vaine, for ſhe ſunge no other ſonge: and hauing cryed that they burnd her, ſhe gaue vp the ghoſt. After her death, God declared that ſhe

she spoke into these thinges thorough
idle rauing: for as they went about to
winde her vp and to burie her, her
body was found all black, as if it had
bene burned in the same instant. The
rest made their profit hereof, for fea-
ring to fall into the same misfortune,
they made from that present a firme
purpose, neuer to defer their Confession: gentle Reader, doe thou the like.
Extracted out of the historie of the Societie
of Iesus anno 1609. in the life of Michael
Ayatumus, a younge Phillippine scholer, of
a holie life.

§. 4. *Of Generall Confession.*

It is good for the most part, to make
a generall confession of our whole
life, and afterwardes euery yeare to
make one, begining from the last, so
to supply the defaults which might
haue hapned in the former: for it often
hapneth, that the Confession is of no
value, ether because of the Confessar,
who is not approued ordinarilie to
heare

heare Confeſſions: or becauſe he is not thy paſtor, nor appointed by him, nor priuiledged by the Pope to heare Confeſſions euery where: or elſe becauſe he is very ignorant, or becauſe he was confeſſed without any ſorrow, or purpoſe to amend him, and to flie the immediat occaſions to fal againe: not to make reſtitution & the like: or for that he hath cōcealed volūtarily ſome ſinne in Confeſſion: or becauſe he had not a will to accept or fulfill the penance, which the Confeſſar enioyned him.

In all theſe caſes, the Confeſſion is voide. And for as much as theſe faults arriue often, it is therfore good, ſomtimes to make general Cōfeſſions. And, notwithſtanding this were not, yet are there ſundrie other reaſons which moue vs therto, which one may ſee elſe where. *As fa. Coſterus l. 1. Of the Sodalitie c. 4. Fa. Puentes, in his booke of Perfection 3. treatiſe c. 7. and heretofore §. 4. of this cap.l. 1. examp. 4.*

§. 5. Of

§. 5. Of Satisfaction, the third part of the
Sacrament of Penance.

For as much as ordinarily with the
fault, all the paine is not pardoned,
which one hath encurred by the sinne,
and that satisfactorie workes, haue
much more efficacie, being done by
the ordonance of the Confessar, as
well by reason of the act of obedience,
which is of inestimable valor, as for
the virtu which they receiue of the Sacrament, and from the merits of Iesus
Christ, applied vnto vs by meanes
therof, one ought to receiue with a
cheerfull hart, the penance enioyned
by the Confessar, how great and hard
soeuer it be, and to endeuour to accomplish it with the soonest.

It is not enough for him who doth
penance, saith S. Ambrose, to wipe
away his sinnes by teares, but he must
moreouer labor to couer them by good
workes. *l. 2. de pœnit. c. 5. & l. 1. c. 16.*
To a great wound (quoth he) must be
applied

applyed a great plaister, and a great sinne requireth great satisfaction. *Ad Virg. laps. cap. 8. & lib. 1. de pænit. cap. 2.*

See touching satisfactiō, most worthie examples, out of the flowers of the liues of Saints of Ribadeneira, of the Emperor Othon and Theodosius, of Henrie 2. kinge of England, in the places cited heretofore. *l. 1. c. 6. §. 6. & l. 2. c. 6. §. 1. sect. 1.*

§. 6. *Of Indulgences.*

Indulgences is the remission of the temporall paine, due by reason of the actuall fault, which is made by the application of the satisfactions, which are in the common treasurie of the Church: to wit, of the merits of our Lord, and of the Saintes; of which treasurie, the Pope hath the keyes, giuen by our Lord himselfe vnto S. Peter and his successors. *Mat. 16. 18.*

The fault being forgiue, yet that there remayneth some paine to be suffered,

S   is

is apparant by the *12. cap. of the 2.*
booke of Kinges, where the sinne of
murder and of adulterie, hauing bene
forgiuen Dauid, yet God did chastice
him with temporall paine in the death
of his sonne. He did as much to Adam,
Gen. 3. & Sap. 10. to Moises sister *Num.*
12. and to a Prophet *3. Reg. 13.*

And albeit these paines may be pardoned, as well by the satisfactorie
workes enioyned by the confessar, as
by those which one doth voluntarily
of him selfe, yet ordinarily all the paine
is not remitted by such like workes: whence it followeth, that the rest
is to be paid in Purgatorie, vnles we
haue recourse to the treasure of the
Church by Indulgences. Wise and
well aduised is he, who by a way so
easie, doth free him selfe from a pay-
ment, which else he is to make by fire,
and by such a fire, as that of Purgatorie is.

E X-

EXAMPLES.

1. S. Francis hauing obtained of our Lord and of Pope Honorius the third, a plenarie indulgence for his Church of our Lady of Portiuncula neere to Asissium, the bruit being spread euery where abroad, a hundred and twentie Sclauonians were moued from heauen to trauell thither, as they did. It came to passe, that a woman fel there soare sick, and hauing ended her deuotions, died. The rest being embarked to returne into their contrie, she appeared to them, saying. Feare yee not, for I am one of your compaine sent by our blessed Lady for to tell you, that by the benefit of the Indulgences, which I gayned together with you at our Ladies of Portiuncula, I am departed directly to heauen, without passing thorough Purgatorie. Which hauing said, she disappeared, leauing all these good pilgrimes

great-

greatly comforted . See you the efficacie and virtu of Ind lgences'? *Taken
out of the annales of the Friar Minors 10.
1.l.2.cap.5.*

2. Our Lord hath maruelously
praised Indulgences to S. Bridgit, as
appeareth by the 102. cap. l. 6. of her
Reuelations.

§.7. *Of the paines of Purgatorie.*

The Apostle S. Paul, speaking of
the diuersitie of those, who build spi-
ritually in this worlde , saith, that he
who dyeth with smale sinnes *shall be
saued, yet so as by fire.* Vpon which wordes S. Aug. discoursing in *Psal.37.* saith.
Because it is written we shal be saued,
therfore we despise the fire of Purgatorie: yes truly we shall be saued by
fire , but by a fire more greuous and
painfull , then all whatsoeuer a man
can suffer in this life. *The same S.Greg.
saith vpon the 3. penitential psalme.Vene-
rable Bede vpon the same psalme. S. Anselme*

ſelme vpon the 1. Cor. 3. S. Bernard ſerm.
de obitu Humberti.

S. Thomas houldeth , that the paines of Purgatorie are greater, then are the paines of all the Martyrs, yea then thoſe which Ieſus Chriſt him ſelfe ſuffered in his moſt holy and painfull paſſion. *3. p. q. 46. art. 6. ad 3.*

EXAMPLES.

1. S. Antoninus writeth, that a certaine perſon giuen to debauchement, was viſited of God , with a longe and painfull ſicknes; At the laſt, looſing his patience, he inſtantly beſought of God that he might dye; & behould an Angel appeared vnto him, who gaue him his choice, ether to remayne two yeares more in this infirmitie, & then to goe directly to heauen , or elſe to dye that very houre, and be three dayes in purgatorie . This ill aduiſed perſon, choſe rather to dye, and to endure for three dayes the paines of Purgatorie;

S 3 He

He died then, and an houre after, the same Angell came to visit him in his paines, and asked him how he found himselfe. Ah (quoth he) you haue deceiued me, for you promised me that I should be but three daies in Purgatorie, and behould I haue already bene here many yeares. No, (replyed the Angell) I haue not deceiued you, but it is the greuousnes of the paines that doe deceiue you, for you haue not as yet bene here but only an houre. Alas bringe to passe then (quoth hee) that I may returne to life againe, and I am readie to endure my sicknes, not two yeares only, but euen as long as euer it shall please God: which was granted him, and neuer after did he complaine of his paines. *S. Antoninus 4. p. Sum. tit.* 14. *cap.* 10. §.4. *Ribad.l.* 1. *de tribulat. c.* 7.

The greuousnes of these paines may be further proued, by all the reuelations which venerable Bede alleadgeth in the 3. and 5. booke of his historie,

torie, Denis the Carthufian, and S.
Bridgit.

§. 8. *Of prayers or suffrages for the departed.*

It is a holie and healthfull cogitation to pray for the dead, that they may be loosed from sinnes. 2. Mac. 12. 46.

It is *holie,* becaufe it commeth from a holy begining, which is charitie. It is *healthfull,* firft to the departed, for it deliuereth them from their paines. 2. To him who doth it, for as much as he by this meanes, encreafeth his owne merits, and confequently his glorie, and maketh him felfe as many friends and interceffors with God, as he afifteth foules.

Againe, that which is faid of praier, may be alfo vnderftood of faftinge, almes, pilgrimages, and whatfoeuer good worke offered to God to this intent, but aboue all, the holy facrifice of the Maffe.

I am of the minde, faith S. Am-

S 4 brofe

brose (speaking to Faustinus of his sister deceased) that we should not so much weepe for her, as asist her with prayers, and recommend her soule vnto God. *lib. 2. ep. 8.*

S. Aug. saith. We must not dout, that the dead are holpen by the prayers of the Church, sacrifices, almes &c. *Ser. 32. de verb. Apost.*

Saint Chrisostom saith. Let vs asist the dead, not with teares , but with prayers and almes. *Homil. 41. in 1. Cor.*

An Angel in the historie of venerable Bede , came to tell in the behalfe of God to a holy personage, that the prayers of the liuing, almes, fastinges, and principally the sacrifice of the Masse, did succour sundry faithfull soules departed, to the end they might be deliuered before the day of iudgment, *lib. 5. hist. Ang. cap. 13.*

Who seeth not then , that it is the duty of a good Christian, in the morning at his arising, and in the euening before

before his ſleeping, hearing, or ſaying Maſſe, to pray for the ſoules detayned in this fire, which we haue
ſeene in the precedent paragraph, to
be ſo terrible? but aboue all for thoſe
of our parents, & to whom for ſundrie
reſpects we may be obliged; and ſomtimes ▬▬ the day time, to aſiſt the
by ſome good worke.

If in this life we ſaw ſome one of
our friendes amidſt a fire, from whence
he could not deliuer him ſelfe, and
yet that we might doe it eaſily, could
we be ſo cruell to him, as not to aſiſt
him? With ſuch meaſure (ſaith our
Lord) as you ſhall haue meaſured vnto
others, it ſhall be meaſured to you a-
gaine. *Mat.7.2. Marc.4.24.*

EXAMPLES.

1. A certaine religious of S. Francis, albeit of a holie life, appeared the
yeare 1541. vnto a nouice, who prayed for him, ſaying that he was in

Purgatorie, for hauing bene negligent to pray for the departed. *Franc. Gon-zaga de orig. Seraph. relig. part. 4. in prouincia Canariæ conu. 7.*

2. Brother Bertrand, prouinciall of the Dominicans, said Masse euery day for the expiation of his ſinnes, but very seldome for the dead. And when vpon a day he was asked the reason, he answered, that the soules that were in Purgatorie, were assured of their saluation, and therfore had not so great neede of prayers as the liuing had. The night following, one that was dead appeared vnto him ten seuerall times, beating with his hande vpon his coffin, as it were in threatning of him: whence he conceiued so great a feare, that the day did no sooner appeare, but he went and said Masse for the dead, and all the rest of his life after, he employed him selfe to asist the deceased. *Lib. 1. Chron. frat. Præ-dic. c. 27. & Theod. de Apoldia lib. 3. vita S. Dominici cap. 8.*

S. Chri-

3. S. Chriſtine natiue of S. Trou in Hasbaye being dead , her ſoule was led by Angells into a place, which by reaſon of the horrible torments which they there endured, ſuppoſed her ſelfe to be in hell, but one of the Angels tould her, that it was Purgatorie. Frō thence they led her to heauen, before the throane of the moſt holy Trinity, who put it to her choice , ether to remayne in heauen for all eternitie, or to returne to her body, to deliuer by good workes, all thoſe ſoules which ſhe had ſeene in Purgatorie , and afterwards to come to heauen , loaden with the more merits . She accepted this laſt condition, and immediatlie entred againe into her body, whilſt Maſſe was ſaid, the body being ſet in the midſt of the Church. Afterwards, vntill her death, ſhe ſuffered ſo many and ſo horrible torments, that ſhe merited the name of Chriſtine the admirable. *Thomas à Cantipr. in her life, and Surius tom 3.c.23.of Iune.*

4. S.

4. S. Leibertus Bishop of Cambray, praying vpon a day in the churchyard of S. Nicholas of the same cittie, for the soules of those, whose bodies were buried in that place, saying. *Animæ omnium fidelium defunctorum requiescant in pace* . The soules of all the faithfull departed, rest in peace, this voice was heard in the ayre most intelligibly, *Amen. In the Martyrologe 23. of Iune* .

See the life of S. Lidwine, and the discourse of the commemoration of the faithfull departed, in the flowers of the liues of Saintes; *by Ribad. 2. of Nouember* .

THE VII. CHAPTER.

Of satisfactorie workes, Fasting , Almes, and Prayers.

THe Archangell Raphaell in the 12. of Tobie, teaching young Tobias the practise of of good workes, said

said vnto him . That prayer accompanied with fasting and almes, was very healthfull and profitable . Yea all the satisfactorie workes which we are able to doe in this life, are referred to these three: for which cause S. Aug. saith . Behould all the iustice of man in this life , fastinge, almes , and prayer . Will you that your prayer flie vp to heauen? Giue it two winges , fastinge and almes. *S. Aug. in psal. 42.*

§. 1. *Of Fasting.*

The Church commands vs to fast the Lent, the four Ember daies , and certaine vigills: that is to say , not to eate then but one meale a day , and to abstaine also from flesh; and in Lent, from flesh and egges : which hath bene practised euen from the Apostles times. *68. canon. Ap. S. Hier. ep. 54. ad Marcellam.*

She also commandeth, that the Fridayes and Saturdayes, and the Rogation

tion dayes, we abſtaine from fleſh.

She declareth the vtiliṭies of Faſtinge, in the preface of the Maſſe in Lent, taken from S. Gregorie . 1. That it repreſſeth the fleſh and vices. 2. That it eleuateth the ſpirit. 3. That it acquireth virtues and merits . For which cauſe the holy ſcripture recommendeth the ſame ſo much vnto vs. *Ioel. 2. pſal. 101. & 34. Luc. 5. Mar. 2. & 9. & 17. Luc. 4. 2. Cor. 11. and the holie Fathers S. Baſil hom. 1. & 2. de Ieiun. Aug. ſer. 55. de temp. Amb. ſer. 23. 25. 34. 36. & 37. And our Lord him ſelfe hath both honored and recommended it by his example. Mat. 4.*

EXAMPLES.

1. The prophet Daniel by faſting, obtained the knowledge of thinges to come. *Dan. 9.*

2. The Niniuites appeaſed the anger of God. *Ionas 3.*

3. Elias and Moyſes by the faſt of fortie

fortie dayes, obtayned the companie and familiaritie of almightie God. *3. Reg. 19. 11. Exod, 24. & 25. & 33. 11.*

4. Eleazer a gentleman of note, being nintie yeares olde, choſe rather to looſe his life after diuers greuous torments he had endured, then to eate ſwines fleſh, contrary to the commandement of God. *2. Mac. 6. 18.*

5. The ſeauen Machabean bretheren, together with their mother, did the ſame. *2. Mac. 6. 18.*

6. The Emperor Iuſtinian, ſeeing his people afflicted with famin, cauſed the butcherie in Conſtantinople to be opened, in the ſecond weeke of Lent, and gaue permiſſion to buy and ſell fleſh, but the good people choſe rather to die by hunger, then ether to buy or to ſell fleſh. *Niceph. lib. 17. cap. 32.*

At Vratiſlaw or Breſlaw in Sileſia, an hereticall Miniſter, to deride and mock at Catholique religion, hauing put a peace of meate into his mouth vpon a Friday, his mouth remayned
open

open and wiftly gaping, without being able to fhut it againe, nether by force, nor yet by art. *In the hiftorie of the Societie. Anno 1592.*

8. A woman in the fame place, hauing put flefh into her mouth vpō a Saturday, fell downe ftarke dead. *Ibidem.*

9. At Poldachie, a cittie of Polognia, in the yeare 1585. a young man eating flefh vpon a Friday, was poffeffed of the diuill, who a litle after, ftopt his throate and kild him out right. *In the fame hift. anno 1585.*

10. A married man, mockinge at the faft of Lent, which S. Elphegus bifhop of Winchefter in England had recommended, died fodainly the night enfuing, according to the prediction of the Saint. *Baron. tom. 10. annal. ecclef. anno. Dom. 947.*

§. 2. *Of Almes.*

Redeeme thy finnes with almes (faid Daniel to Nabuchodonofer) *and thine iniquities with the mercies of the poore.*
Dan.

Dan. 4. 24.

Bleſſed is the man that vnderſtandeth concerning the needie and the poore, in the euill day our Lord will deliuer him. pſal. 40. 1.

Loe this was the iniquity of Sodome thy ſiſter, pride, fulnes of bread and abundance, and the idlenes of her and of her daughters, and they raught not the hande to the needy and the poore. Ezech. 16. 49.

Almes giuing is a marke of predeſtination, according to S. Paul, for in the 3. of the Coloſ. verſ. 12. he ſaith. *Put yee on therfore as the elect of God, holy, and beloued, the bowells of mercie.*

I remember not to haue read (ſaith S. Hierom) that any one came to an euill death, who gladly during his life, practiſed the workes of mercie, becauſe ſuch an one hath many interceſſors: and it is impoſſible, that the prayers of many ſhould not be heard. *S. Hier. ad Nepotian. And the ſame S. Aug. ſaith. ſerm. ad fratres in Eremo.*

Heare for the laſt S. Chriſoſtom. Almes

Almes (faith he) is one of the greateſt friendes of God, and which is alwayes neere vnto him. She hath in ſuch ſort gained his grace, that all whatſoeuer ſhe asketh of him, and for whomſoeuer, ſhe doth obtaine without difficultie. She it is that vnbindes the bādes, the ſhackles, and manacles of ſinners, ſhe expels darknes, and puts out the fire, for which reſpect, ſhe enters with all aſſurance into heauen, for that the gates of this great pallais, are inſtantly open to her, and as if it were the Queene her ſelfe, none nether porters nor gard, dare ſay vnto her, who art thou? whence comeſt thou? but contrariwiſe all the courtiars of heauen, doe goe before her to entertayne her. *S. Chriſoſtom. Hom. 9. in Matt.*

EXAMPLES.

1. S. Catharine of Sienna, hauing giuen a ſiluer Croſſe vnto a poore bodie,

die, our Lord appeared vnto her the night following, saying: that he would shew that Crosse at the day of iudgement to all the worlde. *Ant. Senen. in her life.*

2. S. Iohn the Almes-giuer (so stiled because of the continuall almes which he bestowed) called the poore his Lordes, for as much (quoth he) as they had the power to helpe him, that he should not be shut out of the kingdome of heauen. *Ribad. in his life.*

3. S. Lewis kinge of France, and B. Amædes Duke of Sauoye , were wont to serue the poore bare-head: & this latter called the his hunting houndes, where with he hunted after, and caught the kingdome of heauen. *In their liues.*

4 Robert kinge of France, as Hegaldus writeth, and after him cardinall Baronius, the yeare of our Lord 1033. whersoeuer he went, drew allwayes after him , great wagons all full of poore people, and when any asked him

why

why he did so. I goe(quoth he) to be-
siege the cittie of paradise with these
troupes : God hath said, that he will
open the gates of paradise to the riche,
who haue opened to them their harts
and their treasures. Who then shall
enter into heauen, if this armie shall
not enter, and I also who am the Co-
lonnel of the company?

See the liues of S. Martin, S. Francis, S. Edward Kinge of England, and
S. Oswald: of S. Gregorie pope, S. Iulian bishop of Guence, S. Nicholas, S.
Bernardine, S. Iohn Chrisostom, with
infinit others, and you shall see them
all maruelloussy addicted to this virtu.
Is it not true then, that Almes giuing
is a marke of predestination?

5. Euagrius philosopher, being conuerted to the faith by the Bishop Se-
nesius, gaue him three hundred crownes of gould for an almes, receuing an
obligation from the bishop vnder his
hande, to receaue them againe in heauen. Being dead, he appeared to this
bishop, willing him to goe vnto his

graue and to open it. The which he did, and found his obligation in the handes of him that was dead, wherin was written that he held him ſelfe wel content, for he had receiued his mony in heauen. *Sophron. in prat. ſpirit. cap. 195. Ioan. Zonaras 3. annal.*

6. S. Gregorie writeth, that two Martyrs appeared after their death in the habit of pilgrimes to a deuout matrone; and as ſhe gaue them her almes according to her cuſtome, they ſaid vnto her; You helpe vs now, and we will alſo helpe you at the day of iudgment. *Hom. 32. in euang.*

7. The like did certaine Charterhouſe Monkes martyred vnder Henrie the eight, to a deuout woman at the houre of her death, which had ſomtimes aſiſted thē in the time of their priſonment. *P. Cornelius in Deut. cap. 26, 12.* See the happy death of Peter Velleio, a Portugal marchãt, for the almes which he had beſtowed vpõ the bleſſed father Zauerius. *In his life lib. 4. cap. 3.*

§. 3. *That*

§. 3. *That we neuer loose any thinge, no not in this present life, by giuing almes.*

He that giueth to the poore, shall not lack: he that despiseth him that asketh, shall sustaine penurie. *Prou. 28.27.*

Giue, and it shall be giuen to you. *Luc. 6. 38.*

Giue to vsurie vnto God (saith S. Amb.) he will keepe your pawne most faithfully, and will restore you, your mony augmented with vsurie. *lib. de virg.*

The fauors of benefactors, returne to those who giue them. Hast thou giuen the poore to eate? Thou hast prouided well for thy selfe, for that which thou hast giuen, will returne vnto thee with increase. *S. Basil. hom. 6. in ditescentes.*

EXAMPLES.

1. S. Iohn the Almes-giuer, the more almes he gaue, the more did God enrich

enrich him where with to giue ; in ſo
much as, it ſeemed that there was a
certaine holy ſtrife betwixt God and
S. Iohn, which of them ſhould giue
moſt; S. Iohn to giue vnto the poore,
and our Lord to giue vnto S. Iohn.
For ſo he hath aſſured vs, that God
did alwaies reſtore him the double of
that, which he had giuen for the loue
of him . Going one day vnto the
church, he met a gentleman, which
beſought him to aſſiſt him, ſaying that
theeues had robd him of all he had.
He commanded fiftene poundes of
gould to be giuen vnto him . The
ſteward thinking it to be too much,
gaue vnto him no more then fiue . At
his going out of the church, a Lady
gaue him a bill to receiue fiue hundred
poundes of gould, and to diſtribute it
to the poore : in reading wherof the
Holy Ghoſt diſcouered vnto him, that
his ſteward had cut off two thirds of
the almes which he had commanded
him to giue vnto this gentlemã. Which
hauing

hauing auerred, he fharply reprehended him, and knew by the Lady that
gaue him the bill, that at the firft fhe
had an intention to giue vnto him,
fifteene hundred poundes of gould,
and had fo written within the bill,
and that afterwards not knowing
how, fhe found the thoufand blotted out. *Surius tom. 1. ex Simon. Me-*
taphraft. & Bredembach. lib. 6. collat.
cap. 10.

See the like cafe arriued to S. German bifhop, in *Surius tom. 4. lib. 2. cap.*
11. *Iuly* 31. And to S. Marcellus Abbat.
In the fame Surius, *Decemb. 29. cap. 1.*

2. In the cittie of Nifibie, a chriftiã
woman councelled her husband being
a pagan, to giue to the God of the
chriftians, by the handes of the poore,
fiftie crownes (which he intended to
put out to vfurie) telling him, that
God would affuredlye pay him the
double vfe of his mony together with
the capitall. He did fo, and after three
monthes, he went and found out the
fame

ſame poore, begging at the portall of
the church, to ſee if they would rendar
him his mony. But inſteed of reſtoring
to him, they put forth their handes a-
gaine to receiue of him, wherat he was
offended with them. And as he returned home all heauie, he eſpied one of
his peeces of gould vpon the ground,
tooke it vp, & carried it vnto his wife,
and bought therwith bread, wine, and
a fiſhe. And as he emptied out the ger-
bage of the fiſh, he found within her
guttes a pretious ſtone, the which he
ſould to a gould-ſmith the ſame day,
for three hundred crownes. This miracle touched him at the very hart, and
was the cauſe that he became a Chriſtian. *Sophron. in prat. ſpirit. cap. 185.*

3. S. Boniface biſhop of Ferento in
Italy, being yet but a litle childe, was
wont to giue his apparrel to the poore,
for which his mothes often chid him.
Vpon a day as ſhe was out of doores,
he called in the poore, and gaue them
all the wheate that was in the garner.

T   Which

Which his mother finding at her returne, she began to cry and to lament, saying that she had lost the whole reuenue of a yeare. The litle Saint endeuored to confort her, but seeing that he profited nothing, he besought his mother to goe out of the garner, and then began to pray to God vpon his knees. This done, he calls his mother backe againe, and behould (a thinge most maruellous) she found all her garner fild with most goodly and most excellent graine. This taught her, that to giue almes, doth not empouerish: for which cause, she from that time gaue her sonne leaue, to giue to the poore whatsoeuer he would. *S. Greg. dial. l. 1. c. 9.*

§. 4. How *rigorously God hath punished those, which had no pittie of the poore.*

He that *stoppeth his eare at the cry of the poore, him selfe shall also cry, and shall not be heard. Pro. 21. 13.*

Iudg-

Iudgment shall be done *without mercie to him , that hath not done mercie.* *Iac. 2. 13.*

Thou hast not shewed mercy (saith S. Basil) thou also shalt not finde mercie. Thou hast not opened thy house to the poore, and God also wil not open his kingdome to thee. Thou hast not giuen temporall bread , and thou shalt not haue eternall life. Assure thy selfe , that the fruites which thou shalt reape, shall be like to the seede which thou hast sowen. Hast thou sowen bitternes ? thou shalt likewise reape bitternes. Hast thou sowen crueltie? thou shalt likewise reape crueltie. Thou hast fled mercie, and mercie likewise wil fly from thee. Thou hast abhorred the poore , and he likewise shall abhorre thee , who for thy sake made him selfe so passing poore. *S. Basil orat. ad diuites.*

EXAMPLES.

1. Hatto, of Abbot of Fulde, made

T 2   Arch-

Archbishop of Mayence, fild his barne
with an assembly of poore (sayinge
that he would giue them almes) and
then set fire at the four corners therof,
and burned them all, saying that they
were Rattes, which eate and consumed the corne of the riche . This
crueltie escaped not vnpunished, for
before three yeares after were expired, he him selfe was eaten of Rattes, nether he, nor any of his people, being able to preuent it . *Ioan.*
Trithemius in Chron. monast. Hirsau. ad
an. Dom. 967. Munsterus & Maria Scot.
lib. 3. Genebrard l. 4. Chro. an. 970.

2. A poore man asking an almes of
the master of a Ship , he was refused
by him, saying, that he had nothing
in his Ship but stones: and at the same
instant, all therin was turned into stones. *S. Greg of Tours. lib. de gloria Conf.*
cap. 108. recounteth this as an eye witnes.
And Sigebertus in Chron. an. Dom. 606.
Baron. tom. 8. an. Dom. 605.

3. A certaine riche man at Constantinople,

tinople, being sorrie for that he had giuen a summe of mony in an almes, had no sooner receiued his mony, but he died sodainly. *Baron. tom. 7. annal. ecclef. an. 553.*

4. A couetous person, who would not heare the cries of the poore, as Masse was said for him after his death, at eache *Dominus vobiscum*, the Bishop saw the Crucifix vnfasten its handes from the Crosse, and stoppe its eares. Was not this to confirme that which we alleadged out of the wiseman hertofore, that *he that stoppeth his eare at the cry of the poore, him selfe shall also cry, and shall not be heard? Pro. 21. 13.* nor they who cry or pray for him? *Ioan. Duegnius Hisp. in speculo tristium.*

§. 5. *Of Prayer.How excellent, profitable, and necessarie it is.*

Prayer (accordinge to S. Greg. of Nice) is a discourse and colloquy of the soule with almightie God, touchinge

T 3   that

that which concernes its health and perfection. *lib.de orat. Dom. cap.1.*

It is an eleuation of the foule into God (faith S. Iohn Damafcen) to enter into amorous difcourfe with him. *lib. 3. de fide cap. 14.* It is the key of heauen, faith S. Aug. *ferm.226. de temp.* It is the beft pofeffion that one can haue in this human life, faith Saint Ephrem. *tract.de orat.*

How happie is a foule, which may in euery houre as ofté as it lifteth open heauen, and haue free acceffe to the fecret cabinet of God him felfe, and there difcourfe familiarly with him? O, if the fauorits of the worlde could doe the like with their Prince, how happie would they repute them felues to be? For which caufe alfo, all the Saints haue made fo great account therof, as we fhall hereafter fee; The profits thereof, will appeare by the effects.

Amen, Amen I fay to you, if you aske the Father any thinge in my name, he will

will giue it you, said our Sauiour to his Apostles. *Ioan. 16. 23.* And in another place. *Aske, and it shall be giuen you. Luc. 11. 9.*

The necessitie thereof is the same, that ayre and breath is for the body. The body can not liue without ayre and breathing, nor the soule without praying. For which reason it is that our Sauiour said. *It behoueth to pray alwaies without ceasing. Luc. 18.*

Be not hindred to pray alwaies, saith the wiseman. *Pro. 18. 22.*

The Apostle recommendeth the same in sundry places. *Phil. 4. 6. Coloss. 4. 2. 2. Thess. 5. 16.* And *S. Peter in his 1. ep. c. 4. 7.*

Prayer is also as necessarie for man (saith S. Iohn Chrisostom) as water the fishe. *lib. 2. de orando Deum.*

EXAMPLES.

1. Will you haue a proofe of its excellencie & efficacie? As long as Moyses praied, and stretched vp his armes

T 4   to)

to heauen, his people had the vpper
hande of their enemies, and cut them
quite in peeces. *Exod.* 17.

How many times hath he held the
armes of God, when he was angrie, by
his prayer? *Exod. 32. psal. 105.*

2. The Prophet Ieremie, praying
for the Ifralites, God faid vnto him.
Pray not for them, and hinder me not.
Ierem. 7.

3. Iofua by his prayer, ftaid the
Sunne and the Moone, vntill fuch time
as he had ouercome his enimies. *Io-*
fua. 10;

4. Ifay made the Sunne goe back
to the point, where it had bene ten
houres before, in fauor of the Kinge
Ezechias. And this Kinge by his praier,
draue away death which was about to
giue him his laft blow, and lenghtned
his life fifteene yeares. *4. Reg. 20.*

5. S. Dominick confeft to a certaine Prior of Cifteau, neuer to haue
asked ought of God, which was denied him. And when the Prior faid
vnto

vnto him. Why then doe you not demand of him, Doctor Conrade? It is a
thinge hard to obtaine (replied the
Saint) but if I shall aske it him, I doe
not dout but to obtaine it. He prayed
all the night ensuinge, and (a thinge
most admirable) in the morning Conrade came vnto the Church, and cast
him selfe at the Saintes feete, asked
the habit of religion, and obtayned it.
Ribadeneira vpon his life.

Is it any maruel thē, that praier being
so excellēt, so profitable, & so effectual,
all the Saints haue loued it so much?

6. Reade the life of S. Anthonie, and
of S. Arsenius, you shall see them passe
the whole nightes, without stirring
from off their knees, and to complaine
of the Sunne beating vpon their eyes,
that it tooke from them the repose and
sweetnes of their soule. *Ribad. ex Athanas. & Cassiano.*

7. S. Simeon Stillites praied cōtinual-
ly both day and night; one while standing vpright, another while prostrate;

T 5　　　　and

and praying vpright, made so many reuerences, that one of the seruants of Theodoret, hauing vndertaken to nūber them, counted in one day to the number of twelue hūdred fortie four, & then was wearie of counting more. From the Euensonge of the principall feastes, vntill the morrow morning, he stood vpright, with his handes lifted vp to heauen, without being wearie, nor suffering him selfe to be opprest with sleepe. *Theodoret Cyri. epist. lib. 9. cap. 27.*

8. S. Apollonius, Abbot of two hundred monkes in Thebaidis, prayed a hundred times a day, and a hundred times a night. *Ruffinus lib. 2. cap. 7. Pallad. cap. 52.*

Abdias writeth as much of S. Bartholomew Apostle, S. Antoninus of S. Martha, Palladius of S. Macarius; and what shall I say of S. Iames the Apostle, who by the vse of praying, had his knees as hard as a Camels skin.

9. A certaine Cobler named Zacharie,

charie, was wonte night by night, to
goe and ſalute the moſt B. Sacrament
in the church of S. Sophie in Conſtantinople, and there to make his praiers.
A holy man named Iohn, who alſo
paſſed the nightes in prayer at the por-
talls of the Churches, praying on a
night at the portall of S. Sophie, ſaw
a light to come which ouertooke him:
and the better to conſider what this
man came to doe, he hid him ſelfe aſide
in a corner. Zacharie being come to
the church doore, he there made a ſhort
prayer, and then the ſigne of the Croſſe
vpon the dore, and at the ſame inſtant it opened to him: and the ſame
hapned to two other dores. Being entred into the church, he went before
the high Altar, and after that he had
ended his prayer, he returning home
to his houſe, all the Dores ſhut them
after him of their ſelues. *Raderus in his*
Rowe of Saintes, taken forth of the
Greeke Calendar.

§. 6. *Of the conditions required to pray protfiably.*

You aske and receiue not, becaufe you aske amiſſe. ſaith S. Iames. *cap.* 4. *3.*

To aske aright, we muſt obſerue four pointes.

1. To be in good eſtate. *If our hart doe not reprehend vs, we haue confidence towards God* (ſaith S. Iohn) *and whatſoeuer we shall aske, we shall receiue of him.*1. *Iohn.3.22.* And our Lord ſaid to his Apoſtles; *If you abide in me, and my wordes abide in you, you shall aske what thinge ſoeuer you will, and it shall be done to you. Iohn.15.10.*

Offer ſacrifice no more in vaine (quoth God by his prophet) *incenſe is abhomination to me; when you shall ſtretch forth your hādes, I wil turne away mine eyes frō you, for your handes are full of blood. Waſh you, be cleane, take away the euill of your cogitations from your hartes. Iſay.1.13.*

2. The ſecond point is, to conſider the greatnes of the Maieſtie of almightie

mightie God , to whom we ſpeake.
What meanes is there (ſaith S. Baſil)
to pray without diſtraction ? And he
anſwereth ; If we remember that we
are before the maieſtie of God . *lib.* 1.
Hexam. & in reg. breu. 201. *& 306.*

3. Aske nothing, but what is ether
profitable, or neceſſarie, to thy ſaluation. And that which is indifferent, as
health , proſperitie &c. aske it alſo
with condition : for example , Lord
giue me health , if it be to thy greater
glorie, and my ſaluation.

This is the confidence which we haue
towards him , that whatſoeuer we ſhall
aske according to his will, he heareth vs.
1. *Ioh.* 15. 14. *And the will of God* (ſaith
S. *Paul*) *is your ſanctification .* 1. *Theſ.*
4. 3.

4. To aske all in the name, and by
the merits of Ieſus Chriſt . *Amen I ſay*
to you, if you aske the Father any thinge in
my name, he will giue it you. Iohn 16. 23.

EX-

EXAMPLES.

.1. God the Creator, receiued the gift of Abel, but that of Cain was reiected, becaufe Cain offred it with a hart, full of enuie and rancor againft his brother. *Gen.* 4.

2. At Touloufe in France, a young man being in quarrel & enmity againft an other, albeit he frequented the churches, and recited there fundry prayers, yet neuer could he for the fpace of feauen monthes, once recite the Pater nofter, vntill fuch time as following the councell of a father of the Societie, he was reconciled to his enemie. *In the annales of the Societie anno* 1584.

3. I *will fpeake vnto God* (was Abraham wont to fay before prayer) *I that am but duft and afhes. Gen.* 18. 27.

4. S. Hierom writing to Saluina fayeth, that Nebridius was wont to aske nothinge in his prayer, but that which

which God knew to be best for him. *Epist. 9.*

5. Another holy person was wont to pray reciting A. B. C. and after at the end said. Lord doe thou ioyne the letters together, I aske thee only that which is most agreeable to thee, and most expedient for me, and what this is, thou knowest better then I. And S. Macarius said, that this maner of praier was the best; Lord giue me what thou wilt, and what thou pleasest. *Salmeron tract.12.de orat. Christi in horto.*

6. Iacob being reuested with the garments of his eldest brother Esau, receiued the benediction of his father Isaac. *Gen. 27.* If we will receiue the blessing of our celestiall father, we must approache vnto him, with the garments and merits of our eldest brother Iesus Christ. It is the practise of the Church, neuer to conclude any praier in the diuine office, or in the Masse, but. *Per Dominam nostrum Iesum Christum &c.*

THE

THE VIII. CHAPTER.

Of Communion.

THe holie Church obligeth *(a)* e-
uerie Chriſtian, who hath attai-
ned to the vſe of reaſon, to receiue at
the leaſt once a yeare, and that about
Eaſter: but this is not to ſay, that ſhe
is not maruellous deſirous *(b)* that we
receiue the ſame more often, and that
becauſe of the neceſſitie which the
ſoule hath of this nouriſhment, and
of the greate vtilities ſhe receiueth
therby. (a) *Concil. Lat. can.* 21. (b.)
Concil. Trid. Seſſ. 22. c. 26.

§. *Of the neceſſitie and vtilitie of Com-*
munion.

Amen I ſay to you, vnles you eate the
fleſh of the Sonne of man, and drinke his
blood, you ſhall not haue life in you. Saith
our Sauiour in S. Iohn. *cap. 6. 53.*

The bread which I will giue, is my fleſh
for

for the life of the worlde. I*bid.* 51.

He that eateth my flesh, and drinketh
my blood, abideth in me, and I in him.
I*bid.* 56.

I am stricken as grasse, and my hart is
withered, because I haue forgotten to eate
my bread. *psal.* 101. 5. that is to say, the
holie Eucharist.

To communicat euery day (saith S.
Aug.) I nether praise, nor yet dispraise,
but I councell and exhorte, to communicat euery Sonday. *Lib. de eccles. dog-
mat.* The same S. Hierom saith, *in
apolog. ad* P*amachum.*

O sacred báquet (singeth the church)
wherin Christ is receiued, the memory
of his passion is renewed (a) the minde
is fild with grace (b) and a pledge of
future glorie is giuen vnto vs. (a) *Basil. ser.* 1. *de baptis. cap.* 3. (b) *Amb. in
psal.* 18. *ser.* 15. *v.* 4. *Concil.* T*rid.* S*ess.* 13.
cap. 2.

It is the viaticum of our pilgrima-
ge (a) which is giuen vnto vs, as the
manna to the Isralites (b) to passe
happely

happely the defart and warfare of this life, vntill we arriue to the celeftiall Hierufalem, bringing to vs all confolation (*c*) vertu and graces. (a) *Concil. Nice. can.* 12.2. *Arelat can.* 12. *Chrifoft. l. 6. de facerd. Paulin. in vita Ambrof. Greg. hom. 4. in Euang.* (b) *Exod.* 16. *Deut.* 3. (c) *Sap.* 16. *Ioan.* 6.

Heare what S. Ambrofe faith. Our Lord in the Eucharift, is vnto vs all in all. If you will heale your woundes, he is the medecin. If you be thirftie, he is the fountaine. If you be loaden with finnes, he is iuftice. If you ftand in neede of afiftance, he is virtu. If you feare death, he is life. If you will goe to heauen, he is the way. If you fly darknes, he is the light. If you are hungrie, he is foode. Taft then and fee how fweet our Lord is. *S. Amb. de virginit. ad Marc. for. l. 3. tom. 4.*

EXAMPLES.

1. A certaine woman, hauing bene fiue weekes without communicating,

ap-

appeared like a Mare . *Pallad in hist.*
Lausiac. sect. 17. c. 19.

2. Sister Agnes Abbesse , hauinge
forbidden S. Lutgarde to communicate euery Sonday, was at the same instant stricken with sicknes, whereof
she could not be healed , till after she
had reuoked that sentence. *Surius tom.*
3. c. 12.

3. S. Gertrude praying for one of
her religious, who thorough an indis-
creet zeale diuerted her fellowes to
frequent the cōmunion, our Lord said
vnto her, that all his delight was to be
with men, and that therfore this religious did ill, in withdrawing others
from the communion . *Lud. Blos. in*
Monil. spirit. c. 6.

4. S. Bonauenture, out of reuerence
and humilitie , abstayninge sundrie
dayes to say Masse , as he heard the
same, the priest hauing broken the holie Hoste, one peece therof flew to the
mouth of S. Bonauenture . Then giuing thankes to God, he vnderstood
that

that thofe were more agreable vnto him, who approached to the communion by loue ,. then thofe who for feare abftained from it: which he hath fince committed to writinge . *In the treat. of fpirituall exercifes, intituled Fafcilulus cap. 7. & lib. 2ᵢ de prof. relig. cap. 78.*

5. A litle childe, after he had communicated, was caft by his owne father, being a Iew, into a burning fornace , without receiuing any hurt. *Gregor. Turon. lib. 1. de gloria mart. cap. 10. Nicephor. Ecclef. hift. lib. 17. cap. 25.*

6. S. Liberalis, receiuing the comunion euery Sonday , tooke no other kinde of fuftenance, and was in good health. *Marul. lib. 4. cap. 12. & Pet. de Natal. lib. 4. cap. 93.*

7. Iulia Zerbina at Parma, liued alfo many monthes, without other fuftenance then the B. Sacrament. *Orlandinus in the hift. of the Societie lib. 2. of the yeare 1539.*

Who

Who sees not then, that the holie Eucharist, is the true nourishment of a Christian man, and a soueraigne remedie against all danger? and that therfore it is wisely done to approach often therunto.

§. 2. *Of the preparation and deuotion requisite to communicat well.*

Let a man proue him selfe (that is to say examine him selfe, and if he see him selfe in mortall sinne, that he confes him selfe) *and so, let him eate of that bread, and drinke of the chalice.* For he that eateth and drinketh vnworthely (in mortall sinne) *eateth and drinketh iudgement to him selfe* (that is to say, his condemnation) *not discerninge the body of our Lord . Therefore are there among you, many weake and feeble, and many sleepe* (that is to say, are in the death of sinne.) These are the wordes of the Apostle. 1. *Corinth.* 11. and so explicated *by Theophil.* Saint *Anselme.* Saint *Greg. lib. 2.*
                                        cap.

c. 1. in l. 1. Reg. serm. 1. temp. Concil.
Trid. Seff. 13. c. 7.

Now four thinges are requisite to communicate well.

1. Faith. *1. Tim. 3. S. Basil. quest. 172.*
in reg. breu ; That is to say, to beleue the reallitie of the pretious body of Iesus Christ in the holy Sacrament.

2. Penance and Confeffion.

3. An attention of foule, & deuotiõ excited by prayers and meditations.
Chrisost. hom. 83. in Mat. & 3. ad Ephes.
60. & 61. ad pop.

4. A decent cariage and comportment, to be fasting, chaste, modest, humble, hauing our face, mouth, and handes cleane. *S. Aug. ad Ian. epist. 118.*
cap. 6. Orig. hom. 5. In diuers. euang. locos.

O what horrible indignitie is it, to beleeue that Iesus Christ is in the most holie Sacrament, and yet to presume to receiue him, hauing thorough mortall sinne, the diuell harboured in his foule ?

E X-

EXAMPLES.

1. A holy Bishop hauing asked of God to know the interior estate of two of his subiects, which were reported to be adulterers, as they communicated, he saw the one of them to haue his face black, and his eyes full of blood: and the face of the other, bright and shining, and al his garments as white as snow. And not knowing what it ment, an Angell could him, that the first was an adulterer, and was yet in sinne. The other, albeit he had likewise committed adulterie, yet had he cleansed him selfe by Confession before communion. *In vitis patrum pag.* 2. §. 156. The same also Saint Euthymius Abbat, saw in some communicants, as Surius writeth in his in life *Ian.* 20.

2. Widekindus Duke of Saxonie, being come disguised into the campe of Charlemaigne, saw the priest vpon Easter day giue to those that did communicat,

municat, a very beautifull litle childe, who entered into the mouth of some, with a face laughing, and into others with a countenance frowning, and as it were by force. *Albertus Crautz. l. 2. de hist. de Sax. c. 23.*

3. A young man in Guienna anno 1600. communicating in mortall sinne, had neuer power to open his mouth. Wherat the priest amazed, asked of him if he were confest, who answered with teares, no: *Florimond Reimond tom. 1. of the begining of heresie lib. 2. cap. 12. S. Grég. of Tours, writeth the like historie, lib. de gloria mart. c. 89.*

4. Kinge Lotharius, hauing for a long time kept a concubine, came to Rome to Pope Nicholas to be absolued, assuring that he had put her from him, which notwithstanding he had not done. The Pope to proue his saying, caused him to communicat with all the Lordes of his trayne. A strange case, the kinge died within a few daies after at Placentia, and within the yeare, all

all the others of his company. *Sigebert.*
in chron. anno 870.

5. At Dulaca, a cittie of the Phillippine Iſlandes, a younge man, receiuing the B. Sacrament in mortall ſinne, felt inſtantly moſt ſtrange paines thoroughout his body. He caſt vp the holy Hoſte in a priuie, and the paine ceaſed; our Lord chooſing rather to be in that dirt, then within that ſinfull ſoule. Within a while after, he fell againe to his former ſinnes, and went notwithſtanding vnto the communion, and behould he was at the ſame inſtant, as ſeaſed with a fire in his throate, he withers, and conſumes quite away, which his parents them ſelues perceiued well, and yet deſcouered not the cauſe. He communicats againe, and behould an infinite number of litle flies which fly to his mouth, and gaue him ſo many prickes with their ſtinges, that at the laſt he knew him ſelfe, confeſt him, and preſently all thoſe litle flies, and

V   all

all his paines departed. *In the annales of the Societie anno 1605.* O the blindnes and obstinacie of the sinner! O the admirable patience and benignitie of God!

THE IX. CHAPTER.

Of hearing sermons, or the word of God.

BLessed is the man, *whom thou shalt instruct o Lord, and shalt teache out of thy law. psal. 93. 12.*

Blessed is the wombe that bare thee, and the pappes that thou didst suck (said a woman vnto our Lord after his sermon) *yea rather* (quoth he) *blessed are they that heare the word of God and keepe it. Luc. 11. 28.*

He saith yet more in another place. *He that is of God* (that is to say, according to the explication of the holy fathers *(a)* he that is predestinat to eternall life) *he heareth the wordes of God,*

ther-

therfore *you heare not* (quoth he to the Iewes) *becaufe you are not of God.* Iohn *8. 47.* (a) *Aug. tract. 42. in* Ioan. *Greg. hom. 12. in* euang. *Ber. fer. 1. in Septuag.*

Certainly (faith S. Iohn Chrifoftome) I haue great proofes of your profit and fpirituall aduancement, to fee you euery day to runne with fo great promptitude, and to be fo greedie and defirous, to feede and fill your felues with fpirituall doctrine. For euen as the appetit to corporall meate, is an argument of the good conftitution of the body: euen fo the defire of fpirituall doctrine, is an euident figne of the good conftitution and health of the foule. *Chrifoft. hom. 32. in Gen.*

The wordes of fermons, are called by our Lord, the wordes of God, becaufe it is God who fpeaketh by their mouthes. *He that heareth you, heareth me.* Luc. *10.*

And Mat. *10. 20. It is not you that fpeake, but the fpirit of your Father that fpeaketh in you.*

V 2   We

We giues thankes to God without intermission, because that when you had receiued of vs the word of the hearing of God, you receiued it not as the word of men, but (as it is indeed) the word of God. 1.Thef. 2. 12.

EXAMPLES.

1. S. Ephrem being one day in praier, he heard a voice which said vnto him. Ephrem eate; What shall I eate (quoth he) and who shall giue me foode? Goe to Basil (replied the voice) he will teache thee, and will giue vnto thee the euerlasting bread. He arose, goes seeke S. Basil, and found him preaching in the church. *Surius* 1. *of Feb.*

2. S. Gregorie of Nice, and Metaphrastes write, that S. Ephrem saw a Doue to prompt vnto S. Basil, all that he preached. And Amphilochius addeth, that he saw the tongue of S. Basil all on fire.

3. An Arrian heretique, and a great enimie

enimie of our faith, was conuerted to the truth, for that he perceiued whilſt S. Ambroſe preached, an Angell to dictat into his eare, all that which he ſaid. *S. Paulinus in his life.*

§. 1. *Of the efficacie of the worde of God.*

Why, are not my wordes as fire, ſaith our Lord, and as a hammer breaking a rocke? *Ierem. 23. 29.*

They are alſo called *Trumpets*. *Iſay 58. Ioſue. 6.* By the trumpets which the prieſts cauſed to be ſounded, the walles of Hiericho were ouerthrowē: a moſt aſſured preſage, that at the voice and ſound of the preachers (the true trumpets of the church) the walles and ramparts of our vices, ſhould be ouerthrowen.

EXAMPLES.

1. A certaine woman that had poiſoned her husband, hearing S. Hughe
biſhop

bishop of Grenoble preache, felt so greiuous a sorrow in her hart, for hauing committed so great a sinne, that without regarding where she was, she confest it aloud and publiquely. *Ribad. in the life of S. Hughe.*

2. S. Vincent Ferrier, being about to preache, he perceiued two wicked persons which were a leading to the galloufe, he made them to be brought vnto him, and a cloth to be put before their face. Then he preached of the malice and deformitie of sinne, and of the paines of hell, and that with such feruour and efficacie, that these two theeues touched with repentance for their sinnes, began to sweate, and to smoake or reake, as if they had bene burnt, and their faces being difcouered, they were seene become as black as coales. *Platus de bono stat. relig. l. 2. c. 32.*

O what reformation would there be both in townes and villages, if sinners would frequent sermons and
                                                cate-

catechifmes! But alas it is to be feared,
left that which our Lord faid to his
Apoftles , arriue not to fundry Chriftians . *Whofoeuer shall not receiue you,*
nor heare your wordes, amen I fay to you,
it shall be more tollerable for the lande of
the Sodomites and Gomorrheans , in the
day of iudgment, then for that cittie. Mat.
10. 14.

THE X. CHAPTER.

Of the fingular deuotion , which the good
Chriftian ought to haue to our B.
Lady.

ALL the holy Saintes haue bene fo
affected to the mother of God, &
haue thought fo highly of the defire
which God hath of her honor and her
feruice , that they haue bene bould to
affure , that who fo fhall be truly deuout vnto her, fhall be neuer damned,
but that fhe will obtaine him of her
Sonne, all that which fhall be neceffary

for

for him to be faued . They proue the fame by the wordes of the wife man. *Prou. 8. 34.* faying. *Blessed is the man that beareth me , he that shall finde me, shall finde life , and shall draw saluation of our Lord.*

For this caufe, S.Epiphanius calleth the holie virgin , the roote and feede of glorie. *orat. de Annunt.*

And in Eccles. 24. 24. I am the mother of beautifull loue , and feare , and of knowledge , and of holie hope , in me is all grace of way and truth , they that explicate me , shall haue life euerlastinge .

S. Anfelme and S.Bonauenture lib. 1.phar. cap. 5. fay . *Sicut o beatissima &c.* Euen as , o blessed virgin , all auerted from thee, and despiced of thee, must needes perish: euen fo all conuerted to thee, and respected of thee, it is impossible they should perish.

Heare S. Bernard. God hath placed the whole plenitude of all good thinges in Marie, that we should know, that

that if there be any hope in vs, any
grace of heauen, any hope of ſaluation,
all this comes from God by the handes
of Marie. *Ser. de nat. virg. Mariæ.*

And in another place. She is called,
the Queene and mother of mercie, becauſe we beleeue, that ſhe openeth
the bottomles depth of diuine mercie
to whom ſhe will, when ſhe will, and
after what maner and faſhion ſhe will;
in ſo much, that euen the moſt enormous ſinner, cā not periſh, if this Saint
of Saints, honor him with her interceſ-
ſion & aſſiſtance. *Serm. 1. in Salue regina.*

Who hath euer (ſaith a certaine holie perſonage) reclaymed thy moſt
powerfull fauour with a faithfull hart,
and hath bene reiected? Neuer, neuer
hath one bene heard of. *Eutichianus in
vita Theoph. anno 600. The ſame, Saint
Bernard ſaith, in the ſermon vpon the Aſſumption.*

EXAMPLES.

1. *My mother aske* (ſaid king Salomon

to Berſabee) *for it behoueth not that I turne away thy face.* 3 *Reg.* 20. Salomon was a figure of the Sonne of God, and Berſabee of our B. Lady.

2. *When Ieſus therfore had ſeene his mother* (from the Croſſe wheron he was nayled) *and the Diſciple ſtandinge whom he loued, he ſaith to his mother.* *Woman, behould thy Sonne. And after that he ſaith to the Diſciple, behould thy mother.* Ioan. 19. 26. From which houre, S. Iohn tooke her for his mother. Our Lord recommended vs alſo then vnto his mother in the perſon of S. Iohn. Haue we not then iuſt occaſion, to hould her for our mother as well as hee?

3. S. Thomas of Aquin aſſured before his death, neuer to haue asked ought of our Lord, by the meanes of our B. Lady, which he obtained not. *Ribad.* 7. *of Marche. The ſame is reade alſo of S. Dominick .* Ibid. 4. *of August .*

4. Theophilus hauing giuen his
                                                        ſoule

ſoule vnto the diuell, and ſigned the
gift with his owne hande, had recourſe vnto our Lady, and praied vnto
her ſo feruently and ſo efficatiouſly,
that the diuel was forced to bring him
back againe his bill. *Metaphraſt. 4. of*
Feb. and S. Antoninus. Which the B.
Cardinall Damian admiring, ſaith.
What may be denied thee, o moſt
holy virgin, to whom was not denied
to pluck Theophilus out of the very
throat of hell? Certainly nothing is
impoſſible for hee, ſith thou canſt
from the very bottom of the bottomles depthe, raiſe vp the deſpaired, to
lift them vp into the boſome of glorie.

5. See ſuch other like examples,
in the hiſtorie of Loretto, by *Hora-*
tius Turſelinus lib. cap. 4. cap. 33. In
Ceſarius, lib. 6. mirac. cap. 26. 27.
In Delrio diſq. magic. lib. 6. cap. 2. S.
3. q. 3.

6. A certaine Hermit vpon a day,
ſaw our Lady ſitting vpon a ſumptuous throane, and at her feete, S.

V 6　　　Wadrus

Wadrus and S. Aldegundus, who befought her to doe iuftice vpon Theo-
doric Count of Auefne, who vniuft-
lie vfurped the goods of the Church.
Our Lady anfwered them, that his
wife helde her handes, for as much
as euery day fhe offred for him fixtie
Aue Maries. *In the 3. volume of the*
annales of Hainnau cap. 19.

7. Lewis kinge of France and Emperor fonne of Charlemaine, bore alwaies the picture of our Lady, hanging at his neck (as did alfo S. Heduuige Dutcheffe of Polognia Sur tom.
5.) and if he were ether wearie of hun-
tinge, or ftayed amongft the thic-
kets, he faftned this picture vpon
fome tree, and offered vp his praiers
vpon both his knees. *In the hiftorie of*
France. Canif. l. 5. cap. 29. & Crautz.

7. Andronicus, Emperor of the
eafte, being reduced by a fodaine
accident to the point of death, and
feeing that he could not receiue the
moft pretious body of our Lord for
his

his voyage foode, he put within his mouth a golden image of the moſt holy virgin, which he alwaies bore about his neck, and ſo meltinge into teares, dyed. He beleeued that the B. mother would make his excuſe towards her Sonne, and that he ſhould not be excluded heauen, preſenting at the gate thereof, the picture of her who was the Queene of heauen, and hauing his hart all grauen with the markes of her deuotion. *Binet in his treatiſe of deuotion to our Lady.*

8. The B. mother of Tereſa of Ieſus, being appointed prioreſſe of the Incarnation at Auila, before ſhe began any thinge touching her office, placed in the Prioreſſes chaire, an image of wood of our B. Lady, and offered vp vnto her, the whole houſe and the keyes therof. This act was ſo aggreable to our B. Lady, that within a few daies after (as ſhe her ſelfe hath left in writinge) ſhe ſaw at the beginning of the *Salue*, the

the mother of God come downe from
heauen into the same chaire, with a
great multitude of Angells who said
vnto her, that she had done right well
to set her in her place, and that for this
fact, she would present their prayers
and praises vnto her Sonne. *Rib. l. 3.
cap.* 1. *of her life.*

9. A certaine religious man of the
order of S. Francis, had a custome neuer to take his refection, if first he had
not said his Beades once to our B.
Lady. One day being set at the table,
he called to minde, that he had not
discharged that day, that pious dutie.
Hauing then obtained leaue of the
Gardian to goe forth, he went and
said his Bedes in the Church; and as
he staied somwhat longe, another
went for to call him. Who as he entred into the Church, he saw our Ladie, accompanied with a multitude of
Angels, who gathered from the mouth
of this religious as he said his Beades,
most faire Roses, the which they placed

ced about our Ladies head : and at e-
uery time that he pronounced in the
Aue Marie the name of Iesus , our
Lady and the Angells bowed downe
their heades . *Extracted out of the Chro-*
nicles of the Friar Minors. Part. 3. l. 1. c.
36. & 37.

10. A Sodaliste of our B. Lady , in
the yeare 1586. confest at his death, that
he had bene presented before the iudgment of God , and in great danger of
being saued, had he not bene sodainly
asisted by our B. Lady. *Franciscus Ben-*
cius in the annales of the Societie, anno
1586. and Ioannes Bonifacius in the histo-
rie of the virgin l. 4. c. 18.

12. Martin Guttrich an heretique,
hauing heard in the sermon of Doctor
Frederick Fornerus preacher of Bam-
berge , that none could die ill , who
deuoutly serued our B. Lady , and
dailie offered vnto her sonne Aue Maries, he began from that very time, to
say vnto her euery day , seauen in he
morning, and as many at night, which
he

he continued for three whole yeares: at the end whereof being fallen sick, our B. Lady appeared vnto him, warning him to be confest, and to receiue the B. Sacrament, tellinge him, that she had obtained of her Sonne, that he should not die in his wicked heresie, in requitall of the seruice that he had done her, and that she would come and fetche him, at the same instant that she was deliuered of her Sonne: as it came to passe, for he deceased on Christmas night, betwixt twelue and one aclock, the yeare of our Lord 1607. This historie was written more at large by the preacher aforsaid, as an eye witnes, in a letter sent to a certaine friend of his at Monich. the 4. of Ianuarie 1608.

If an heretique hath merited so much fauour of the mother of God, for some few Aue Maries, which he recited during his heresie, what oughtest thou to hope for (true Christian

ſtian Catholique) if being in the ſtate of grace , thou rendreſt vnto her e-uery day , ſome pious ſeruice reci-tinge the Roſarie, or the Bedes, or at the leaſt a litle Coronne of twelue Aues , interpoſing three Paters, in honor of the crowne of twelue Star-res or fauours, wherwith the moſt holy Trinitie hath crowned her ſou-le ? And how much more , if ranc-king thy ſelfe in ſome Sodalitie of hers , thou reſolueſt to be particu-larly and ſingularly deuout vnto her? Wilt thou be aſſured more and more , one day to rendar and giue vp thy ſoule betwixt her armes ? Put thy ſelfe in the companye of thoſe, who pray one for another to this purpoſe, reading the Litanies of Loretto , with ſome other prayers vnto S. Ioſeph.

Loe here that which I had to im-part vnto thee , touching the maner to liue Chriſtianly, that is to ſay, to liue in ſuch ſort, that thou mayeſt, as

a true

a true soldiar of Iesus Christ, hauing driuen away sinne from thy soule, trampled vpon the diuell, the world, and the flesbe thy mortall enimies, hauing gotten many merits and virtues by the exercise of good workes, thou maist one day at the last, ascend vpon a chariot of honor, and triumphantly enter into euerlastinge glorie and felicitie, Amen.

To the greater glorie of God, and of his glorious mother the Virgin Marie.

APPROBATIO.

Ego infrascriptus testor me perlegisse libellum inticulatum, *The Christian Catholike,* Per R P Philippum Doultreman Societatis Iesu Sacerdotē Gallicè compositum, & in linguam Anglicanam per Ioannem Heigham traductum, nihilque in eo, contra fidem Catholicā aut bonos mores deprehendisse, sed magnam potiùs vtilitatem & consolationem Catholicis Angliæ alaturum fore. Quare securè imprimi potest. Datum Audomari in Collegio Anglorum Soc. Iesu, die 18. Aug 1622.

Hugo Buccleus Soc.
Iesu Sac.

THE

A TABLE.

THE II. BOOKE.

§ I.

A TABLE.

THE III. CHAPTER.

Of the three Theologicall virtues, Faith, Hope, and Charitie, pag 289.

The

A TABLE.

§ 5. Of

A TABLE.

FIN.